Sami Hadawi

PALESTINIAN RIGHTS AND LOSSES IN 1948

A Comprehensive Study

Part V: An Economic Assessment of
Total Palestinian Losses
Written by Dr Atef Kubursi

Saqi Books

Library of Congress Cataloging-in-Publication Data
Hadawi, Sami.
    Palestinian rights and losses in 1948.
1. Jewish-Arab relations—1917-
2. Jewish-Arab relations—Economic aspects—Palestine.
3. Palestinian Arabs—Economic conditions. I. Title.
DS119.7.H3214   1988   333.3'095694   87-20519

British Library Cataloguing in Publication Data
Hadawi, Sami
    Palestinian rights and losses in 1948: a comprehensive study.
    1. Palestine-History-1929-1948
    2. Israel-Arab War, 1948-1949
    I. Title
    956.94'04   DS126

ISBN 0-86356-157-8

First Published 1988 by
Saqi Books, 26 Westbourne Grove,
London W2 5RH.
© Saqi Books 1988

Photoset by
Hassib Dergham & Sons
Beirut

Printed in Great Britain by
Billing and Sons ltd,
Worcester.

To His Royal Highness Prince Hassan bin Talal, the Crown Prince of the Hashemite Kingdom of Jordan, without whose interest, guidance, and support, this Study would not have been possible.

Contents

★ Acknowledgements	XI
★ Palestine Land Measurements and Currency	XIII
★ Preface	XV

PART ONE
THE SEEDS OF CONFLICT

Chapter 1: Palestine under the Ottoman Turks	3
Chapter 2: British Pledges of Arab Independence (1915)	11
Chapter 3: British Commitment to a Jewish National Home in Palestine (1917)	15
Chapter 4: British Military Administration (1918 to 1920)	19
Chapter 5: The Palestine Mandate Period (1920 to 1948)	23

PART TWO
THE LAND PROBLEM

Chapter 6: The Soil of Palestine	31
Chapter 7: Palestine System of Land Tenure	35
A. The Ottoman Land Code	35
B. Palestine Land Legislation	42
Chapter 8: Palestine System of Land Taxation	45
A. The Ottoman System	45
B. The British Administration	46
Chapter 9: Government Laws Regulating the Acquisition of Arab Land by Jews	55
A. The Land Transfer Ordinance (1920)	55
B. The Transfer of Land Ordinance (1920-21)	56
C. Protection of Cultivators Ordinance (1929)	56
D. The Cultivators (Protection) Ordinance (1933)	57
E. The Land Transfer Regulations (1940)	58

Chapter 10: Jewish Acquisition of Arab Land   61
Chapter 11: Palestinian Opposition to Jewish Land Purchase   69

PART THREE
PALESTINE AFTER THE MANDATE

Chapter 12: Palestine and the United Nations   79
    A. The Plan of Partition (1947)   79
    B. The Armistice (1949)   81
    C. UN Resolutions on Palestine   82
Chapter 13: Israeli Seizure of Arab Property   85
    A. Immovable Property   85
    B. Looting of Arab Movable Property   87
Chapter 14: The Palestine Conciliation Commission   89
    A. Appointment, Tasks, and Responsibilities   89
    B. The 'Global' Assessment of Palestinian Losses (1951)   93
    C. Identification and Valuation of Individual Immovable Property (1964)   94
    D. Commentary on Assessment and Identification of Ownership   96
    E. Blocked Bank Accounts   102

PART FOUR
EXAMINATION AND REVISION OF UNITED NATIONS DOCUMENTS

Chapter 15: Identification of Arab Land Ownership   105
    A. General Remarks   105
    B. Examination of the Work of the Land Expert   110
    C. Revised Identification of Ownership Basis of Immovable Property   111
    D. Conclusion   112

PART FIVE
AN ECONOMIC ASSESSMENT OF TOTAL PALESTINIAN LOSSES IN 1948

Chapter 16: Palestine Losses: an Overview   117
    A. Introduction   117
    B. The Theoretical Basis for Compensation   118
    C. Previous Valuations of Palestinian Losses and their Deficiencies   121
    D. Plan of Part Five   122
    F. A Synopsis of the Results   122
Chapter 17: Alternative Assessments of Palestinian Losses: an Analytical Review   123
    A. Introduction   123
    B. The UN Palestine Conciliation Commission Estimates of the Value of 'Abandoned' Property   123

	C. The League of Arab States Estimates	128
	D. Professor Yusif Sayigh's Estimates	132
	E. Concluding Remarks	136
Chapter 18:	German Reparation Payments and Restitution of Property to Jews	139
	A. Introduction	139
	B. The Luxembourg Agreement and the Israeli-German Treaty	139
	C. Restitution for Lost Property	140
	D. Indemnification for Persecution of Persons	141
	E. Jewish Classification of Damage	142
	F. Concluding Remarks	143
Chapter 19:	The Typology of Palestinian Losses: a Re-evaluation	147
	A. Introduction	147
	B. Ownership of Capital	149
	C. Concluding Remarks	159
Chapter 20:	Valuation of Palestinian Urban and Rural Real Estate Losses	161
	A. Introduction	161
	B. A Methodological Note	162
	C. A Note on the Data	166
	D. Valuation of Rural Land	167
	E. Valuation of Urban Property	177
	F. Concluding Remarks	181
Chapter 21:	Palestinian Losses: a Final Balance Sheet	183
	A. Introduction	183
	B. Distribution of Losses by Item	184
	C. Relationship of Our Estimates to Previous Estimates	186
	D. The Capitalized Income Approach versus the Itemized Approach	188
	E. Concluding Remarks	188

Maps

A. Ottoman Administrative Districts (1914)	193
B. The Eastern Arab World	194
C. Syria (1916)	195
D. Partition of Syria and Iraq under the Sykes-Picot Agreement (1916)	196
E. Zionist Proposals for a 'Zionist State' as Submitted to the Paris Peace Conference 1919	197
F. British and French Mandates over the Eastern Arab World (1920)	198
G. Mandated Palestine 1920 to 1948	199
H. Palestine, Classification of Soil	200
I. Palestine Land Sales Restricted Zones (1940)	201
J. Land in Jewish Possession or Occupation (1945)	202
K. Palestine – Map of Partition (1947)	203
L. Jerusalem International Zone (1947)	204

M. Palestine as a Result of Armistice Agreements (1949) — 205
N. Jerusalem According to the General Armistice Agreement (1949) — 206

Appendices

I. UN Working Paper on Principles of 'Return and Compensation of Refugees' — 209
II. UN Working Paper on Principles of 'Historical Precedents for Restitution of Property' — 214
III. Findings of Land Expert on 'Individual Arab Property in Urban Areas' — 221
IV. Findings of Land Expert on 'Individual Arab Land in Rural Areas' — 223
V. Territories Excluded from Revised Study — 224
    The West Bank — 225
    The Gaza Strip — 229
VI. Jewish Land Holdings in the Israeli-Occupied Territory Excluded from the Study — 230
VII. List of Arab Towns and Villages Part of whose Inhabitants Reported to Have Remained in their Homes in 1948 — 242
VIII. Revised Survey of Land and Property Claimed by the Palestinians: — 246
    A. In Urban Areas — 247
    B. In Rural Areas — 248
    C. As Arab Land in Jewish Settlements — 306
IX. 'Focus' by Federal Republic of Germany on 'Restitution in Germany' dated No 1/May 1985 — 308
X. Valuation of Land in Rural Areas — 315
XI. Valuation of Property in Urban Areas — 316

Notes

319

Acknowledgements

I wish to thank all those who assisted in one way or another in making it possible for this long overdue Study to be published.

I acknowledge the kindness and assistance of Dr Alf M. E. Erlandsson, Chief of the United Nations Archives in New York, and of his staff; and the unfailing help they extended to my two researchers in their access, examination, and extraction of information from the records of the Palestine Conciliation Commission.

I am also grateful to Raji Musleh and Leila Mehdi who carried out the laborious and most intricate work of examining the United Nations documents and extracting therefrom the information required for the Study.

I recognize with deep gratitude and appreciation the assistance I received from my colleague in the project, Dr Atef Kubursi, Professor of Economics at McMaster University in Hamilton, Ontario, and President of Econometric Research, Ltd, who shouldered the bulk of responsibility for an extremely arduous and complicated task of assessing Palestinian losses. This required meticulous planning and execution in the face of great odds and difficulties. Mention must also be made of those who assisted him, particularly David Butterfield, Winifred Crowther, Betty May Lamb, Doug Welland, and Ibrahim Hayani.

Lastly, my thanks are due to Dr Roy Karaoglan who co-operated with Dr Kubursi during the final stages of the work, and to Dr Yusif Sayigh who from time to time gave us the benefit of his expert advice.

Palestine Land Measurements and Currency

The land measurements and currency used in this Study are the metric dunum and the Palestine pound (£P) at its value when the British Mandate over Palestine came to an end in May 1948. These then stood at:

Land measures
1 metric dunum = 1,000 square metres
1,000 metric dunums = 1 square kilometre
2,590 metric dunums = 1 square mile

Currency
£P1 = 1,000 mils
or £1 sterling
or $ US 4.03

Preface

*'Those who deny freedom to others
Deserve it not for themselves,
And, under a just God,
Cannot long retain it.'*

Abraham Lincoln (1859)

General Remarks
For thirty-five years I have been endeavouring to arouse interest in the Arab world for action to be taken in the matter of identifying and assessing the losses — material and otherwise — suffered by the Muslim and Christian indigenous inhabitants of Palestine as a result of the partition of their homeland and the creation of the state of Israel in 1948.

I wrote articles in the press, compiled and published in pamphlet form statistical information relating to land ownership in Palestine, and drew attention to the other — visible and invisible — losses sustained by the refugees.

In the meantime, the UN General Assembly established the Palestine Conciliation Commission and, among other things, entrusted it with the task which, summarized, was as follows:

1. To investigate which refugees wished to return to their homes and to arrange in the interval to safeguard their rights and interests in the properties which they left behind;
2. To investigate which refugees did not wish to return to their homes and, if they were property owners, to assess the value of their properties with a view to the payment of compensation; and
3. To investigate all other losses sustained by the refugees, whether they were

property owners or not, and to assess their nature, extent, and value for the purpose of payment of compensation.

Because of my knowledge and experience gained in the service of the Palestine government, I was selected in 1952 to act as Land Specialist to the Palestine Conciliation Commission for the Study being conducted at United Nations Headquarters in New York within the framework specified by the General Assembly. The investigation was later completed by a Mr Frank Jarvis of Great Britain as Land Expert, and his report was published by the Commission in 1964. The whole question of property, restitution, losses, and compensation was subsequently declared complete and the documents deposited in the archives of the United Nations.

In 1980, I had the honour of meeting His Royal Highness Crown Prince Hassan of the Hashemite Kingdom of Jordan, and when he heard of my project and unsuccessful endeavours, he graciously agreed to extend to me his personal support in my undertaking to examine the United Nations documents and assess the extent of the value of the various categories of losses suffered by the Palestinians in 1948.

The work carried out by the Land Expert of the Palestine Conciliation Commission when examined was found to fall short of the Commission's terms of reference as outlined above because it dealt — and only partially — with one aspect of the problem and ignored the more important and essential issues defined by the UN General Assembly. An interim commentary on the activities of the Commission was prepared at the request of His Royal Highness and published in September 1981. Entitled *Land Ownership in Palestine* it draws attention to the omissions and failures of the Palestine Conciliation Commission. This was subsequently followed by the launching of this comprehensive Study.

In planning the implementation of the project, we were guided by the claim for reparations, indemnification payments, and restitution of property which the Institute of Jewish Affairs of the World Jewish Congress submitted to the Allied Powers in 1944 for crimes committed by Nazi Germany against the Jews. In this connection, see Appendices II and IX.

The Study is not designed to argue the political or humanitarian issues involved in the Palestine problem, nor is it intended to suggest a solution to the conflict. It is confined to the nature and extent of the losses suffered by the Palestinians in 1948. The Study does, however, touch upon certain other matters where these are considered relevant and helpful to a presentation of the Arab case.

Furthermore, it should be noted that the Study is not intended to be a claim for compensation payments of the value of immovable property abandoned by the refugees in their flight in 1948. The Palestinians, whatever the ultimate consequences, remain adamant in their refusal to accept compensation and thereby surrender their rights and interests in their ancestral homeland. However, the Study does not exclude the possibility of restitution of immovable property to its rightful owners and the payment of compensation for the other colossal losses – material, physical, and psychological – suffered by the Palestinians, just as the Jews and the state of Israel were compensated by the West German government for crimes committed by the Nazi regime during World War II.

In the meantime, the Study provides a record of what the Palestinian ordeal involved and how it has affected the lives of the original inhabitants and their descendants; it should form a basis for any just and equitable solution to the problem if and when this becomes possible.

The passage of time, the death of the older generations, the changes which have occurred in the topography of the country, and the impossibility of carrying out an inspection on the ground, make it close to impossible to reach figures nearer to reality. Notwithstanding existing discrepancies and deficiencies, the team of economists and researchers did what was humanly possible to arrive at a reasonably accurate assessment.

Whatever criticism may be levelled at the Study, the fact remains that a whole nation has been uprooted and incurred losses that cannot be assessed in material terms. The Study will serve as a record of fact until justice is reached.

It should also be noted that this Study is limited to the situation as it existed in Palestine in 1948 and does not consider what occurred later as a result of the 1967 Israeli war of aggression and the occupation of the West Bank and the Gaza Strip. These will require a separate investigation and assessment.

Summary of Conclusions

Finally, the Study shows that the estimated population of Palestine in 1948 was 2,115,000, of whom 1,415,000 (about two-thirds) were Muslims and Christians, and 700,000 (about one-third) were Jews.

The total land area of the country is 26,320,000 metric dunums, of which 92 per cent is considered to have been Arab-owned against only 8 per cent in Jewish ownership and occupation in 1948.

The value of the losses suffered by the Palestinians as a result of their flight in the face of terror, expulsion, and dispossession, was first assessed in Palestine pounds, the currency of the country in 1948. Later the US dollar was used.

Chapter 21 of the Study shows that the assessed value of the losses of every description suffered by the Palestinians, as a result of the partition of their homeland and the creation of the state of Israel in 1948, amounted to $169,000 million.

In conclusion, monetary compensation alone will not remove a grievance or an injustice or make the problem 'go away', and no one knows this better than the Jews who suffered so much as a result of the crimes against humanity committed by the Nazis. But monetary compensation and restitution of legitimate rights and property, accompanied by a change of heart, will go a long way towards creating an atmosphere of goodwill whereby the aggressors and their victims who, out of necessity must live side by side, will be able to accommodate to each other as good neighbours in a genuine spirit of peace and harmony. Towards this end the present Study aspires.

Sami Hadawi
Toronto, Canada

Part One

The Seeds of Conflict

I
Palestine under the Ottoman Turks

The struggle in Palestine between Arabs and Jews has been, and still is, fundamentally over *land*. Without land there could not have been a Jewish state. Therefore, the process of accumulating land was for the Jews a premeditated and determined effort which began in the late nineteenth century under the declining Ottoman administration and spanned six decades, accelerating under the British Mandate. The Jewish task of land purchase was successful because of propitious political, economic, and social circumstances in the region. The success can be attributed essentially to the facts that the land system inherited from the Turks was vulnerable and open to manipulation; that the Palestine Arabs were still mainly a tribal society, fragmented and without a coherent political infrastructure able to defend its interests and oppose the Zionist organized take-over of land; and that the British Mandatory power failed to protect Arab rights, and instead enacted legislation favourable to Jewish goals.

Palestine in the late nineteenth century and the early twentieth century was predominantly an agricultural society and its system of land tenure was based on the Ottoman Land Law which was excessively complicated in theory but which in practice granted rights of ownership, usage, and disposition freely. Since Palestine was considered conquered territory by the Ottomans, absolute ownership of land was vested in the state.

Administratively, Palestine was divided into a *vilayet* (administrative division) extending in the north from Sidon (now in Lebanon) to the south of Nablus and administered by the government in Beirut; the territory from that point southward, including the city of Jerusalem, to the borders of the Sinai Peninsula comprised the *sanjak* (district) of Jerusalem and was administered directly by the central government in Istanbul; while the territory along the eastern borders of the River Jordan formed the southern part of the *vilayet* of Syria and constituted the *sanjaks* of Hauran and Ma'an, administered from Damascus. At no time was this latter territory, now comprising the Hashemite

Kingdom of Jordan, a part of Palestine, and any claim that it was is erroneous and politically motivated [see Map A].

The majority of the population in Palestine at the time was Sunni Muslims. Small numbers of Shi'a Muslims and Druze existed, while about 16 per cent of the population was Christian (Greek Orthodox, Armenian, Roman Catholic, Greek Catholic, and Protestant). The Jewish community varied between 24,000 persons in 1882 and 56,000 in 1918. Both Christians and Jews were free to practise their religions, and they exercised a certain degree of autonomy under the chief ecclesiastical leaders of the various religious sects.

The majority of the Muslim population was engaged in agriculture and lived in villages. Apart from the peasant farmers, there was a sizeable number of nomad bedouins who lived mainly in the Naqab (or Negev), the territory stretching south of the town of Beersheba to the Gulf of Aqaba. The urban population, consisting of Muslims, Christians, and Jews, was engaged in commerce and catered to the foreign pilgrims and tourists who visited the Holy Places annually.

Most social patterns of behaviour under Turkish rule relied upon kinship, village and family ties, and personal connections. The dominant families were those that relied principally on the strength of their long-established local position. Members of these families were recruited into the governing class of the Ottoman Empire. Furthermore, Palestine had a kind of feudal system consisting of a small number of landowning families and a backward peasantry; the *Ulemas* (interpreters of Muslim laws and traditions) occupied a strong position, for they alone could confer legitimacy on Ottoman government acts.

Albert Hourani analysed the relations of mutual dependence between the Turkish Sultan and the notables in these words:

> The political influence of the notables rests on two factors: on the one hand, they must have access to authority, and so be able to advise, to warn, and in general, to speak for society or some part of it at the ruler's court; on the other, they must have some social power of their own, whatever its form and origin, which is not dependent on the ruler and gives them a position of accepted and 'natural' leadership.[1]

The decline of the Ottoman Empire gave the European powers the opportunity to penetrate the domain of what became known as 'the Sick Man of Europe' through their religious orders. France established itself as the so-called protector of the Catholic communities in Lebanon, Syria, and Palestine, while the Orthodox Christians came under Tsarist Russian protection. The British, on the other hand, were mainly concerned with the security of the Suez Canal and the route to India. They believed that if they were to support Jewish immigration to Palestine, they would insure their position against Muhammad Ali, then the ruler of Egypt, and his successors. This was apparent in the following dispatch from Viscount Palmerston from London to the British Ambassador in Constantinople:

> ... the Jewish People if returning under the sanction and protection and at the invitation of the Sultan, would be a check upon any future evil designs of Mehemet Ali or his successors.[2]

Notwithstanding British and Zionist approaches, Sultan Abdul Hamid continued to resist a mass immigration of Jews to Palestine despite offers of financial benefits from the leaders of the Zionist movement.

Professor Halil Cin writes in this connection:

> In fact, in order to both protect its economic interests and frustrate the Zionistic attempts, the Ottoman Government re-defined in the 1870's the legal status of Palestine and took all the necessary measures against its abuse for any insidious purpose. The Ottoman policy concerning the legal arrangements finds its most explicit expression in the following statement by Abdul Hamid II: 'If we wish to preserve the Muslim Arab superiority in Palestine, we must rule out the idea of the Jewish settlement. Otherwise, since the Jews will possess in a short time all the power in the area they are settled in, it will mean that we have signed the death warrant of our fellow Muslims.'[3]

Professor Cin goes on to say:

> The transformation by the Ottoman Government of the *Berr'ush-Sham* territory, especially of Palestine, into the status of State land, was prompted by various administrative and political considerations. In the first place, it was necessary to transform the territory into State land in order to prevent the infiltration of Jewish settlers into the region... The sale of private property was not subject to the control of the government, and hence the Sublime Porte could not interfere in the purchase by the Zionists of private property willingly put on sale by the owners themselves. Therefore, Sultan Abdul Hamid, who was fully aware of this Zionist strategem, purchased by using his own private resources as much of Palestine as possible in order to frustrate the Zionist attempts for the ownership of the region.[4]

As for the state land,

the Zionist leader Dr. Theodor Herzl applied to Sultan Abdul Hamid for the sale of some of this land to the Jewish settlers. The Sultan's reply on this matter was as follows: 'I would not sell even one inch of the land, for this homeland is not mine but belongs to all the Ottoman people. My people conquered this land by shedding their blood, and it is with their blood that they have made it fertile. Before it can be taken away from us, it shall be flooded again by our blood. We can give it away only by what we took it. Members of my Syrian and Palestinian troops fell one by one in action at Plevina. I would never dream of selling one inch of this land. Let the Jews keep their billions. Only when my Empire falls can they usurp Palestine, but as long as we live and this Empire lives, only our bodies can be partitioned. I cannot allow the operation of a living body.'[5]

During his exile in Salonica, the Sultan cried out the following warning: 'The Jews have an aim in our homeland. They want to purchase Jaffa and Jerusalem.'[6]

Again in his book *My Political Memoirs*, Sultan Abdul Hamid observed as follows: 'The Zionist leader Herzl can never persuade me by his arguments. The Zionists want not only to be engaged in farming in Palestine but also to set up a government there and elect their own political representatives. I do well understand the implications of their most inordinate speculations. Yet they are behaving foolishly if they think that I am going to consent to their plans. Just as much as I respect the Jews within our Empire, so much I detest their speculations on Palestine.'[7]

The assassination of Tsar Alexander II in 1881, and the pogroms which followed, had set in motion a mass exodus of Jews from Russia, and Palestine had taken its fair share. The objectives of the early Jewish immigrants to Palestine, it should be noted, were not regarded by the Arab inhabitants as nationalistic or politically motivated. They were considered as purely religious and philanthropic; therefore the indigenous inhabitants harboured no animosity or opposition to them. On the contrary, because of their ordeal in Russia and Christian Europe, the Arabs felt sympathy for the 'People of the Book', as the Holy Koran of Islam describes the Jews and Christians. Zionist ambitions were then not generally known, while the inhabitants felt secure in their homes and property.

However, it soon became clear to the unsuspecting Muslims and Christians of the country that the immigrating Jews were not the old pious class who came to the Holy Land to pray and die, but rather a new breed of determined groups with the ulterior motive of eventually turning Palestine into an exclusive Jewish state. This they planned to do by acquiring possession of the lands of the country as a first step.

Part One: The Seeds of Conflict

It is generally believed that Palestinian opposition to the sale of Arab lands to Jews began only after World War I with the disclosure of the Balfour Declaration of 1917. In fact, Arab opposition to Jewish immigration and land purchases started and began to grow in intensity before political Zionism was officially launched in 1897, and consequently long before the outbreak of World War I in 1914, as the following brief notes indicate.[8]

The new Jewish immigrants were settled mainly on the land, and received financial support from Baron Edmond de Rothschild, who, in 1917, received the letter from the British government containing the Balfour Declaration. A campaign of purchase of Arab land was inaugurated, and some of the wealthy Arab landowners were influenced to sell land to the new Jewish immigrants at the tempting prices offered, with the result that 'the eviction of the peasants from the land caused serious clashes' between Arab and Jew. In other instances, lands were sold by the Turkish government to the Jews because the Arab peasants were unable to pay their taxes; and on other occasions, the peasants fell victim to money-lenders who charged usurious interest rates and in turn sold the land to Jewish purchasers. As a result, conflict between Arab and Jewish farmers began to appear as early as 1886. The apprehensions of the Arab farmers were shared by the Christian class of tradesmen and professionals in towns and cities who also feared the threat of economic competition.

On 24 June 1891, the Muslim notables of Jerusalem petitioned the Turkish Grand Vizier urging that 'Russian Jews should be prohibited from entering Palestine and from acquiring land there'. And in 1897, the Mufti of Jerusalem presided over a commission which scrutinized applications for transfer of land in the area and was able to stop all purchases by Jews for the next few years.

The conflict over the eviction of Arab peasants from lands bought by Jews continued during the last decade of the nineteenth century. The pattern of reaction among the rural population towards the new colonists was described as being one of initial resentment, suppressed or open hostility, giving way in time to resignation and outward reconciliation.

The year 1897 saw the emergence of political Zionism – as distinct from spiritual Zionism – during a conference held in Basle, Switzerland, where the Zionist programme was formulated and the principles for the establishment of the World Zionist Organization were laid down.

The announcement had a profound effect on the people of Palestine who saw dangers to their very existence inherent in it. By 1908, resentment against the Jewish immigrants had reached a peak and overflowed into indignation against the Arab feudal landowners who profited financially from the sale of land to the Jews at high prices.

Consequently, an anti-Zionist movement developed. Evidence of strong opposition to Zionism began to appear; people who co-operated with the

Zionists were unequivocally denounced; the press was extremely vocal against Zionism; and anti-Zionism played a prominent role in the campaign of most candidates to the Ottoman Parliament.

During debates in the Turkish Parliament, the Palestinian deputies urged the government to take measures against Jewish immigration and land purchases. They were reinforced by telegrams of protest from Jaffa against the continued purchase of land by Jews, and Parliament urged that steps should be taken against Jewish immigration and land purchases.

In May 1910, the Arab press attacked the Sursok family of Beirut for their intention to sell their extensive land holding in Marj ibn 'Amer in Palestine to the Jews. The inhabitants of Haifa and Nazareth protested, accusing the Zionists of seeking to deprive the local population of its land; while the *El-Carmel* newspaper warned against mortgaging any land with the Anglo-Palestine Company because of its Zionist identity. Once again a group of Arab deputies in the Turkish Parliament demanded an assurance that Jews would not be permitted to take possession of the lands of the local population and that mass Jewish immigration would not be tolerated.

Throughout the summer of 1913, Syria witnessed a general campaign of protest against the sale of state land in the Beisan area to Jews. The protesters explained that the land in question was usurped from them and registered in the name of the previous Sultan, and that the state was now contemplating selling it to the foreigners. The protesters reminded the Sultan that it was the duty of the ruling authorities to safeguard the interests of their subjects whom they tax and conscript. They concluded by stating that they would 'prefer to die defending our nation and our possessions rather than emigrate to unknown destinations and perish from starvation'.[9]

The Zionist leaders were aware of the growth of Arab opposition to their movement, but they preferred to ignore it and to rely on determination and economic means to acquire the lands of Palestine whether the Arabs agreed or not. The Palestine correspondent of the Hebrew newspaper *Ha'olam*, the central Zionist organ, made this pertinent comment which went unheeded:

> The greater force in Palestine is the Arab.... We forgot altogether that there are Arabs in Palestine and discovered them only in recent years.... The greatest enemies of Jewish efforts are the Christian intellectuals among the Arabs.[10]

There is a misconception in the minds of many people whereby the Jews, in addition to their biblical and historical claims to Palestine, actually purchased the majority of its lands and that these were sold willingly by the local inhabitants. This is not so, either before or during the British Mandate period.

Part One: The Seeds of Conflict

The maximum area of land the Jews were able to purchase by 1918 did not exceed 650,000 dunums out of a total area of 26,320,000 dunums. However, notwithstanding the support the Zionists received during the period of the British Mandate, maximum Jewish land holdings on the date the state of Israel was created in 1948 stood at only 1,492,000 dunums, or 5.67 per cent of the total area.

2
British Pledges of Arab Independence (1915)

The turning-point in the history of Palestine came during World War I. Notwithstanding the fact that the Arabs enjoyed with the Turks complete political independence and equality, exercised their full civil and religious rights, and shared with the Turks the rights of sovereignty over the various territories comprised within the Ottoman Empire, they wished to establish for themselves an independent Arab state like the Balkan states which broke away from Turkish domination.

Both the British and Turkish governments made overtures to the Arabs to join their ranks in the world war which was then raging. In the end, the British succeeded and an agreement was concluded between Sharif Hussein of Mecca, as the representative of the Arab peoples, and Sir Henry McMahon, British High Commissioner in Egypt, on behalf of his government.

The proposal as originally submitted by Sharif Hussein was that Great Britain would, in return for Arab aid in the war against Turkey, pledge its support of Arab independence within a territory defined as:

> ... bounded on the north by Mersina and Adana up to the 37° latitude, on which degree fall Birijik, Urfa, Mardin, Midiat, Jezirat (Ibn 'Umar), Amadia, up to the border of Persia; on the east by the borders of Persia up to the Gulf of Basra; on the south by the Indian Ocean, with the exception of the position of Aden to remain as it is; on the west by the Red Sea, the Mediterranean Sea up to Mersina. [See Map B.][1]

A correspondence of ten letters ensued culminating in a British promise of Arab independence couched in the following terms as communicated to Sharif Hussein by Sir Henry McMahon:

> The two districts of Mersina and Alexandretta and portions of Syria lying to the west of the districts of Damascus, Homs, Hama, and Aleppo cannot be said to be purely Arab and should be excluded from the limits demanded.
>
> With the above modification, and without prejudice to our existing treaties with Arab chiefs, we accept those limits.
>
> As for these regions lying within those frontiers wherein Great Britain is free to act without detriment to the interests of her ally, France, I am empowered in the name of the Government of Great Britain to give the following assurances and make the following reply to your letter: 'Subject to the above modifications, Great Britain is prepared to recognize and support the independence of the Arabs in all the regions within the limits demanded by the Sharif of Mecca.' [See Map C.][2]

The extent and value of the Arab contribution to the Allied cause was commented upon by military correspondent Captain Liddell Hart on two occasions:

> Strategically, the capture of Aqaba removed all danger of a Turkish raid through Sinai against the Suez Canal or the communications of the British army in Palestine... its capture ensured that the 'Arab Ulcer' would continue to spread in the Turks' flank, draining their strength and playing on their nerves.[3]
>
> In the crucial weeks while Allenby's stroke was being prepared and during its delivery, nearly half of the Turkish forces south of Damascus were distracted by the Arab forces.... What the absence of these forces meant to the success of Allenby's stroke, it is easy to see. Nor did the Arab operation end when it had opened the way. For, in the issue, it was the Arabs who almost entirely wiped out the Fourth Army, the still intact force that might have barred the way to final victory. The wear and tear, the bodily and mental strain on men and material applied by the Arabs... prepared the way that produced their [the Turks'] defeat.[4]

Ironically, while the British were negotiating with Sharif Hussein, they were at the same time secretly conniving with the French government on how to divide liberated Arab territory between them. The Sykes-Picot Agreement[5] which eventually resulted [see Map D] was described by author George Antonius as:

> A shocking document. It is not only the product of greed at its worst, that is

Part One: The Seeds of Conflict

to say, of greed allied to suspicion and so leading to stupidity; it also stands out as a startling piece of double-dealing.[6]

The capture of Jerusalem on 9 December 1917 had a great moral effect on the Arabs who saw signs of ultimate Turkish defeat and the realization of their dreams of freedom and independence.

On 11 December 1917, General Allenby, as Commander-in-Chief of the British Expeditionary Forces, entered the Holy City, walked on foot into the Old Sector, and had delivered from the steps of the Citadel a message 'To the inhabitants of Jerusalem the Blessed and the people dwelling in the vicinity', part of which stated:

> Since your City is regarded with affection by the adherents of three of the great religions of mankind, and its soil has been consecrated by the prayers and pilgrimages of multitudes of devout people of these three religions for many centuries, therefore do I make known to you that every sacred building, monument, holy spot, shrine, traditional site, endowment, pious bequest, or customary place of worship, of whatsoever form of the three religions, will be maintained and protected according to the existing customs and beliefs of those to whose faiths they are sacred.[7]

As the war entered its final stage, rumours began to spread of Allied duplicity. These disturbed the Arabs. Sharif Hussein, who by now had declared himself king, approached the British government and demanded an explanation. It made four attempts to allay Arab fears: the Hogarth Message of 4 January 1918;[8] the Bassett Letter of 8 February 1918;[9] the Declaration to the Seven of 16 June 1918;[10] the Anglo-French Declaration of 7 November 1918.[11]

In summary, all these were assurances and affirmations of support for the fulfilment of the pledges and promises, given by the British government to Sharif Hussein, on Arab independence within the territory defined in the Hussein-McMahon correspondence. The Anglo-French Proclamation, like the other assurances, defined war aims as the setting up of national governments freely chosen, their only concern being to support such 'governments and administrations' and to grant them recognition 'as soon as they are actually established'. But the general armistice was signed four days later and wartime promises became subject to the post-war realities of power. The promises to the Arabs were broken to satisfy British aims in Palestine, Trans-Jordan, and Iraq, and French aims in Lebanon and Syria.

After the war, a controversy arose between the Palestinians and the British government over whether Palestine was or was not included in the British pledge of Arab independence. As it turned out, in 1939, the Maugham

Commission[12] was appointed to study the Hussein-McMahon correspondence[13] and to express its opinion as to whether or not Palestine was included. Sir Michael McDonnell, former Chief Justice of Palestine, was invited to attend and participate in the meetings of the Commission. He expressed the opinion publicly that 'Palestine *was* included'; otherwise, he said, why:

> speak of the districts of Damascus, Homs, Hama, and Aleppo, not one of which is east of Palestine and all of which go northward in that order away from Palestine? Why say nothing of the Sanjaks of Hauran and Maan to the west of which the whole of Palestine lies? Why not, if Palestine was to be described, speak of Lake Hule, the River Jordan, the Lake of Tiberias, and the Dead Sea as the eastern boundaries? To suggest that an area of the size of Palestine and of the importance of the Holy Land, if not excluded by the fact that it did not lie west of the districts of Damascus, Homs, Hama, and Aleppo, was intended to be excluded by a side wind by the reference to the interest of France which, at that very time, the British government was refusing to admit, is an argument that will not hold water.

The Commission's findings were:

> His Majesty's Government were not free to dispose of Palestine without regard for the wishes and interests of the inhabitants of Palestine, and that these statements must be taken into account in any attempt to estimate the responsibilities which – upon any interpretation of the Correspondence – His Majesty's Government have incurred toward these inhabitants as a result of the Correspondence.[14]

3
British Commitment to a Jewish National Home in Palestine (1917)

Zionist political ambitions in Palestine began to take shape at the turn of the century, following the publication of Theodor Herzl's book, *The Jewish State*.[1]

The Zionist claim to Palestine is based on the premise that the 'Divine Promise' in the Holy Bible applies only and solely to those who describe themselves as Jews without regard to the Arab inhabitants of the country,[2] and that the Jews of today are Semitic in origin and can claim descent from Abraham.[3]

Efforts with Sultan Abdul Hamid of Turkey to secure Palestine for the Jews failed, but the occasion presented itself with the outbreak of World War I and at a time when Great Britain was hard pressed by the exigencies of the conflict. The Zionists represented to the British government the advantages of winning world Jewish support by helping them to meet Zionist ambitions in Palestine.

These efforts succeeded and, in a letter dated 2 November 1917, British Foreign Secretary Arthur James Balfour informed Lord Rothschild that:

> His Majesty's Government view with favour the establishment in Palestine of a national home for the Jewish people, and will use their best endeavours to facilitate the achievement of this object, it being clearly understood that nothing shall be done which may prejudice the civil and religious rights of existing non-Jewish communities in Palestine or the rights and political status enjoyed by Jews in any other country.[4]

Reading through the *first* clause of the Declaration which referred to the establishment of 'a Jewish national home', the British government took the unique step of recognizing that all those who called themselves 'Jews' had an unqualified right to Palestine – a land they had never seen – against the consent of the indigenous inhabitants and contrary to the principles of citizenship applicable in the rest of the world whereby a person can claim a right to a

15

homeland only through birth or residence under certain specific conditions.

With regard to the *second* clause which prescribes that 'nothing shall be done to prejudice the civil and religious rights of the existing non-Jewish communities', it will be observed that the Muslim and Christian inhabitants of the country are mentioned in such a way as to give an entirely false picture of their position and their indubitable right to it. Although constituting 92 per cent of the total population in 1917, the Palestinians are referred to as 'the existing non-Jewish communities'. This tended to give the erroneous impression that they were an insignificant minority occupying a position subordinate to the Jewish minority. This clause, by purporting to protect the rights and interests of the Palestinian inhabitants as 'the existing non-Jewish communities', in reality aimed at eventually robbing them (as in fact happened in 1948) of their right to the country of their birth as owners and occupiers.

As regards the *third* clause concerning the rights of Jews in other countries, the Declaration gave them the homeland of another people while safeguarding their own rights in their countries of origin. This is most unusual, as can be seen in the case of Rabbi Meir Kahane, an American citizen born in Brooklyn, New York, who now sits as a member of the Israeli Parliament and whose proclaimed platform is the expulsion of all the Palestinians of the West Bank and the Gaza Strip from their homes and country.

The Declaration was described as a document where one nation solemnly promised to a second nation the country of a third. What was unique about it is that Great Britain was not in occupation of the country and did not even have any control over it.

The indifference and lack of integrity with which Palestinian rights and interests were handled by Arthur Balfour when he was informed of Arab objections to the Declaration, are damaging to the image of the British government and people, who had made pledges and promises to Sharif Hussein in return for Arab support in the war against Turkey but had broken them after the Arabs had fulfilled their share in the bargain. Lord Balfour bluntly explained the position of the British government when he said:

> In Palestine we do not propose even to go through the form of consulting the wishes of the present inhabitants of the country.... The four great Powers are committed to Zionism. And Zionism, be it right or wrong, good or bad, is rooted in age-long traditions, in present needs, in future hopes, of far profounder import than the desires and prejudices of the 700,000 Arabs who now inhabit that ancient land.[5]

In 1921, a controversy arose as to the exact meaning of the terms of the Balfour Declaration and what it had actually promised. The Jews claimed that it meant the eventual establishment of a Jewish state and the expulsion of the Arab inhabitants from the country. This was officially disclosed by Dr Eder, a member of the Zionist Organization in Palestine, when he appeared before a British military court of inquiry appointed to look into the causes of the riots of that year. Dr Eder then stated:

> There can be only one national home in Palestine, and that is a Jewish one, and no equality in the partnership between Jews and Arabs, but a Jewish preponderance as soon as the members of the race are sufficiently increased.[6]

In 1922, the British government attempted to appease the Palestinians with a statement that 'the terms of the [Balfour] Declaration do not contemplate that Palestine as a whole should be converted into a Jewish national home.'[7] But the Palestinians were not convinced that their rights and interests were not being prejudiced as they watched, and made every effort to resist, the catastrophe prepared for them in the 'national home' policy that gradually crystallized into a 'state' within a span of thirty years.

The territory to which the Balfour Declaration referred was not defined at first. But Lloyd George, then Prime Minister, described it as 'from Dan to Beersheba', which later became the boundaries of Mandated Palestine. The Zionists were not satisfied, and in a memorandum to the Paris Peace Conference dated 3 February 1919,[8] attempted to enlarge the boundaries to include land beyond the 'from Dan to Beersheba' limits [as shown on Map E].

Comparing the proposed extended limits with the situation on the ground, it will be observed that they include the West Bank and the Gaza Strip (occupied in 1967), the Golan Heights (occupied in 1967-73), and the southern part of Lebanon up to Sidon (occupied in 1982). Circumstances beyond their control forced the Israelis in 1985 to withdraw from Lebanon, but this does not mean that they have relinquished their policy of expansion, as laid down and officially declared in 1943 to include:

> A sovereign Jewish state which would embrace Palestine and probably Trans-Jordan; an eventual transfer of the Arab population from Palestine to Iraq; and Jewish leadership for the whole Middle East in the fields of economic development and control.[9]

4

British Military Administration (1918 to 1920)

The defeat and surrender of the Turkish army in World War I brought jubilation to the Arabs who now looked forward to a bright future of freedom and independence after four hundred years of foreign domination.

But their enthusiasm was soon dampened and shrouded with uncertainty as they learned that the Allied Powers had no intention of fulfilling the pledges and promises given to Sharif Hussein and were, in fact, preparing for them a new form of colonialism under what they described as the 'Mandate' system to be supervised by the League of Nations.

On 28 June 1919, the Treaty of Versailles and the Covenant of the League of Nations were signed. Article 22 of the Covenant provided:

> 1. To those colonies and territories which as a consequence of the late war have ceased to be under the sovereignty of the States which formerly governed them and which are inhabited by peoples not yet able to stand by themselves under the strenuous conditions of the modern world, there should be applied the principle that the well-being and development of such peoples form a sacred trust of civilization and that securities for the performance of this trust should be embodied in this Covenant.
> 2. The best method of giving practical effect to this principle is that the tutelage of such people should be entrusted to advanced nations which by reason of their resources, their experience, or their geographical position, can best undertake this responsibility, and which are willing to accept it, and that this tutelage should be exercised by them as mandatories on behalf of the League.
> 3. The character of the Mandate must differ according to the stage of the development of the people, the geographical situation of the territory, its economic conditions, and other similar circumstances.

4. Certain communities formerly belonging to the Turkish Empire have reached a stage of development where their existence as independent nations can be provisionally recognized subject to the rendering of administrative advice and assistance by a Mandatory until such time as they are able to stand alone. The wishes of these communities must be a principal consideration in the selection of the Mandatory.[1]

The fourth clause created what became known as the 'A' Mandates, to which the Palestine Mandate eventually belonged.

The answer of the Arab Congress, meeting in Damascus, to Article 22 of the Covenant was included in 'The Damascus Programme of the General Syrian Congress' which read as follows:

1. We ask absolutely complete political independence for Syria within these boundaries: On the north, the Taurus system. On the south, Rafah and a line running from Al-Juf to the south of the Syrian and the Mejazian line from Aqaba. On the east, the Euphrates and Khabur rivers and a line extending east of Abu Kamal to the east of Al-Juf, and the Mediterranean Sea on the west.

2. We ask that the government of this Syrian country should be a democratic civil constitutional monarchy on broad decentralization principles, safeguarding the rights of minorities, and that the king be the Emir Feisal, who carried on a glorious struggle in the cause of our liberation and merited our full confidence and entire reliance.

3. Considering the fact that the Arabs inhabiting the Syrian area are not naturally less gifted than other more advanced races, and that they are by no means less developed than the Bulgarians, Serbians, Greeks, and Roumanians at the beginning of their independence, we protest against Article 22 of the Covenant of the League of Nations, placing us among the nations in their middle stage of development which stand in need of a Mandatory Power.

4. In the event of the rejection by the Peace Conference of this protest for certain considerations that we may not understand, we, relying on the declaration of President Wilson that his object in waging war was to put an end to the ambition of conquest and colonization, can only regard the Mandate mentioned in the Covenant of the League of Nations as equivalent to the rendering of economic and technical assistance that does not prejudice our complete independence. And desiring that our country should not fall a prey to colonization, and believing that the American Nation is farthest from any thought of colonization and has no political ambition in our country, we will seek the technical and economic

assistance from the United States of America, provided that such assistance does not exceed twenty years.

5. In the event of America not finding itself in a position to accept our desire for assistance, we will seek this assistance from Great Britain, also provided that such assistance does not infringe on the complete independence and unity of our country, and that the duration of such assistance does not exceed that mentioned in the previous article.

6. We do not recognize any right claimed by the French government in any part whatever of our Syrian country and refuse that she should assist us or have a hand in our country under any circumstances and in any place.

7. We oppose the pretensions of the Zionists to create a Jewish Commonwealth in the southern part of Syria, known as Palestine, and oppose Zionist migration to any part of our country, for we do not acknowledge their title, but consider them a grave peril to our people from the national, economical, and political points of view. Our Jewish compatriots shall enjoy our common rights and assume the common responsibilities.

8. We ask that there should be no separation of the southern part of Syria, known as Palestine, nor of the littoral western zone, which includes Lebanon, from the Syrian country. We desire that the unity of the country should be guaranteed against partition under whatever circumstances.

9. We ask complete independence for emancipated Mesopotamia and that there should be no economical barriers between the two countries.

10. The fundamental principles laid down by President Wilson in condemnation of secret treaties impel us to protest most emphatically against any treaty that stipulates the partition of our Syrian country and against any private engagement aiming at the establishment of Zionism in the southern part of Syria: Therefore we ask for the complete annulment of these conventions and agreements.[2]

President Wilson's 'Fourteen Points'[3] included 'the rejection of any territorial acquisition by conquest and the recognition of the right of self-determination of peoples'.

In regard to non-Turkish nationalities in the Turkish territories occupied by the Allied Forces, the President said that they should be given 'an absolute unmolested opportunity of development'. In his address on 11 January 1918, he stressed that:

> peoples and provinces are not to be bartered about from sovereignty to sovereignty as if they were mere chattels and pawns in a game, even the great game, now forever discredited, of the balance of power; but that

every territorial settlement involved in the war must be made in the interests and for the benefit of the populations concerned.[4]

At the same time, the President appointed the King-Crane Commission to visit the area, investigate the situation, and make recommendations. Summarized, these included: *a)* that Syria, including Palestine and Lebanon, be kept a unity according to the desires of its majority; *b)* that the extreme Zionist programme for Palestine be seriously modified in regard to unlimited Jewish immigration which seeks to make Palestine a distinctly Jewish state.

The Commission went on to say that the Balfour Declaration in favour of 'a national home for the Jewish people' was not equivalent to making Palestine into a Jewish state; nor could such a state be created without the gravest trespass upon the 'civil and religious rights of existing non-Jewish communities in Palestine'. This fact was repeatedly exposed in the Commission's conferences with Jewish representatives, for 'the Zionists looked forward to a practically complete dispossession of the present non-Jewish inhabitants of Palestine, by various forms of purchase'. Subjecting the Palestinians

> to unlimited Jewish immigration, and to steady financial and social pressure to surrender the land, would be a gross violation of the principle [self-determination] just quoted, and of the peoples' rights, though it kept within the forms of law.... One effect of urging the extreme Zionist program would be an intensification of 'anti-Jewish feeling both in Palestine and in all other portions of the world which look to Palestine as the *Holy Land*'.[5]

The Syrian protest and the recommendations of the King-Crane Commission went unheeded by the Paris Peace Conference, and the League of Nations proceeded to implement the provisions of Article 22 of the Covenant as if all was well.

The territory known as 'Syria' was split up into four separate Mandate sections with Lebanon and Syria placed under a French administration, and Palestine, Trans-Jordan, and Iraq under the British. The inhabitants were not even given any say in the selection of their Mandatory Power [see Map F].

So began the conflict. Its end is not in sight in an area of the world where peace had prevailed despite the four hundred years of Turkish occupation and rule.

5

The Palestine Mandate Period (1920 to 1948)

The newly created 'Mandate' system now being applied to their territories had not been foreseen by the Arabs in general and the Palestinians in particular. They had fought for freedom and independence only to find themselves once more in the clutches of a foreign power with their destiny in the balance.

The competition between them and the Zionists was uneven: the Palestinians found themselves separated from their mother country, Syria, and did not have the ability or means to stand alone against a formidable enemy who had international support and the financial means to reach its goal.

To start with, Sir Herbert Samuel was appointed High Commissioner for Palestine; Norman Bentwich became Attorney General, responsible for the enactment of legislation; Albert Hyamson was Director of Immigration, with the last word on immigration policy; and Max Nurock was senior Assistant Secretary, watchdog on what was going on in the offices of the central government. All these officials were known to be active Zionists who co-operated with their counterparts in the Zionist Organization of Palestine to carry out the policy of the Balfour Declaration.

The Palestinians, on the other hand, throughout the period of the Mandate, did not have a single senior official in the central government with comparable responsibilities. All were subordinate, complying with instructions from a higher official.

The effect of the Zionist officials on the situation in Palestine was commented upon by Kenneth Stein who recently conducted a study on the land question in Palestine. Because of its importance, it is reproduced in full. He said:

> The Jewish leadership, with its diverse and pluralistic origins, used the articles of the Mandate to enhance its special status. The land sphere was just one area in which the Zionists utilized their consultative prerogatives,

which they were given in Article 4 of the Mandate. Zionists influenced the appointments of key officials, wrote documents, and drafted the terminology used in the Balfour Declaration, the articles of the Mandate, the 1920 Land Transfer Ordinance, the 1926 Correction of Land Registers Ordinance, successive pieces of legislation for the protection of cultivators, the MacDonald Letter, and the definition of a landless Arab. Each time a major British statement on land or policy was issued in Palestine – including the Shaw Report, the Hope-Simpson Report, the French Reports, and the Peel Report – the Zionists issued their own verbal reply. Zionist input into policy concerning land began with Chaim Weizmann's opposition to loans for the fellaheen in 1918 and continued beyond the Jewish Agency's scrutiny of landless Arab claims in the 1930's. The appointment of Norman Bentwich as attorney general, which was a position of influence in the Land Registry Department in the 1920's, as well as Judge A.H. Webb's appointment to evaluate landless Arabs, aided Zionist fortunes in the land sphere. Although some Zionists did not like Sir Herbert Samuel's public policy of political neutrality from 1920 to 1925, the fact that a Jew and a Zionist was the first high commissioner in Palestine meant that the growth and development of the Jewish national home was not inhibited during the Mandate's formative years.

The Zionist successes and the Palestinian Arab inability to thwart Jewish land purchase were indicative of the differences in background and experience between the two groups. First, the Zionists brought with them immigrant baggage that included survival against nefarious regimes and bureaucracies of eastern and western Europe. Many Zionists were accustomed to using wily, manipulative, innovative, and calculating methods to survive. The Arabs' primary experience was of survival against nature, and they had little experience in confronting the bureaucratic and legislative machinery introduced by the Ottomans and the British. They were used to working through traditional hierarchical channels. Second, most Zionists were accustomed to verbal negotiations and written evidence in defending and expanding their communal status in Palestine, and the Arabs lacked verbal and writing skills. Third, high literacy levels helped the Jews use their knowledge of the Arab community for their own purposes.[1]

One of the first actions of the British government in Palestine even before the Mandate was approved was the closure of the Ottoman Agricultural Bank on the instigation of Chaim Weizmann, as Kenneth Stein has pointed out. The reason behind this was to put pressure on Arab farmers to sell their land to the Jews. The Bank was not reopened after the war when the need was greatest; on

Part One: The Seeds of Conflict

the contrary, the Palestine government insisted on the collection of arrears and loans as they fell due.

Describing the situation in Palestine on the eve of Easter 1920, the Palin Commission Report stated in this respect:

> The incident of the veto on the Agricultural Loans, however, had a far greater effect in inflaming the growing irritation of the population against the Zionists.... The people at once came to the conclusion that the Zionists had interfered in order that they should be left in great straits and should ultimately have to sell their lands to the Zionists at any price.[2]

The text of the Mandate was approved by the Council of the League of Nations on 24 July 1922, and came into force officially on 29 September 1923, and applied to the territory as delineated on Map G. The area amounted to 10,163 square miles of land and 272 square miles of inland water comprising Lake Tiberias (or the Sea of Galilee), half the Dead Sea, and Lake Hule, making a total area of 10,435 square miles or 27,027 square kilometers.

The Mandate embodied two main objectives: 1. to give effect to the provisions of Article 22 of the Covenant of the League of Nations which provide that 'the well-being and development' of the people of the mandated territory 'form a sacred trust of civilization', and that the existence of the people of Palestine 'as an independent nation was provisionally recognized'; 2. responsibility for putting into effect the provisions of the Balfour Declaration of 2 November 1917 for the establishment in Palestine of 'a national home for the Jewish people, it being clearly understood that nothing shall be done which may prejudice the civil and religious rights of existing non-Jewish communities in Palestine, or the rights and political status enjoyed by Jews in any other country'.

These objectives were merged into Article 2 of the Mandate which was worded to read as follows:

> The Mandatory shall be responsible for placing the country under such political, administrative, and economic conditions as will secure the establishment of the Jewish national home, as laid down in the preamble, and the development of self-governing institutions, and also for safeguarding the civil and religious rights of all the inhabitants of Palestine, irrespective of race and religion.

It provided further in Article 6:

> The Administration of Palestine, while ensuring that the rights and

position of other sections of the population are not prejudiced, shall facilitate Jewish immigration under suitable conditions, and shall encourage, in co-operation with the Jewish agency referred to in Article 4, close settlement by Jews on the land, including State land and waste lands not required for public purposes.[3]

In 1948, when the Mandate came to an end, the population was estimated to have reached a total of 2,115,000 persons, of whom 1,415,000 were Muslims and Christians, and 700,000, that is about one-third of the total population, were Jews.[4]

It is important to remember these figures because Zionist claims have often been made that the Jews were in history the majority of the inhabitants, and the slogan used was, 'Give a country without a people to a people without a country'. Perhaps this was why the British government ignored the Muslim and Christian inhabitants and referred to them in the Balfour Declaration as 'the existing non-Jewish communities'.

Evidence of the number of Jews in earlier periods is given here to prove that the Arab population had at all times constituted the majority in the country.

Firstly, according to Harry Luke and Edward Keith-Roach:

> Throughout the Middle Ages, the Jewish population in Palestine remained a negligible quantity. Benjamin of Tudela visited the country in 1170-1 and found only about 1,440 Jews. Moses ben Nahman Girondi in 1267 reports the existence of only two Jewish families in Jerusalem, engaged as Dyers; as a result of Moses ben Nahman's efforts, one of the old synagogues in Jerusalem was rebuilt, more families settled in the town, a rabbinical college was set up, and Jewish students began to resort to Jerusalem from neighbouring countries. Apart from Jerusalem, Jewish centres developed in Safad, Acre, Ramle, and Sarafand. During the following century, the condition of Jews greatly improved, both numerically and economically, and at the beginning of the fifteenth century, the immigration of Jews from Germany is first reported; these founded a settlement in Jerusalem which was afterwards destroyed by the native Jews. It was the expulsion of the Jews from Spain (1492) and Portugal (1495) which first created a 'return' on a considerable and effective scale.[5]

Secondly, according to David Millard, writing in 1843:

> I am satisfied that the actual number of Jews in the Holy Land has often been over-rated. From the best source of information I was able to consult,

Part One: The Seeds of Conflict

I am convinced that their present number in Palestine does not exceed 12,000 to 14,000. The highest of these estimates was given to me by the Rev. Mr. Nicholayson, missionary to the Jews at Jerusalem, and the lowest by the Rev. Eli Smith, missionary at Beyroot, who has resided in Syria many years and has travelled in all parts of Palestine. Both these gentlemen assure me there has been no recent increase of Jews in the Holy Land by emigration. Even under the late government of Mehemet Ali (of Egypt), which was protective to both Jews and Christians, there were no movements among the Jews to return to the Holy Land.[6]

Thirdly, the Palestine government estimated the Jewish population in Palestine between 1882 and 1918 to be as shown in Table 5.1.

Table 5.1: Jewish Population of Palestine

1882	— 24,000
1895	— 47,000
1900	— 50,000
1910	— 81,000
1914	— 85,000
1916-18	— 56,000[7]

Both the Balfour Declaration and the Mandate provided for a concept of political equality, and the British government, as the Mandatory power, reaffirmed its dual obligation to the Jews and the so-called 'non-Jewish communities' in a number of its policy statements on Palestine. Ultimately, the government found out that this dual policy was not working because the obligation on the establishment of 'a Jewish national home' was not equivalent to protecting 'the civil and religious rights' of the existing non-Jewish communities. The first was referred to as a statement of right; the other was a statement of sufferance.

Therefore, unable to reconcile the two responsibilities, the British government decided to give up the mandate to the newly established United Nations Organization which replaced the defunct League of Nations, the architect of the mandate system.[8]

Part Two

The Land Problem

6

The Soil of Palestine

Palestine was predominantly an agricultural country, and its land varied from plains, to hilly rocky regions, sand dunes, salty areas, and marshes. Yet, significantly, agriculture during the Ottoman period was the mainstay of the economy of the country.

Free-flow irrigation was limited and existed only in the Jericho Valley below sea level, in the Hule Basin in the north, and along the coastal plains of the Jaffa and Acre districts. Therefore, agriculture depended largely on rain and dry farming which made crop rotation essential to allow the land to rest and regain its vitality.

Modern agricultural techniques, such as mechanical ploughing and harvesting and fertilization, were not available, and probably were yet unknown even to the Turkish overlords. The age-old cattle-drawn plough was the only implement available and natural manure was burned in village ovens as fuel for baking bread. This practice was eventually prohibited by the Mandatory administration.

Despite these primitive methods, Palestine was capable of producing for export citrus fruits, olive oil, raisins, figs, and barley. The Palestine citrus was recognized to be of superior quality which made the Jaffa orange famous in the European markets, and the type of barley produced in the plains of the Gaza-Beersheba region of the south was regarded as high grade and best suited for the production of beer.

The Turks made no effort to improve the agricultural capabilities of the Arab regions of their empire; on the contrary, they used every effort to impoverish the farmers in order to subdue their political ambitions. They went a step further in World War I, cutting down the olive trees in Palestine and the cedar trees in Lebanon to use as fuel to run their locomotive trains, and rounding up the cattle on which the Arab farmers depended for their livelihood.

By the time the Turkish army surrendered and left the country, the Palestine farmers found themselves much poorer: they had been burdened by the British administration with the payment of current taxes and arrears of loans contracted during the Ottoman period. This placed a financial strain on farmers that compelled many to sell their lands to the Jews.

According to government records, the rural lands of Palestine were divided into four distinct soil zones: the *Coastal Plains*, which consist of first-class fertile land with an abundance of underground water and a plentiful rainfall; this territory was highly developed and contained large stretches of citrus groves; the *Hill Country* is land varied even within narrow limits, and agriculture was dependent solely on rainfall. Owing to the nature of the terrain, the olive became the principal tree of the countryside and a large proportion of the existing groves goes back as far as the time of the Christian Crusades. Other types of deciduous fruit trees also covered the hillside, prominent among these, next to the olive, was the vine; the *Jordan Valley*, below sea level where cultivation depended on the existence of streams or water pumped from the River Jordan. The moderate temperature and humidity during the winter months produced vegetables and fruits at a time in the year when these commodities were not available in other parts of the country; the *Southern Region (Naqab or Negev)*, equal to about half the territory of Palestine, which, except for small regions suitable for patch cultivation when there was a sufficient rainfall, consisted mainly of 'deeply eroded uplands and rift valleys'. Generally, the government regarded this area as unsuited for any form of irrigation scheme because of the nature and topography of the terrain, despite claims to the contrary.

In the statistics of *A Soil Survey of Palestine* supplied by the government to the Anglo-American Committee of Enquiry which visited Palestine in 1946 to study and make recommendations for a settlement of the Palestine problem, the government divided the soil of the country into three main categories [see Map H] as shown in Table 6.1.

It will be observed that the majority of the land in Palestine was considered by the government to be of the 'poor-quality' type. But this did not mean that such land was not capable of cultivation by the Arab majority.

Part Two: The Land Problem

Table 6.1: The Soil of Palestine

		predominant use	area (*dunums*)[1]
I.	*Good-quality Land*		
	1. High-class land, level or gently undulating, with fertile soils and an adequate water supply.	Intensive citrus, fodder, and vegetable cultivation.	1,184,000
	2. Good land, with loamy soil, similar to (1), but with lower rainfall.	Citrus, cereals, and vegetables.	824,000
	3. Good land, with deep alluvial soils, suitable for a wide range of ground crops, and where irrigation is available for intensive farming.	Cereals, fodder, and deciduous fruits.	1,264,000
			3,272,000
II.	*Medium-quality Land*		
	4. Uplands of limestone with steep and terraced slopes, much shallow and rock outcrop, with tracts of deeper soils in valleys.	Cereals, olives, vines, and deciduous fruits.	4,920,000
	5. Uplands, similar to (4) but with more bare rock, steeper slopes, and less cultivable land.	Cereals, olives, vines, and deciduous fruits.	2,388,000
	6. Semi-desert lowlands, with good loess soils, but cultivation limited by low and very variable rainfall.	Barley, wheat, and melons.	2,476,000
			9,784,000

III. *Poor-quality Land*

7. Lowlands, with limited seasonal crops and grazing, some broken land and some highly saline soil and extensive stretches of cultivable land if irrigated.	Seasonal pasture with patches of irrigation on favourable sites.	424,000
8. Dry eroded hills:		672,000
a) Northern Belt, with sufficient moisture for patches of cultivation where sufficient soil.	Seasonal grazing and patch cultivation.	
b) Wilderness, with very arid conditions.	Limited seasonal grazing.	2,280,000
9. Coastal sand dunes		344,000
10. Southern desert (Negev), deeply eroded uplands and southern rift valleys.	Desert with scanty patches of cultivation only when rainfall is sufficient.	9,544,000
		13,264,000
Grand Total:		26,320,000 *dunums*

7

Palestine System of Land Tenure

A. The Ottoman Land Code[1]

The system of land tenure applied in Palestine during the four hundred years of Ottoman occupation was, in theory, excessively complicated, but, in practice, it was like any other system where the people enjoyed full and unfettered rights of ownership, usage, and disposition. The system was based on the Ottoman Land Law which, it is presumed, went back to the ancient law of Genghis Khan. Later, some of the principles of Muslim religious (*shari'a*) law were absorbed. A distinction was, however, made between Muslim lands, or the lands under Arab suzerainty in the time of the Prophet Muhammad, and the lands conquered since the beginning of Muslim expansion. The Muslim lands were allodial and the conquered lands were feudal. Palestine was considered conquered territory by the Turks, and the absolute ownership of land was vested in the state.

The Ottoman government continued the practice of the previous rulers of divesting itself of a temporary right of user conditional upon numerous feudal burdens. At first a direct grant of this right was made to feudal lords in consideration of military service. The lords had the lands cultivated by slaves. Later, military fiefs were abolished and the slaves became direct tenants. Feudal burdens were gradually removed and a limited right of disposition was assimilated to the restricted right of user.

The land tenures of Ottoman law comprised various modes of user, the features of which were set out in the Ottoman Land Code. Not all of these modes of user were actually found in Palestine. Most of the land was held under two distinct tenures commonly referred to as *mulk* and *miri*. *Mulk* means 'property'. The tenure called *mulk* is a private ownership tenure. Land so owned may be called 'allodial' land. It is held in absolute ownership. The holder has almost unfettered freedom in regard to its use and disposition. *Miri*, on the other hand, was a conditional usufruct tenure of land held theoretically by grant from the state. The holder or possessor is a usufructuary whose tenure resembles a leasehold, subject to certain limitations on the use and disposition of the land and to the payment of certain fees. The interest is indeterminate, assignable, and hereditary. The extent of *mulk* or allodial lands in Palestine was limited, and was usually found in the old cities or in garden areas. Rural land in this category is rare.

Although the state land tenure of Palestine is of feudal origin, comparisons with other feudal tenures which it resembles are misleading. The law and practices regulating land tenure in Palestine are far removed for instance from English land law which is also of feudal origin.

Palestine land law was rendered more difficult to understand by the difficulty of translating Ottoman legal terms into English. The terms *mulk* and *miri* have not an exact counterpart in English legal terminology. Their translation as 'freehold' and 'leasehold' or as 'estate in fee simple' and 'estate tail' is misleading. 'Allodium' and 'feudum', or 'allodial land' and 'feudal lands', are only nearer approximations. Similarly, the terms 'vacant' for *khali*, 'communal profits-a-prendre' for *matruka murafaqa*, or 'easements in common' for *matruka mahmiya*, must all be considered as terms suggested as giving a meaning nearest to the Turkish. It is essential to master the characteristics of the various categories in order to understand the land tenure of Palestine.

The Ottoman Land Law classified land under five kinds or categories. These, with suggested approximate counterparts in English, are:

1. *Mulk* (private or allodial land);
2. *Miri* (state or feudal land);
3. *Waqf* (land assured to pious foundations or revenue from land assured to pious foundations);
4. *Matruka* (communal profits-a-prendre land or land subject to public easements in common);
5. *Mewat* (dead or undeveloped land).

A more logical classification, based on the provisions of the law, would be in two kinds, *mulk* and *miri*, with subdivisions:

A. *Mulk* (allodial or private land)
1. *Mulk* (allodial land proper);
2. *Waqf sahih* (allodial land in mortmain tenure).

B. *Miri* (feudal or state land)
1. *Miri khali* (vacant state land);
2. *Miri taht et-tasarruf* (private usufruct state land);
3. *Miri matruka murafaqa* (communal profits-a-prendre state land);
4. *Miri matruka mahmiya* (common *easement* or *servitude* state land).

Part Two: The Land Problem

The elements of land ownership under Ottoman land tenure were: 1) the bare ownership (*raqaba*); 2) the enjoyment or user (*tasarruf*); 3) the disposition (*ihala*).

In a general way the category indicated the mode of tenure, the amount of control which the state retains over the land, and the extent of the rights of user and disposition of which the state has divested itself in favour of private, communal, or general public interests. These divested rights were lapsable, in which event they reverted or escheated to the state. If the state retained a vestige of control, though it divested itself of the usufruct user and disposition rights, the land still remained state land. If the state divested itself of all its rights, the land became *mulk* (allodial land).

Mulk (Allodial Land Proper)
Mulk (allodial) land proper assumed its character when all the three elements of the ownership were vested in the holder. The owner could use and dispose of his land freely and was not obliged to cultivate or use the land profitably (in contrast to the case of a usufructuary of state land). *Mulk* could be made *waqf* (mortmain) by dedication under the religious law to charitable purposes. Succession to *mulk* was laid down by the religious law. The owner could also devise it by will, subject to the rights of legal heirs. Where there were no heirs and no outstanding debts, *mulk* property could be devised without interference from the state. Where an owner died intestate and without heirs, *mulk* land escheated and became vacant state land. As the list of heirs entitled to succession under religious law was almost inexhaustible, this eventuality was remote. The law applicable to *mulk* proper was the Muslim religious law or the ecclesiastical law of the community of which the owner was a member.

Waqf Sahih (Mortmain Land)
When *mulk* (allodial land proper) was dedicated to pious uses, it became *waqf sahih* (mortmain land). The dedication might be by deed or devise, and was irrevocable: the land must remain to the dedicated use in perpetuity. *Waqf* (mortmain) lands of the Muslim community were regulated by the Muslim religious law. These provisions were spread over several books on Muslim law. Commonly relied upon was Umar Hilmi's *A Gift to Posterity on the Laws of Evqaf*. *Waqf* (mortmain) lands belonging to non-Muslim communities (whether or not originally constituted under Muslim religious law in Ottoman times) were regulated by the ecclesiastical laws of the respective communities.

Miri (State Land)
State lands of all categories were regulated by the special land laws known as: 1. the Imperial Land Law of 1274 AH; 2. the Land Law of 1275 AH; 3. the Law as to *Miri* (usufruct title deeds of 1326 AH).

These were amended by laws generally referred to as the Provisional Land

Laws enacted up to 1331 AH (1913 AD). The ordinances enacted by the government of Palestine did not greatly modify the Ottoman land tenure.

Khali (Vacant) Land

Khali (vacant), as distinct from *matruka* (common) land, is land not allocated by the state to any interest. So long as this land remained idle, the state, could, if it so desired, allow the inhabitants of the vicinity to graze their flocks, fell wood, or draw water therefrom gratuitously. But, in actual fact, owing to the hunger for land in Palestine, this category of land simply did not exist because the Arab farmers made use, in one way or another, of every dunum of land within the boundaries of their villages.

Miri (Usufruct Land)

Land assumed the status of *miri* (usufruct) land when the *tasarruf* (usufruct) was allocated by the state to any private interest under grant *(ihala wa tafwidh)*. The usufruct in state land comprised the rights of user and disposition with certain limitations. The grant of the usufruct was express or presumed. It was express when it was embodied in a state deed of grant or in an official register. It was presumed as a 'lost grant' *(haq el qarar)* from the incident of undisputed possession for a period of ten years or more, if the possessor could, in addition, establish legal origin, such as evidence of acquisition from a predecessor with a good title. Acquisitive prescription was foreign to Ottoman land tenure. In Palestine, because of historical events, by far the greatest number of grants were presumed. Most Ottoman registrations of *miri* (usufruct) titles in Palestine were based on a presumed or lost grant.

The grant of *miri* land was conditional on the payment of consideration to the state (with the exception of waste land revived with the prior leave of the state, in which case it was granted gratuitously). The consideration was twofold. The first consideration consisted of an 'immediate payment' *(mu'ajala)*, also called the 'price of the land' *(tapu misl* or simply *tapu)*, and was sometimes referred to as the 'fair price' *(badl misl)*. The second consideration was referred to as the 'deferred payment' *(mu-ajjala)* more commonly known as the annual tithe *('ushr)*. The immediate payment was a one-time payment made as an entrance fee. Under the Ottoman regime it was assessed by local experts on the basis of the fertility and situation of the land, i.e. of its economic value. But during the period of the Mandate the immediate payment was assessed by a commission and the Director of Land Settlement. The *mu-ajjala* (deferred payment) was a proportionate fee (originally paid in kind and later in money) on the annual produce of the land, basically a tenth or tithe, or its equivalent where the land was used for purposes other than crop raising. The Palestine government abolished the tithe, replacing it with land taxes based on the value of the land with no relation to its produce.

Part Two: The Land Problem

The grant of the *tasarruf* (usufruct) was also, legally speaking, conditional on the land being maintained under effective cultivation or other profitable use. This was to ensure the collection of the tithe by the state. Originally *miri* (usufruct) lands were granted for ordinary seasonal grain cultivation. In 1913 the uses to which land could be put were extended by the Turkish government to almost every use not repugnant to public policy, provided always that the prescribed taxes and land registry fees were paid and that the land was not alienated to *waqf* (mortmain) tenure by subterfuge, as had happened before.

A usufructuary could in his lifetime dispose of his usufruct right to other interests by transfer (*faragh*) on condition that he obtained the permission of the state and registered the transfer in the Land Registry. *Miri* land could be mortgaged and sold to satisfy a mortgage. The usufructuary could not in any way alienate his usufruct to *waqf* (mortmain) tenure. Usufruct land could, however, be converted into *mulk* (allodial) land if special leave was obtained from the head of state.

The *tasarruf* (usufruct) automatically devolved by inheritance (*intiqal*) to statutory heirs in accordance with the special State Land Inheritance Law. It could not be devised by will. The absence of statutory heirs automatically terminated the grant of *miri* and the land became *mahlul* (option) land, i.e. subject, against payment, to re-grant to persons entitled to statutory options. In actual practice *mahlul* land rarely, if ever, occurred in Palestine.

Co-sharers and those who jointly with the usufructuary enjoyed servient rights of way and water easements had a right of priority to acquire the *miri* land against fair price (*badl misl*) whenever the usufructuary wished to dispose of his rights to others.

If a person possessed *miri* land for more than ten years adversely to another, the latter was debarred from bringing an action for the recovery of the land because of the passage of time (*murur zaman*). This was based on the principle of 'limitation of actions' but it did not necessarily destroy the right of the former usufructuary. It prevented him from asserting his rights through the court. It amounted to extinctive prescription. This rule originated from the time when there were no registrations of land, and gave the active possessors the benefit of the doubt as to legal acquisition.

Duly incorporated bodies (other than pious foundations constituted under religious law) had practically the same rights as private individuals in regard to the enjoyment of *tasarruf* (usufruct) in *miri* land. Ordinary trading companies could acquire land as might be required for higher purposes. During the British Mandate period, companies dealing specifically with land were required to obtain a special licence from the High Commissioner.

Miri (usufruct) land could be held jointly by two or more co-sharers, so long as the shares were defined. There were two kinds of joint holding: ordinary partnership *(ishtirak)* and village or clan partnership *(masha')*. In the case of ordinary partnership, the land did not necessarily have to be distributed periodically for purposes of cultivation. In the case of village or clan partnership *(masha')*, the land was distributed periodically (usually once in two to four years) for cultivation, which meant that a usufructuary cultivated sometimes in one locality and sometimes in another. This mode of tenure must be distinguished from the communal *(matruka)* tenure. Clan partnership applied strictly to usufruct land, that is, for ordinary agricultural purposes, and each shareholder had a definite share which could be freely acquired or disposed of.

Miri (usufruct) land had to be registered in the Land Registry. But, owing to the failure of the Ottoman land registration machinery, the majority of the lands of Palestine were found on British occupation to be unregistered or under imperfect and obsolete registration. In 1928, the Palestine government enacted the Land (Settlement of Title) Ordinance which made it mandatory for all types of land to be entered in the Land Register. By the end of the Mandate in 1948, about 25 per cent of the lands of the country had been surveyed and registered.

Matruka (Common Land)
According to Article 5 of the Ottoman Land Code, *matruka* land was of two kinds:

1. *Matruka murafaqa* (communal land) where the profits-a-prendre user was assigned *(takhsis)* by the state to any specified communal interest. There was very little such land in Palestine. The assignment of the profits-a-prendre user must in every case be expressed. In Turkish days the assignment was invariably conveyed by letters patent of assignment in the form of imperial receipt *(firman humayun)*. Limitation of action was not operative as regards such communal land. Any accretions added to communal lands by squatters could be demolished.

2. *Matruka mahmiya* (common lands) were assigned for the inhabitants in general of a village or town or of several villages or towns for pasture purposes. No individual had the right of ownership of such land, but the villages as a whole had the right to benefit from the land in a limited manner. Such land could neither be bought nor sold, and the lapse of time was not considered in relation thereto, according to the provisions of Article 102 of the Ottoman Land Code and Article 1695 of the Mejille. Under Ottoman practices, such land was not required to be registered.

Mahlul (Option Land)
Land assumed the status of *mahlul* when existing usufruct grants over *miri* land lapsed. Usufruct land did not directly escheat to the state, but was open to

statutory options which were exercised within prescribed times by persons of specified classes. If the option was exercised, the grant was made against payment of the immediate consideration. Otherwise, the land was auctioned. Should the auction fail because the highest bid was insufficient, *mahlul* land reverted to the state and became vacant state land.

Waqf Gheir Sahih or Miri Mauquf or Takhsisat Waqf (Quasi Mortmain)
Land of this category was not *waqf* (mortmain) land in the true sense of the word. It was *miri* land of which the state revenues were dedicated to pious uses or the usufruct of which was dedicated to pious foundations. The ownership remained vested in the state. Quasi-mortmain land was held by private usufructuaries in the same way as any *miri* (usufruct) land proper. There were extensive areas of this nature in Palestine. For most of them tithe was paid by the government to ancient imperial Muslim pious foundations instead of being incorporated into the normal state budget. The Palestine government, under an agreement with the Supreme Muslim Council, the authority controlling Muslim pious foundations, commuted the pious foundations tithes to a fixed sum payable annually to the Supreme Muslim Council for the purpose of the Muslim pious foundations. In 1935, the Rural Property Tax Ordinance replaced the tithe tax system, and under an agreement between the Palestine government and the Supreme Muslim Council, the latter became the recipient of £P 30,000 annually in lieu of the *waqf* share in the tithe. When during World War II the government decided as a war measure to double and redouble the rates of rural property tax, the Supreme Muslim Council applied for and received a proportionate increase in its share of the tax.

Mewat (Dead Land)
Such lands were unallocated or waste areas situated beyond the confines of inhabited regions which could only be rendered cultivable by special effort. Such land could be granted gratuitously to usufructuaries if revived with state permission, as an inducement to control developments of waste lands.

While the interpretation placed by the Palestine government on the provisions of the Ottoman Land Code as described above was accurate in so far as the terminology was concerned, it did not reflect the true situation as it existed in actual everyday life. For example, the restrictive provisions relating to possession were never enforced, and people exercised full unlimited rights of ownership, usage, and disposition whether the land was of the *mulk* or *miri* category; and at no time had ownership of the *miri* category reverted to the state because of neglect of cultivation or for any other cause.

This explanation of the facts is important to avoid any impression that the land could revert, under certain circumstances like non-cultivation by the owner for a certain period of time, to the state – an allegation which is often used by the Israeli government to justify its seizure of Arab lands.

B. Palestine Land Legislation

The Mandatory government added a sixth category of land tenure to the five existing since Ottoman days. The Orders-in-Council of 1922 to 1940 provided that all lands which were subject to the control of the government by virtue of treaty, convention, agreement, and succession, and all lands which were acquired for the public service or otherwise, should be regarded as 'Public Land'.

Article 12 of the 1922 Order-in-Council required that all rights in, or in relation to, any public land should vest in trust for the government of Palestine; while Article 13 enabled the High Commissioner to make grants of leases of any public lands, or to permit such lands to be temporarily occupied on such terms or conditions as he might think fit, provided that the grant or disposition was in conformity with the existing law, namely, the Ottoman Land Code and its subsidiary legislation.

The public lands of Palestine as they existed when the Mandate came into force included lands varying greatly not only in physical characteristics, but also in the extent and nature of the ownership and control of government in them. There were large areas in which the precise interest of the state had not been specified.

In the public domain, under the *miri* category, were the lands which the Ottoman government took over from the Sultan Abdul Hamid after the revolution of 1908; these in turn were taken over by the Palestine government. They were called *jiftlik* or *mudawwara*, and were located in the Beisan sub-district and in three villages in the Gaza sub-district. All of them were and continued to be occupied by Arabs who claimed rights in them based on many years of occupation. Full ownership was eventually accorded to the so-called tenants upon payment of *badl misl* (a low unimproved capital value).

When *mewat* land was found during land settlement operations to be free of any private rights, it was registered as *miri* in the name of the government. But, as the government pointed out, it was frequently difficult to assume that there had been no grants in the past; consequently, it was not safe to state that all the empty lands south of Beersheba or east of Hebron, for instance, were *mewat*.

With regard to lands of the *matruka* category, the government regarded these as common or communal lands for the general use of the public, or assigned for the general use of the inhabitants of some village or group of villages for the grazing of flocks, wood-cutting, and other similar purposes. The control of government over such lands was limited to that necessary to enable the villagers to benefit from them in the way intended. Rivers, wadis, drainage channels, and roads were registered as *matruka* controlled by government on behalf of the general public.

Land and property purchased or acquired by government during the period of the Mandate was registered in the name of the High Commissioner in trust for the government of Palestine. Such lands and property were considered to be in the nature of 'private government property', more or less equivalent to the provisions of English law to land in actual possession by the government as against Crown property as a whole.

Following the coming into force of the Land Registration Law of 1858, the Turkish authorities had proceeded to organize local land registry offices in various parts of the Ottoman Empire, but failed to provide a cadastral survey for proper registration. The law required that all future dealings in land were to be recorded in both the land and taxation registers, but it soon became apparent to the cultivators that the registers could be used as a means of identifying properties and owners for the double purpose of taxation and of disclosing the existence of persons subject to military conscription.

For these reasons, only a small proportion of transactions was registered and these chiefly concerned elderly persons, females, foreigners, and those sufficiently influential to be able to avoid military conscription.

Where registration was effected, there were many anomalies. For example, areas were sometimes expressed in quantity of seed required to sow them, or in dunums the number of which was arrived at by the merest guess; or, in other instances, areas were entirely omitted. There were also cases where a loose verbal description of the boundaries was given by reference to the names of owners of adjoining land or physical features such as roads, streams, hills, etc.; there were even instances known to this writer personally, where boundaries were defined by a particular incident which had taken place there at some distant date.

The result was that, in order to avoid taxation, a person owning some hundreds of dunums had them recorded as an area of, say, ten, twenty, or thirty dunums. Uncultivable land and land used by the villagers collectively for the purpose of grazing flocks and gathering firewood was not recorded.

When the British occupied Palestine in 1917 to 1918, the land records which existed were found to be in utter chaos as regards names of owners, areas, and boundaries. Besides, many of the existing records had been removed by the Turkish military authorities to Damascus, Adana, and towns in the interior of Turkey.

In 1928, the Mandatory government enacted the Land (Settlement of Title) Ordinance providing for: *a)* a division of the land, by means of a cadastral survey, into units of registration called parcels according to category and ownership; *b)* judicial investigation of all registrable rights in the parcel; and *c)* the recording in a new land register of the title and other registrable rights affecting the land concerned.

The introduction of land settlement of title operations had a double purpose: the first, with which no one could argue, was to put straight a chaotic situation inherited from the Turks and to enable the cultivator to improve his land; the second had the sinister motive of facilitating and accelerating the process whereby Jews could acquire land with an accurate title in furtherance of the Balfour Declaration policy. Since Jewish interests were principally in the country's more fertile areas, land settlement operations were commenced in the coastal plain used for the cultivation of citrus and vegetable plantations, where disputes over ownership, areas, and boundaries were much less frequent than in the hilly regions. By 1948, when the Mandate came to an end, land settlement operations in the coastal plain had been completed and Jewish land holdings in the country had jumped from 650,000 dunums prior to 1920 to 1,589,000 dunums in 1944.[2]

8

Palestine Systems of Land Taxation

It is important to discuss the land taxation systems applicable in Palestine during the Turkish and British Mandate periods because the work of the Land Expert of the Palestine Conciliation Commission in relation to non-settled rural land was based entirely on the land taxation records of the Palestine government.

A. The Ottoman System
The system of land taxation inherited from the Turkish regime was based on: the *'Ushr* (meaning one-tenth) or Tithe, applicable in rural areas; the *Werko*, or House and Land Tax, applicable in urban areas; the *Musaqqafat*, a Tax on Roofed Buildings.

1. *The Tithe ('Ushr):* Muslim law treated all land in private ownership as subject to payment of either tithe or tribute. The tithe represented the share of the sovereign, or of the community as a whole, in the produce of the soil. It was not a peculiarly Muslim institution. Tribute was no longer exacted by the Turks at the time of the British occupation but tithe was, in principle, still payable by all private owners.

The tithe, as its name indicates, was supposed to be equivalent to one-tenth of produce. The original tithe had, however, been increased from time to time by the Ottoman government for revenue purposes, and at the time of the British occupation, it was collected at the rate of 12 1/2 per cent of the gross yield of the land. Crops were assessed on the threshing floor or in the field, and the tithe was collected from the cultivator.

The tithe, under the Ottoman regime, was frequently not collected directly through a government agency. It was farmed out by public auction, usually to influential persons who were able to provide adequate security. This practice, being open to abuse, was discontinued after the British occupation.

2. *The House and Land Tax (Werko):* the House and Land Tax was levied on immovable property of every description. It was based on capital value and varied from 4 per thousand on *miri* (rural) land to 10 per thousand on *mulk* (town) land and from 4 to 10 per thousand on built-up properties.

This tax had many defects, since, in the absence of a survey, identification of each property was difficult; furthermore, at the time of the British occupation, no general reassessment had been carried out for twenty-five years, and many records had been lost, destroyed, or taken away by the Turks.

3. *The Tax on Roofed Buildings (Musaqqafat):* this tax combined both state and municipal taxes and was payable by the owner at the rate of 12 1/2 per cent.

B. The British Administration

Following the British occupation, certain changes were introduced into the system of land taxation. Farming out the collection of the tithe was abolished, all additional percentages were removed, and the tax on all crops and other produce was reduced to 10 per cent. In regard to the House and Land Tax *(Werko),* this became payable on the basis of the transfer price, or a valuation when properties were transferred, and consequently the tax on transferred properties became much heavier than on others. In the case of properties which were not the subject of a transfer, reliance had to be placed on tax collectors who had been in the employ of the Ottoman government and who knew what total House and Land Tax had been payable by the inhabitants of a village. The village elders provided lists of persons liable and of the amounts payable by them. As for the Tax on Roofed Buildings *(Musaqqafat)* collected by the Ottoman regime at the rate of 12 1/2 per cent, representing both the government and municipal shares, this was first collected by the Palestine administration at the rate of 8 1/3 per cent of the annual value, but from 1926 the rate was raised to 11 per cent of which the government retained 3 1/3 per cent and 5 per cent (later raised to 7 2/3 per cent) was paid to the municipality concerned.

The British Mandatory government recognized the unsatisfactory condition of the land registration and land taxation systems inherited from the Turks, and appointed Sir Ernest Dowson, an authority on land reform, to study and make recommendations on changes. As a result of his visit to Palestine, a new department was established to introduce the recommendations he made. Albert Abramson was appointed Commissioner of Lands, and one of the first officials to join the new department was the writer of this book. He stayed in the department, participated in formulating and implementing the new procedures, and ended up as official valuer for the classification of rural lands and general inspector of assessments in urban areas until the termination of the Mandate in 1948.

Part Two: The Land Problem

As an interim measure, in 1928, the government enacted the Commutation of Tithes Ordinance which replaced the antiquated Turkish tithe system that was based on actual production. The new law had as its basis the payment of a fixed aggregate amount of tax annually, irrespective of whether the land was cultivated or not and the extent of the produce of the farmer in a particular year.

The new tax was related to the average amount of tithe that had been paid by a village as a whole during the years immediately preceding the application of the Commutation of Tithes Ordinance to it, and was distributed by village committees under official supervision on the basis of the assessed productivity of the soil in cereals or fruit trees. The extent of the area cultivated or planted was not taken into account.

In the meantime, preparations were made to introduce new tax legislation in urban and rural areas.

1. *Urban Areas.* In 1928, an Urban Property Tax Ordinance was enacted providing for the replacement of the various city tax laws in force during the Ottoman regime. This new law was generally designed on the principles of the latest laws applicable in certain parts of the British Empire whereby the net annual value of a property was arrived at by deducting from the gross annual value 20 per cent to 33 1/3 per cent for repairs and other charges. In the case of vacant land, the net annual value was presumed to be 6 per cent of the estimated capital value. The maximum rate of tax was 10 per cent of the net annual value of buildings and vacant plots, but in 1931, the rate of tax on industrial buildings in which mechanically driven machinery was used was raised to 15 per cent.

The assessment of property in urban areas was carried out by an assessment committee made up of two government officials, one of whom was a surveyor from the Department of Land Settlement which was responsible for the application of the Urban Property Tax Ordinance, and two non-official members chosen by the municipality concerned.

Every attempt was made to comply with the technical provisions of the ordinance relating to the net annual value, but non-official members on the committee remained influenced by the practices followed during the Ottoman period and refused to apply their assessments on the basis of the actual rental and capital values of the property if sold on the open market by a willing seller to a willing purchaser. They were influenced in their assessments by their excessive tolerance with the property owner who naturally benefited from a low assessment. The only exception was where a property was leased to the government. In that event, the committee had no alternative but to quote the exact rental figure.

Therefore, the net annual value figures appearing in the tax records bear no relation whatsoever to the real capital values of buildings and vacant land if sold on the open market by a willing seller to a willing purchaser, and no sales transactions were ever concluded between the parties on the basis of the net annual values entered in the tax records.

2. *Rural Areas*. In preparation for the introduction of a new system of taxation, two officials (Maurice C. Bennett and Richard Hughes) were appointed Official Valuers to tour the country and, in consultation with the elders of the villages, to classify rural lands according to their productivity value. The categories they used in dividing and classifying the area of a village were roughly as follows:

The village built-up area
The *Hawakir* (garden area used for the production of vegetables and fruits)
The *Mawaris* (first-grade land used for the production of cereals and fruit plantations)
Crop Land (second-grade land used for the production of cereals)
Crop Land (third-grade land used for the production of cereals in alternate or more years)
Crop Land (poor land)
The *Ba'el* (common or communal lands of the village used for cattle grazing and wood-cutting purposes)

The field work was carried out between 1926 and 1934 and the results were shown on village maps divided into fiscal blocks and accompanied by schedules prepared by the Department of Surveys indicating the area of each block. This classification remained unaltered until the land was settled under the Land (Settlement of Title) Ordinance when the classification was revised to apply to the smaller unit of parcel.

In 1935, the Rural Property Tax Ordinance[1] was promulgated to replace the Commutation of Tithes Ordinance except in the Beersheba sub-district where the latter continued to apply until the termination of the Mandate in 1948.

The ordinance provided for the categories shown in Table 8.1.[2]

Table 8.1: Land Categories under the Rural Property Tax Ordinance

category	description
1	Citrus (excluding Acre sub-district)
2	Citrus (Acre sub-district)
3	Bananas
4	Village built-on area or land reserved therefor and any area which in the opinion of the Official Valuer is reserved for the erection of buildings

Part Two: The Land Problem

category	description
5	1st Grade Irrigated Land and 1st Grade Fruit Plantation
6	2nd Grade Irrigated Land and 2nd Grade Fruit Plantation
7	3rd Grade Irrigated Land and 3rd Grade Fruit Plantation
8	1st Grade Ground Crop Land, 4th Grade Irrigated Land, and 4th Grade Fruit Plantation
9	2nd Grade Ground Crop Land, 5th Grade Irrigated Land, and 5th Grade Fruit Plantation
10	3rd Grade Ground Crop Land, 6th Grade Irrigated Land, and 6th Grade Fruit Plantation
11	4th Grade Ground Crop Land, 7th Grade Irrigated Land, and 7th Grade Fruit Plantation
12	5th Grade Ground Crop Land, 8th Grade Irrigated Land and 8th Grade Fruit Plantation
13	6th Grade Ground Crop Land, 9th Grade Irrigated Land, and 9th Grade Fruit Plantation
14	7th Grade Ground Crop Land and 10th Grade Irrigated Land
15	8th Grade Ground Crop Land
16 A	Forests and Uncultivable Land
16 B	Roads, Railways, Rivers, and Lakes
17	Fish Ponds

The first thirteen categories were taxed according to the estimated productivity of the soil, and supposedly in some relation to the net annual yield. Generally, the rates of tax per dunum approximated to 10 per cent of a low estimated net annual value of the several categories of land. Categories 14, 15, and 16 were exempted from taxation. But in 1943, the government decided, as a war measure, to levy a tax on categories 14 and 15 and to impose a tax on fish ponds which were then coming into existence in Jewish settlements. Category 16 remained exempt until the termination of the Mandate.

The soil of Palestine differed considerably even within the limits of a single village, particularly in the hill regions; and the possible uses of certain lands depended largely on the availability of rainfall. It was for these reasons that the government decided upon as many as sixteen categories of land for the purpose of taxation. Classification was less rigid than it might have been since it bore no relation to actual capital value; thus two plots of land with the same productivity but in different locations (and of different capital value) were taxed alike. Land in category 16, even though it might have great potential value as building land, if in close proximity to a city or town, was not liable to tax.

Government classification of 'cultivable' land came under intense criticism from two Jewish agricultural land experts.

Maurice Hexter of the Jewish Agency condemned the government classification of 'cultivable' land before the Royal (Peel) Commission, because, he said:

> The figures, based on a fiscal survey, were necessarily falsified by the natural desire to evade the tax. They were compiled by surveyors unable to classify cultivability, and limited to recording areas actually under cultivation, omitting fallow lands. The estimate of government excludes all or nearly all land requiring considerable capital outlay; thirdly, it excludes all land under water, such as Hule; fourthly, it does not distinguish between quality and productivity of the soil; fifthly, the figures are still estimates; sixthly, their present basis seems to us no more than the estimates which they displace; and lastly, the definition is unrelated to realities, because it omits, as it shows by its very contents, technology, capital, education, skill, and markets.[3]

A. Granovsky, another critic of the government classification of 'cultivable' land, came to the same conclusions as Mr Hexter, and said:

> In order to test the accuracy of the survey statistics, Jewish Agency experts classified the lands of two villages into the prescribed categories. In one village, near Jerusalem, where the survey made for the introduction of the rural property tax had shown 2,794 dunums, or 51.8 per cent, of the lands uncultivable, the Jewish Agency experts could find only 975 dunums, or 18.8 per cent, of uncultivable land. In the second village, near Haifa, where 2,185 dunums, or 28.1 per cent were registered as uncultivable by the government, the Jewish Agency experts found no more than 726 dunums, or 9.3 per cent, of such land.

Mr Granovsky then remarked:

> It would also seem that the terms 'cultivable' and 'cultivated' were often used interchangeably during the survey, and that only such lands were registered as 'cultivable' as were then actually under cultivation. That this was an erroneous appraisal is proved by the very fact that many new stretches of land have since been brought under tillage. With the extension

Part Two: The Land Problem

of the cultivated area, the area of the cultivable lands has also been enlarged. The total area of cultivated lands has been extended year by year, and thus considerably enlarged in the course of time. While this was true, the tax records carried the same figures of 'cultivable' land as originally classified.

Mr Granovsky then quoted as an example the figures for 1930-31 which, he said, showed that:

> The whole area under cultivation was 3,866,189 dunums, while by 1934-35, it has been extended to 4,529,906, that is to say, 663,717 dunums, or 17 per cent more of the land was being worked. These figures apply only to winter and summer fruits and to vegetables, while the *krab* areas, that is to say, the lands which it is customary in Palestine to leave lying fallow every other year, were not taken into account.[4]

As the Official Valuer of the Palestine government between 1935 and 1948, the writer can vouch as to the accuracy of the arguments of the two Jewish Agency experts. Soon after taking office, he became personally aware of the anomaly, which he then attributed to the lack of understanding of the surveyor in the field of the difference of meaning between the terms 'cultivable land' and 'cultivated land'. Thus, where a surveyor found a piece of land under actual cultivation at the time of inspection, he recorded it as 'cultivable'; where he found the land not under cultivation on the date of inspection, he recorded it as 'uncultivable' although it may have been first-grade cultivable land.

The matter was reported to the central government with a proposal for the revision of the classification of land, but the government response then was that the expenditure involved would more than outweigh the anticipated increase in the incidence of the tax. Two years later, the Mandate over Palestine came to an end.

The villagers whose cultivable lands were placed in a non-taxable category were naturally pleased and raised no objection. The effect was that their names in some instances did not appear at all in the tax records, and if they did, their holdings were placed in a non-taxable category.

This account of the situation as it existed in 1948 is important to the present examination of the United Nations documents, but nothing can be done to make the figures correspond with reality at this late date.

As regards the Beersheba sub-district, also known as the Naqab, or Negev, this comprises about half the territory of Palestine. The territory was never surveyed by either the Ottoman government which occupied Palestine for four hundred years, or by the British Mandatory during its thirty years of administration. The only available plans of the region were those prepared by a British archaeological survey party before World War I including, incidentally, Lawrence of Arabia, who became interested in the Arabs from that period and played a major role in Arab-British relations. Hence, there are no reliable records of land classification or registers of ownership except for the area in and around the town of Beersheba.

The first estimate of the 'cultivable' lands of the Beersheba sub-district was put at 1,500,000 dunums; the government Department of Surveys admitted this was mere guesswork. When Sir John Hope Simpson visited Palestine in 1930 to study the land situation, the estimate quoted to him was raised to 1,640,000 dunums. Even that was inaccurate because it did not take into account the crop rotation system used in the region. The figure of 1,640,000 dunums was retained and was eventually quoted in the 1943 edition of *Village Statistics*, a publication which was first prepared for the Royal Commission. The 1945 edition, however, raised the area of cultivable land to 2,000,000 dunums as a result of a visit the writer made to Beersheba in 1944 in his capacity of Official Valuer in charge of the classification of land under the Rural Property Tax Ordinance. He met the district authorities to discuss the possibility of applying to the sub-district the provisions of the Rural Property Tax Ordinance so as to bring it into line with the rest of the country. That year happened to be one of abundant rainfall which encouraged the bedouins of the area to plough almost all land capable of being cultivated. On the basis of the schedules of production prepared for the Food Controller as required by the war measures legislation, the cultivated area that year was estimated to be closer to 4,000,000 dunums, that is double the figure which appeared in the 1945 edition of *Village Statistics*.

This encouraged the Official Valuer to assume that the earlier estimates of the Department of Surveys took into account only the land actually cultivated in any one year. Since 'cultivable land' in the context of the Rural Property Tax Ordinance meant land capable of being cultivated, not land under actual cultivation, the Official Valuer decided to prepare the fourth edition of *Village Statistics* to show an increased figure of 4,000,000 dunums as the cultivable area of the Beersheba sub-district. In fact, the edition for the year ending in 1947 was prepared in draft form but was not printed or published because of the termination of the Mandate in May 1948.

Mr A. Granovsky, writing on behalf of the Keren Kayemeth Leisrael (Jewish National Fund), correctly criticized the Palestine government's figure of 1,640,000 dunums, and said:

> What applies to the rest of the country also applies to the Beersheba sub-district; that the size of its cultivable area is not identical with that already cultivated. In that region, also, the area brought under cultivation becomes

more extensive every year. From the figures of the Agriculture Department of the Palestine Government, it appears that the cultivated area of the Beersheba sub-district was increased by more than 65 per cent during the five years of 1931-1935, thus: 1930-1931 — 1,266,362 dunums; 1931-1932 — 1,380,742 dunums; 1932-1933 — 1,345,429 dunums; 1934-1935 — 2,109,234 dunums.

Mr Granovsky went on to point out:

The experts of the Jewish Agency estimate the cultivable area of the Beersheba sub-district at 3,500,000 dunums, apart from any new tracts which may become cultivable in the future when supplies of underground water are found and provision is made for storing the rain-water which now runs off unused.

He concluded by challenging the official definition of the term 'cultivable'.[5]

Sir John Hope Simpson supported the Jewish Agency contention when he said: 'There is practically an inexhaustible supply of cultivable land in the Beersheba area', given the possibility of irrigation.[6]

It should be noted that in the majority of cases Arab methods of cultivation were still primitive; owing to the hunger for land, especially in the hill regions, the Arab farmer paid no attention to economic considerations and could be seen with his family engaged in the cultivation of small patches of soil between the rocks sometimes by means of a pickaxe, or in terracing still smaller pockets and placing olive-tree shoots in them in the hope that they would survive. Many village families were able to subsist, though miserably, on such marginal land, which, according to government standards, was classified as non-cultivable and therefore, non-taxable. While such land was held in individual ownership, the tax distribution committee failed to enter the land and its owner in the tax distribution list because there was no tax to be assessed; the owner was then only too pleased to be non-liable for payment of the tax. Cases are known to exist in which influential members of the tax distribution committee would include their own lands under the non-taxable category in order to escape taxation.

It can, therefore, be safely stated that except in the salty hills and lands in the vicinity of the Dead Sea, hardly any land in Palestine was not utilized in one way or another as olive orchards, for afforestation, or as grazing land. The vast areas of olive orchards and vineyards which cover the hillsides even in areas with barely any soil are evidence of, and a credit to, the tenacity and skill of the Palestinian Arab farmer. It is significant that the extent of Arab ownership of olive orchards in Palestine in 1948 was 99 per cent.

9

Government Laws Regulating the Acquisition of Arab Land by Jews

The acquisition of land in Palestine, which was the focal point of the Zionist political movement, began in the nineteenth century, and gained momentum after the Balfour Declaration in 1917.

Following the partition of 'Greater Syria' after World War I into the French and British mandated territories, some of the large landowners found themselves residents of one country while their agricultural lands and tenants were in another. Under such conditions, the landlord was no longer able to collect his rent on time, if at all, while the government pressed him for the payment of taxes due on the land. Many landlords were thus compelled to part with their holdings: this was where the Jewish land-broker stepped in with the enticement of attractive prices.

To respond to Arab fears and avoid the disturbances between Arabs and Jews which erupted from time to time, the government was obliged to take action, but its sincerity as an honest trustee continued to be doubted. Five different pieces of legislation were enacted between 1920 and 1940, none of which offered the assurances and protection the Arabs sought and demanded. They were as follows.

A. The Land Transfer Ordinance (1920)
This ordinance was designed to secure the protection of agricultural tenants from eviction when land was sold by the landlord. Its object was political rather than economic, namely, to maintain tenants of long standing on the land, large tracts of which were being sold by absentee landowners to Jews. It provided for the control of land transactions. The consent of the administration had to be obtained for all such transactions; it was given through the district governor, where he was satisfied that the person about to acquire the property (i) was resident in Palestine; (ii) would not obtain property exceeding in value £P 3,000

or in area 300 dunums; (iii) intended himself to cultivate the land immediately. It was also a condition (iv) that the transferor, if in possession, or the tenant in occupation of the property leased, would retain sufficient land in the district or elsewhere for the maintenance of himself and his family.

If an application were rejected by the district governor, an appeal could be made to the High Commissioner, whose decision was final. The High Commissioner also had the power to consent to the sale of large areas of land, if he were satisfied that the transfer was in the public interest.[1]

B. The Transfer of Land Ordinance (1920-21)

This law replaced the earlier ordinance and constituted the Director of Lands as the authority to grant permission for disposition of land instead of the district governor. The Director of Lands was bound to grant that consent if satisfied that the transferor had a title, provided, in the case of leased agricultural land, that he was also satisfied that any tenant in occupation would retain sufficient land in the district or elsewhere to maintain himself and his family.

This ordinance, in fact, remained a dead letter. It could be circumvented in one of two ways: either the landlord who wanted to dispose of his land ejected his tenants as a preliminary operation, and so sold the land with vacant possession to the purchaser, or the landlord or the purchaser induced the tenant to withdraw on payment of compensation. In either case there was no tenant in occupation, and the conditions of the ordinance consequently failed to operate.[2]

C. Protection of Cultivators Ordinance (1929)

This Ordinance cancelled the provisions of 1921 which required that, on sale, arrangements should be made to provide a tenant in occupation with land in lieu of the holding from which he was dispossessed.[3] It appeared to aim to protect the cultivator who had been at least two years in a holding, by requiring the landlord to give him a full year's notice before the tenancy could be terminated or the rent increased, and by providing for compensation for the tenant for disturbance and for improvements which he had carried out himself. It provided further that where the tenant had cultivated a holding for five years or more, the landlord should pay him, as additional compensation, a sum equal to one year's average rent.

In practical effect, this ordinance was of little value in preventing the displacement of tenants. It was extremely difficult for any tenant to establish a tenancy of five years on the same holding. In any case, at best, the ordinance only provided for money compensation, while what was clearly required was not compensation for disturbance, but protection against disturbance.[4]

D. The Cultivators (Protection) Ordinance (1933)
This ordinance remained substantially the law until the termination of the Mandate in 1948. Its salient provisions were as follows:

a) It defined a 'statutory tenant' as any person, family, or tribe occupying and cultivating a holding otherwise than as owner thereof. The term included the relatives of any person occupying and cultivating a holding who might have, with the knowledge of the landlord, cultivated such holding: it included the heirs of a tenant, and also any person who had been hired by the landlord to do agricultural work and receive as remuneration a portion of the produce of the holding which he cultivated.

b) It provided that a 'statutory tenant' who had occupied and cultivated a holding for a period of not less than one year could not, provided that he had paid his rent and that he had not grossly neglected his holding, be evicted therefrom unless he had been provided with a subsistence area which was to be, as far as possible, in the vicinity of the land from which he was being displaced.

c) It provided for the protection of the rights of persons to graze or water animals, or cut wood or reeds, unless provision of equivalent value was secured towards their livelihood, provided that they or their agents had exercised the practice concerned, habitually, at the appropriate season, for not less than five consecutive years within a period of not more than seven years prior to the date when any application was made to a court for their eviction.

Like the laws which it replaced, this new legislation failed to protect the interests of legitimate tenants without prejudicing the rights of the landlords. It encouraged tenants who had entered into a lease agreement with a landlord to refuse to honour their obligations under the lease once they had acquired the rights of a 'statutory tenant', and to avail themselves of the provisions of the ordinance to remain in occupation without paying rent. The ordinance also encouraged trespassers and squatters whom it never intended to protect but who, under the definition of 'statutory tenant', became legally entitled to protection. Such persons entered upon land without the knowledge or consent of the owner, often without paying rent, and sometimes remained on the land not as bona-fide cultivators but rather with a view to exploiting the pecuniary value of their gratuitously acquired rights. The provisions of the ordinance made their eviction by the landlord not only a lengthy process but one which might not always be successful, owing to the difficulty of complying with the legal requirement of finding alternative subsistence areas. Consequently, the landlord was obliged to have recourse either to buying the occupier off the land with no effective guarantee that he would not return and acquire fresh rights and a fresh nuisance value as a 'statutory tenant', or to dispose of the property at any cost and get rid of his troubles. At this stage, the Jewish land-broker, who might have had a hand in setting the situation up, stepped in and made an offer to purchase the land with all its problems. The occupants were then compensated by the new Jewish purchaser, and if they were legitimate tenants, after spending the compensation money, would become either landless cultivators or join the labour market. There was ample evidence at the time of Jewish land-brokers encouraging squatters as a means of compelling the Arab landlord to sell. The government was eventually faced with an acute problem of landless farmers which remained with it until the termination of the Mandate in 1948.

E. The Land Transfer Regulations (1940)[5]

The promulgation of these regulations conformed with the provisions of *The MacDonald White Paper,* 1939 (Cmd. 6019). This drew attention to Article 6 of the Mandate which provided that 'while ensuring that the rights and position of other sections of the population are not prejudiced, to arrange close settlement by Jews on the land', and it pointed out that:

> The reports of several expert commissions had indicated that owing to the natural growth of the Arab population and the steady sale in recent years of Arab land to Jews, there was now in certain areas no room for further transfers of Arab land, whilst in some other areas such transfers of land must be restricted if Arab cultivators are to maintain their existing standard of life and a considerable landless Arab population was not to be created.

The regulations then divided Palestine into three zones (see Map I) as follows:

Zone 'A' (comprising an area of 16,860,000 dunums in the hill country as a whole, together with certain areas in the Jaffa and Gaza sub-districts, including the northern part of Beersheba sub-district): transfer of land save to a Palestinian was prohibited except in certain circumstances.

Zone 'B' (comprising an area of 8,348,000 dunums of the northern plains, eastern Galilee, a stretch of the coastal plain south of Haifa, an area in the northeast of the Gaza sub-district, and the southern part of the Beersheba subdistrict): transfer of land by a Palestinian Arab save to a Palestinian Arab was prohibited, except in special circumstances.

Zone 'C' (comprising an area of 1,292,000 dunums and consisting of the Haifa Bay, the greater part of the coastal plain, an area south of Jaffa, the Jerusalem town planning area, and all municipal areas): transfer of land was unrestricted.

These Land Transfer Regulations came into force after the Jews had come into possession of a sizeable portion of the most fertile lands of the coastal and other plains of the country. The Arabs rejected the new legislation arguing that they had come about too late and did not go far enough. They reiterated their demand that a total prohibition be placed on the sale of land by Arabs to Jews over the entire country, but the government failed to act.

What eventually happened was that certain flaws in the regulations enabled Jews to purchase land in the prohibited and restricted zones under the names of shady Arab land-brokers with monies advanced by Jewish organizations and covered by 'irrevocable powers-of-attorney'. The land would continue to appear in the government records in the name of an Arab purchaser but would, in fact, be handed over to a Jewish organization for the establishment of a Jewish settlement thereon. The government was aware of these clandestine transactions but did nothing to prevent them. Between 1940 when the regulations came into force and 1948 when the Mandate came to an end, at least two such Arab brokers were known to the writer to have lost their lives.

To meet the growing Arab outcry against land sales to Jews and the creation of an additional landless Arab farmer population, the government, in 1942, established a committee composed of the district commissioner of Jaffa as chairman with representatives of the Legal, Land Settlement, and Land Registration departments as members, and the writer as secretary, to examine the provisions of the Cultivators (Protection) Ordinance and to make recommendations.

After hearing evidence from both Arab and Jewish sources, the committee submitted its report (not published) which, among other things, expressed the view that, although before 1933 it was the landlord who had abused the legislation and the tenant who accordingly needed increased protection, since that date it had become the landlord's rights which needed greater protection. The Cultivators (Protection) Ordinance was regarded as an instrument to facilitate the exploitation of landlords by tenants rather than as an instrument for the protection of tenants from the exploitation of the landlords.[6]

No action was taken on the recommendations of the committee, apparently because of the impending termination of the Mandate.

Commenting on the legislation enacted by the Palestine government during the period of the Mandate, author Kenneth Stein stated:

> Jewish land purchase continued despite obstacles thrown in its path by Ottoman prohibitions, exorbitant prices, and a steady increase of British restrictions. The British myopically believed that the passage of legislation and regulations would physically and economically assist the poor Palestinian Arab fellaheen. What was needed was an agrarian policy that

provided credit facilities, agricultural tax reform, modernization of agricultural methods, and more efficient land use. The British had neither the trained personnel nor the political and financial commitment to implement such policies. Instead, solutions through administrative directives and ordinances were considered sufficient. When ordinances dealing with land were decreed in Palestine, they inevitably incorporated Zionist opinion. For example, the Land Transfer Ordinance in 1920 and its amendments did not prevent land speculation, and the Zionists had helped draft them. Under the Beisan Agreement in 1921, the fellaheen in the region could not retain the lands guaranteed to them by the British even when they were available at incredibly low prices, and the Zionists helped rewrite the Beisan Agreement in 1928 in order to gain legal access to these lands. In 1929 and 1933, Arab tenants were not protected by the various editions of the Protection of Cultivators Ordinances that Zionists lawyers had helped to write; and from 1931 to 1936, the landless Arab inquiry did not enumerate property or resettle Palestinian fellaheen on alternative land because of Zionist access to the process. Finally, because small-landowner protection never evolved, the British ultimately imposed legislative restrictions on land purchase through the 1940 land transfer prohibitions. But, like the previous legislative attempts, they proved incapable of stopping the transfer of land because of economic forces.[7]

10

Jewish Acquisition of Arab Land

The abnormality in the principle of acquisition of Arab land by the Jews in Palestine in contrast to the practices in other parts of the world is that such land became extra-territorial, mortmain, and inalienable once it passed into Jewish possession. No Arab was allowed at any time to benefit or gain any advantage from it by way of lease, cultivation, or even labour. This discrimination against the Arabs was one of the reasons why the Palestinians disbelieved the Zionists' professions of friendship and goodwill.

The following Zionist documents in this respect are self-incriminating and show evidence of discrimination:

1. *The Jewish Agency*. The Constitution of the Jewish Agency, signed in Zurich, Switzerland, on 14 August 1929, has the following provisions in its Land Holding and Employment clauses:

> *d)* Land is to be acquired as Jewish property, and subject to the provision of Article 10 of this Agreement, the title to the lands acquired is to be taken in the name of the Jewish National Fund, to the end that the same shall be held as the inalienable property of the Jewish people.
> *e)* The Agency shall promote agricultural colonization based on Jewish labour, and in all works or undertakings carried out or furthered by the Agency, it shall be deemed to be a matter of principle that Jewish labour shall be employed... .

2. *Keren Kayemeth (Jewish National Fund)*. Article 23 of the lease concluded between the Fund and the Jewish lessee reads as follows:

> The lessee undertakes to execute all works connected with the cultivation of the holding only with Jewish labour. Failure to comply with this duty

by the employment of non-Jewish labour shall render the lessee liable to the payment of a compensation of ten Palestinian pounds for each default. The fact of the employment of non-Jewish labour shall constitute adequate proof as to the damages and the amount thereof, and the right of the Fund to be paid the compensation referred to, and it shall not be necessary to serve on the lessee any notarial or other notice. Where the lessee has contravened the provisions of this Article three times, the Fund may apply the right of restitution of the holding without paying any compensation whatever.

[The lease also provides that] the holding shall never be held by any but a Jew. If the holder, being a Jew, leaving as his heir a non-Jew, the Fund shall obtain the right of restitution. Prior to the enforcement of the right of restitution, the Fund must give the heir three months' notice, within which period the heir shall transfer his rights to a Jew, otherwise the Fund may enforce the right of restitution and the heir may not oppose such enforcement.

3. *Keren Hayesod (Palestine Foundation Fund)*. In the agreement for the repayment of advances made by the Keren Hayesod to settlers in the colonies in the maritime plain, the following provisions are included in regard to the employment of labour:

> *Article* 7: The settler hereby undertakes that he will during the continuance of any of the said advances, reside upon the said agricultural holding and do all his farm work by himself or with the aid of his family, and that, if and whenever he may be obliged to hire help, he will hire Jewish workmen only.

In the similar agreement for the *Emek* colonies, Article 11 contains the provision that: 'The settler undertakes to work the said holding personally, or with the aid of his family, and not to hire any outside labour except Jewish labourers.'

These discriminatory provisions are part of a general Zionist policy for dealing with the Muslim and Christian indigenous inhabitants of Palestine. From the beginning of their movement, the Zionists have been plotting not only to acquire the lands of Palestine in one way or another, but also to get rid of the Arab inhabitants. The following selective quotations confirm what the Zionists planned to do:

1. *Theodor Herzl*, the founder of political Zionism, wrote in his *Diaries*, published twenty-six years after his death, that existing landed property was to

be gently expropriated, that any subsequent resale to the original owners was prohibited, and that all immovables had to remain in exclusively Jewish hands.

In regard to the Arab population, they were to be induced to cross the frontier 'unbemerkt' (surreptitiously), after having for Jewish benefit rid the country of any existing wild animals, such as snakes. This population was to be refused all employment in the land of its birth.[1]

2. *Yosef Weitz*, a high official of the Jewish National Fund and an important advocate of the removal of the indigenous Arab population, declared in 1940 that the proper solution was for the land of Israel (Palestine) to be without Arabs, because there is no room for compromise. They must be completely removed, leaving not one village, not one tribe... They must be removed to Trans-Jordan, Syria, or Iraq. This plan was widely discussed in the Palestinian Jewish community and was authorized by the top.[2]

3. *David Ben-Gurion*. In a 1 January 1948 entry in his 'Independence War Diary', he described his military doctrine of attacking defenceless civilian Arabs in these words:

> There is no question as to whether a reaction is necessary or not. The question is only time and place. Blowing up a house is not enough. What is necessary is cruel and strong reactions. We need precision in time, place, and casualties. If we know the family [we must] strike mercilessly, women and children included. Otherwise, the reaction is inefficient. At the place of action there is no need to distinguish between guilty and innocent.[3]

Notwithstanding the Zionists' influence on the Mandatory government and the assistance they received from it, the extent of land in Jewish ownership on the date the Jewish state came into existence was a small percentage of the total. *Village Statistics* 1945, published by the Department of Land Settlement, quotes a figure of 1,491,699 dunums, or 5.67 per cent of the total land area of Palestine, as being Jewish-owned.[4] The *Survey of Palestine* 1945-1946, prepared by the Palestine government for the Anglo-American Committee of Inquiry, stated:

> Between the opening of the land registries in October 1920 and 31st December 1945, Jews had purchased and registered a net area of 938,365 dunums. The assumption that they owned 650,000 dunums prior to October 1920 is generally accepted. The total area now owned by them may, therefore, be put at about 1,588,000 dunums.[5]

A. Granott, an Israeli land expert, also cited a total area of 1,588,000 dunums in the legal possession of Jews at the end of June 1947; he said that 181,000 dunums of this total were held under concessions granted by the Palestine government.[6]

Table 10.1 shows the areas of land purchased annually by Jews and registered in the land registries between the years 1920 and 1945.

Table 10.1: Land Purchased by Jews according to Land Registry

year	dunums
Area owned before 1920 (estimated)	650,000
1920	1,048
1921	90,785
1922	39,359
1923	17,493
1924	44,765
1925	176,124
1926	38,978
1927	18,995
1928	21,515
1929	64,517
1930	19,365
1931	18,585
1932	18,893
1933	36,991
1934	62,114
1935	72,905
1936	18,146
1937	29,367
1938	27,280
1939	27,973
1940	22,481
1941	14,530
1942	18,810
1943	18,035
1944	8,311
1945 (estimated)	11,000
Total	1,588,365[7]

The figures quoted by the three different sources are very similar; and whichever is accepted as representing the extent of Jewish-owned land in Palestine, the fact remains that Jewish land holdings on the date the state of Israel came into existence in 1948 did not exceed 6 per cent of the total land area of Palestine.

As to the allegation that the Palestine Arabs had sold their lands to the Jews, Mr Granott exonerates the Palestinian farmers by providing evidence that the majority of land acquisitions by Jews had been from absentee landowners.

Commenting on 'the distribution of the land from the point of view of its ownership before it passed into the hands of the Jews', Granott states:

> The Jews acquired their land principally from large and medium Arab landowners; the area which was bought from small proprietors was not extensive... although there are no figures covering the whole of the land acquisition, there are more or less precise data on the majority of the lands which in the various periods passed into the hands of the Jews. The figures relate to acquisitions which were made by the big companies and associations—PICA, the Palestine Land Development Company, and the Jewish National Fund.

He then listed Jewish acquisitions up to the year 1936 and pointed out that the figures embrace 'only about half (55.4 per cent) of all the areas which were acquired by Jews'.[8]

According to Mr Granott's tabulation, acquisition of land by the three Jewish companies by the end of 1936 stood as shown in Table 10.2.

Table 10.2: Land Acquisition by the Three Jewish Companies at the End of 1936

	dunums	%
Acquired from large absentee landowners	358,974	52.6
Acquired from large resident landowners	167,802	24.6[9]
Acquired from government, churches, and foreign companies	91,001	13.4
Acquired from fellahin (farmers)	64,201	9.4
Total	681,978	

Mr Granott remarks:

> If we add up all these figures, we shall find that no less than 90.6 per cent of all acquisitions were of land which formerly belonged to large landowners, while from fellaheen only 9.4 per cent was purchased.[10]

The fact that the majority of the lands acquired by the Jews during the period of the Mandate were bought from non-Palestinian absentee landlords is corroborated in a memorandum dated 25 February 1946 submitted by the Arab Higher Committee to the Anglo-American Committee of Inquiry on its arrival in Palestine. Dr Yusif Sayigh, the signatory of the memorandum, listed the

Palestinian Rights and Losses in 1948

areas acquired, as compiled from a field survey conducted at the time, *in only a part of Palestine*, as 461,250 dunums out of a total area of 1,491,699 of which 841,699 dunums were purchased during the period of the Mandate. 'The real total area sold this way', Sayigh explained, 'is definitely more'; he commented: 'The fuller the data, the less the blame to attach to Palestinian Arabs.'

The information contained in the memorandum, because of its importance, is given in Table 10.3.

Table 10.3: Land Sales to Jews in Palestine by Non-Palestinian Absentee Landlords

name of seller	area (dunums)	locality
Lebanese		
Heirs of Salim Ramadan	3,000	Hittin
Heirs of Jammal and Milki	2,500	Nimrin
Ghulmia and Jbara	4,000	Zuq et Tahtani
Emir Chehab family	1,100	Khalisa
Francis family	3,000	Dafna
Shab'a villagers	1,500	Khan el-Dweir
Debki and Shams families	1,600	Ed-Dawwara
Farha family	1,400	Ez-Zawiya
Chehab family	1,300	En-Na'ima
Farhat and Bazza families and Mardinis (of Syria)	9,000	Qaddas
Razza family	3,500	El-Malakiya
Ahmad el-As'ad	2,000	El-Manara & Udeisa
Moitenes villagers	1,200	Jabal Meimas
Father Shukrallah	900	Qaddita
Father Shukrallah	700	Yarda
Deishum villagers	1,100	Hawwara
Ali Salam	41,500	Hula Concession Area
Najib Sursock	26,500	Tell el-Firr & Jalloud
Sursock family	240,000	Marj ibn 'Amer (Plain of Esdraelon)[11]
Zu'rob family	5,000	Hanouta
Quteit villagers	4,500	Samakh
'Oweini family	2,500	Nahariya
Tayyan family	31,500	Wadi Hawarith
	388,800	

Part Two: The Land Problem

name of seller	area (dunums)	locality
Syrians		
Heirs of Emir El-Jazairi	34,000	Kafr Sabt and Sha'ara
Heirs of Emir El-Jazairi	3,000	Kirad El-Kheit, Baqqara, and Ghannama
El-'Akawi family	1,600	El-Khaffas
Emirs Fa'our and Shaman	800	Es-Salihiya
El-Fadl family	1,200	Barjiyat
Za'al Salloum	1,500	Khirbet Es-Summan
Boso family	4,000	Khiyam El-Walid
Qabbani family	10,550	Wad El-Qabbani
	56,450	
Others		
Bahai Persians (Iranians)	8,000	Nuqeib
Comte de Shadid (Egyptians)	8,000	Samakh
	16,000	dunums[12]
Grand Total	461,250	

11

Palestinian Opposition to Jewish Land Purchase

Finding themselves in an inferior political position to the Zionists in British government circles, the Palestinians had to express their opposition and anger against the sale of their lands to Jews in the only way open to them, and that was by violent action.

Disturbances occurred in Palestine in 1920, 1921, and 1929; then a general strike in 1936 crippled the economy of the country for six months; this was followed by an open rebellion against British authority which lasted from 1936 to 1939, and came to an end only because of the beginning of World War II.

Five commissions of inquiry were appointed each with terms of reference to investigate the causes and make recommendations: the Palin Commission in 1920; the Haycraft Commission in 1921; the Shaw Commission in 1929; the Peel (Royal) Commission in 1937; the Woodhead (Partition) Commission in 1939.

The Palin Commission (report not published) dealt with the disturbances which took place on Easter Sunday 1920. In its Report,[1] the Commission attributed the riots to: 1. Arab disappointment at the non-fulfilment of promises made; 2. Arab belief that the Balfour Declaration implied a denial of Arab rights; 3. Palestinian fear that the establishment of a Jewish national home on Palestine soil would lead to their economic and political subjection to the Jews.

In an attempt to appease Palestinian fears, Sir Herbert Samuel,[2] who took office as first High Commissioner for Palestine on 1 July 1920, made public a message from His Majesty King George 'To the People of Palestine' assuring them:

> Of the absolute impartiality with which the duties of the Mandatory Power will be carried out, and of the determination of my Government

to respect the rights of every race and every creed represented among you.[3]

The King's message did little to reassure the Palestinians. In March 1921, another disturbance took place; and this time Sir Herbert Samuel made the following statement:

> I hear it said in many quarters that the Arab population will never agree to their country, their holy places, and their lands being taken away from them and given to strangers. People say that they cannot understand how it is that the British Government, which is famous throughout the world for its justice, could ever have consented to such a policy.
>
> I answer that the British Government... has never consented and will never consent to such a policy... [The Balfour Declaration] means that the Jews, a people who are scattered throughout the world, but whose hearts are always turned to Palestine, should be enabled to find their homes, and that some among them, within the limits that are fixed by the numbers and interests of the present population, should come to Palestine in order to help by their resources and efforts to develop the country to the advantage of all its inhabitants.
>
> If any measures are needed to convince the Moslem and Christian population... that their rights are really safe, such measures will be taken. For the British Government, the trustee under the Mandate for the happiness of the people of Palestine, would never impose upon them a policy which that people had reason to think was contrary to their religion, their political, and their economic interests.[4]

At the same time, the High Commissioner appointed the Haycraft Commission to investigate the causes of the riots. The Commission, reporting in October 1921:

> maintained that the root of the trouble lay in Arab fear of the consequences of a steady increase in Jewish immigration which they regard not only as an ultimate means of Arab political and economic subjection, but also as an immediate cause of Arab unemployment.[5]

A period of uneasy tranquillity prevailed in the country in the years which followed. But on 24 August 1929, the most serious disturbances to date took place; and on 14 September 1929, yet another commission of inquiry was appointed under the chairmanship of Sir Walter Shaw 'to enquire into the immediate causes which led to the recent outbreak in Palestine and to make recommendations as to the steps necessary to avoid a recurrence.'[6]

The Shaw Commission reported on 30 March 1930.[7] Its members were convinced that Zionist land acquisition and Jewish colonization were the foremost Arab grievances, and 'the fears of the Arabs that the success of the Zionist land policy meant their expulsion from the land were repeatedly emphasized.' The Commission went on to say that the Protection of Cultivators Ordinance of 1929 did nothing to check the tendency for Arab farmers to become landless. The Arab position, the Commission pointed out, was now acute and there was no alternative land to which persons evicted could move. In consequence, a landless and discontented class was being created.

The Commission went on to say that between 1921 and 1929:

> There were large sales of land in consequence of which numbers of Arabs were evicted without promise of other land for their occupation. Palestine cannot support a larger agricultural population than it at present carries unless methods of farming undergo a radical change.

Among the recommendations which the Shaw Commission made that relate to land, were: *a)* that the government should lay down more explicit directions as to the conduct of policy on such vital issues as land tenure and immigration; *b)* that a scientific enquiry should be held into land cultivation and settlement possibilities; and that, pending this enquiry, the eviction of peasant cultivators from the land should be checked.

One outcome of the recommendations of the Shaw Commission was the appointment of Sir John Hope Simpson to investigate and report on immigration, land settlement, and development. He arrived in Palestine on 20 May 1930, and his Report was published on 20 October 1930.[8]

Concurrently with the appointment of Sir John Hope Simpson, the British government issued what became known as *The Passfield White Paper*[9] reaffirming the findings of the Shaw Commission and postponing any statement of future policy pending the report of Sir John Hope Simpson on immigration, land settlement, and development.

But the Statement of Policy was rendered ineffective as a result of the issue of a communication which became known as the 'MacDonald Letter', dated 13 February 1931 and addressed to Chaim Weizmann,[10] which annulled the provisions of the White Paper. Kenneth Stein attributes the turn-about in British policy to the 'sympathetic ear' the Zionists had in Ramsay MacDonald. He goes on to reveal that:

> No fewer than five drafts of the MacDonald Letter were written, the first of which was completed on 29 November. Most of the actual drafting of

the letter was done by Zionists. In addition to Weizmann, Leonard Stein, Lewis Namier, and Maurice Hexter made important contributions. The Zionists meticulously expunged from the 'White Paper' all implications that were potentially dangerous to their aspirations.[11]

In his Report, Hope Simpson emphasized the small size of Palestine, an area of only 10,435 square miles, of which more than three-quarters was 'uncultivable' by current economic standards. Of the 'cultivable' land, about 14 per cent had been bought by Jews with the displacement of the indigenous Arab tenant farmers and labourers. This indicated that Zionist plans, which were said to be based on their ability to make the desert blossom, included the acquisition of as much cultivable land as could be bought from Arab landowners. The largest sale, with which the Report dealt in some detail, concerned the Vale of Esdraelon (Marj ibn 'Amer). In ancient times, Esdraelon was the granary of the country, and is regarded by the Palestinians as the most fertile tract of land in Palestine. The bitterness felt owing to the sale of large areas by the absentee Sursock family to the Jews and the displacement of the Arab tenants remained unresolved.

It should be noted that the Sursock family had been granted the title to a large tract of land in Marj ibn 'Amer for 'services rendered' to the Sultan of Turkey. While legal ownership became vested in the Sursocks, in effect, the grant did not alter the existing relationship between landlord and tenant, and the Arab cultivator continued in full possession, paying a portion of his annual produce to the new landlord as rent.

Hope Simpson's Report also briefly drew attention to the customary rights of the nomadic bedouin population of Palestine. He referred to the 1922 census figure of 103,351 belonging to five main tribes and 75 sub-tribes, and reported:

> The majority of these bedouins wander over the country in the Beersheba area and the region south and east of it, but they are found in considerable numbers in the Jordan Valley and in smaller numbers in the four other plains. Their rights had never been determined. They claim rights of cultivation and grazing of an indefinite character over indefinite areas. In any solution of the Palestine problem, they are an element which must be recognized. Also in any plans of development, it will be necessary to consider and scrupulously to record and deal with their rights.

Hope Simpson went on to say:

> Complaints have been made by these people in respect of the Jewish settlements both in the Vale of Esdraelon and in the Maritime Plain. Their

substance was that the bedouin custom over many centuries of taking their stock to the north of Palestine during the summer months when there is no grazing in the south, and grazing 'their flocks and herds on the stubbles after the harvest had been carried out, was being obstructed by the new Zionist settlers'.

One of the other recommendations of the Hope Simpson Report was on the need for a more methodical agricultural development system; and Lewis French, formerly Secretary to the Punjab government in India, was appointed in 1932 to take charge of the formation of a Department of Development for the settlement of such landless Arabs as had been displaced as a result of the sale of their lands to Jews and had failed to find other land on which they could establish themselves or some other equally satisfactory occupation.

Little is known of the activities of this department except that an area of 5,740 dunums of irrigated land was purchased by the government in the Beisan sub-district for the resettlement of the landless Arabs, and an economic survey was carried out on the coastal plain to ascertain what areas were capable of close settlement. One thing, however, is certain: the problem of landless Arabs as a whole remained unresolved until the termination of the Mandate in 1948.

The situation in Palestine continued to deteriorate after Hitler came to power in Germany in 1933 and the Jews began to emigrate. In this, the Palestinians saw a new danger.

On 25 November 1935, the leaders of the five Arab parties presented the High Commissioner with a joint memorandum calling for:

a) the establishment of a democratic government;
b) prohibition of the transfer of Arab lands to Jews and the enactment of a law similar to the Five-Faddan Law of Egypt, also known as Lord Kitchener's Homestead Exemption Law of 1912, which gave small cultivators protection against expropriation of their land and livelihood for debt;
c) the immediate cessation of Jewish immigration;
d) the immediate and effective investigation into illicit immigration.[12]

With no positive response from the government to any of these demands, a general strike was declared that disrupted the economic life of the country for six full months, and was followed by an open rebellion until the outbreak of World War II in 1939.

One of the other measures taken by the Palestinian leadership was the establishment of an Arab National Fund whose objectives were to solicit funds for the purpose of purchasing Arab land which otherwise might go to the Jews. The competition between the Arab National Fund and the Zionist organizations was considerable as each party tried to outbid the other. The former used nationalist slogans to assist it in preventing the alienation of Arab land. The forces against the Palestinian farmer were difficult to overcome. These were expressed in a letter published in the local press in the following terms:

> I sell my land and property because the government compels me to pay taxes and tithes at a time when I do not possess the necessary means of subsistence for myself and my family. In the circumstances, I am forced to appeal to a rich person for a loan which I undertake to refund together with an interest of 50 % after a month or two... I keep renewing the bill and doubling the debt... which eventually forces me to sell my land in order to refund my debt out of which I took only a meagre sum.[13]

With the rebellion in progress and rumours of a world war on the horizon, the British government used its old methods of appeasement, appointing another commission of inquiry on 7 August 1936. This time it was a Royal Commission under the chairmanship of Lord Peel, with the following terms of reference:

> To ascertain the underlying causes of the disturbances which broke out in Palestine in the middle of April; to enquire into the manner in which the Mandate for Palestine was being implemented in relation to our obligations as Mandatory Power towards the Arabs and Jews respectively; and to ascertain whether, upon a proper construction of the terms of the Mandate, either the Arabs or the Jews have any legitimate grievances on account of the way in which the Mandate has been, or is being, implemented; and if the Commission is satisfied that any such grievances are well founded, to make recommendations for their removal and for the prevention of their recurrence.[14]

The Report of the Royal (Peel) Commission was published on 22 June 1937. Simultaneously with the Report, the Mandatory government issued a *Statement of Policy*[15] expressing general agreement with the arguments and conclusions of the Commission.

The findings of the Commission with which this Study is concerned were 'the growth of Arab distrust in His Majesty's Government's ability and will to carry out [its] promises' and 'Arab alarm at the continued purchase of Arab land by Jews'.

In the final analysis, the Commission suggested partition of the country between the Arabs and Jews, but this solution was rejected outright by the Palestinian majority and the rebellion was intensified.

One final attempt was made by the British government to solve the Palestine

Part Two: The Land Problem

issue by the publication of a *Statement of Policy*, which became known as the *MacDonald White Paper*, a few months before World War II broke out. The British government declared:

> Neither their undertakings to the Jews nor the national interests of Britain warranted that they should continue to develop the Jewish national home beyond the point already reached.
>
> The Government therefore decided:
>
> 1. That the Jewish national home as envisaged in the Balfour Declaration and in previous statements of British policy has been established;
>
> 2. That to develop it further against Arab wishes would be a violation of British undertakings to the Arabs, and that such a policy could only be carried out by the use of unjustifiable force;
>
> 3. That, therefore, after the admission of a final quota of 75,000 more Jewish immigrants over a period of five years, Jewish immigration should stop;
>
> 4. That during this period of five years, a restriction should be placed on the acquisition of further land by the Jews;
>
> 5. That, at the end of the period of five years, self-governing institutions should be set up in the country.[16]

Legislation covering the restriction of the sale of Arab land to Jews, referred to in paragraph 4 above, was enacted in 1940. For details, see chapter 9, p. 58.

Arab political activities and rebellion came to a complete halt during the war years, apparently in order not to embarrass the British government in its hour of trial, while Zionist terrorist activities increased significantly and eventually resulted in the British government decision to give up the Mandate over Palestine to the newly established United Nations.

Part Three

Palestine After the Mandate

12

Palestine and the United Nations

A. The Plan of Partition (1947)
How the partition of Palestine was accomplished and the intrigue that went on behind the scene to obtain a majority vote in the UN General Assembly is outside the scope of this Study except to repeat, merely for the record, how James Forrestal, then US secretary of defence, viewed 'the methods that had been used by people outside the executive branch of the [US] government to bring coercion and duress on other nations of the General Assembly [as having] bordered closely onto scandal'.[1]

The Arab states vehemently opposed the proposal of partition on the grounds that it was incompatible with law and justice and contrary to the principles of Western democracy relating to the rights of people to self-determination and freedom; and they warned of the inevitable dangers that partition held, not only for the Middle East, but also for the peace and tranquillity of the world.

Nevertheless, on 29 November 1947, the General Assembly, by a majority of only one vote, recommended the partition of Palestine.[2] Sir Zufrallah Khan of Pakistan told the General Assembly after the 'die had been cast': 'We much fear that the beneficence, if any, to which partition may lead, will be small in comparison to the mischief which it might inaugurate.'[3]

The immediate result of the UN Resolution was to deprive the Palestinians of their homeland, their homes, lands, and other possessions, the travesty with which this Study is concerned.

The effect of the General Assembly Resolution on partition, shown on Maps K and L, provided for the establishment of:

a) a *Jewish state* on 56.47 per cent (15, 261, 648 dunums) of the total land area of Palestine of 26,323,000 dunums, although Jewish land ownership in this territory did not exceed 9.38 per cent (1,383,856 dunums); the population of this state would have been 498,000 Jews and 497,000 Arabs with the Jews established as the ruling class contrary to Western democratic principles;

b) an *Arab State* on 42.88 per cent (11,589,868 dunums) in which Jewish land holdings were a mere 0.84 per cent (95,540 dunums), and the Jewish population would have been only about 10,000 souls;

c) an *International Zone of Jerusalem* on about 0.65 per cent (175,504 dunums) of territory.

As can be observed from the above, the injustice of the General Assembly action was to give the Jewish minority the larger portion of the country, including the most fertile coastal and plain lands and all Arab-owned orange groves, leaving the smaller sector with its hilly and arid regions for the Arab majority. It was a travesty of justice which the Arab majority could naturally not accept or even entertain.

After the adoption of its recommendation, the United Nations took no steps to implement the partition in a peaceful manner. It failed to take appropriate and effective measures to safeguard the lives, property rights, and interests of the indigenous Muslim and Christian inhabitants, thereby opening the way to the disastrous events that followed.

The British Mandatory government moved out of the country on 14 May 1948, before the United Nations had made arrangements for the functioning of the commission provided for in the Resolution of Partition. That Resolution stipulated that the UN Commission would take over progressively 'the administration of Palestine as the Mandatory Power withdraws its armed forces'.[4] The country was left in a vacuum with the forces of law and order collapsing. Fighting broke out between members of the Jewish and Arab communities, the former attempting to occupy as much territory of Palestine as possible before the Mandate ended; the latter unarmed, not organized, and without leadership, making feeble efforts to defend their lives, families, and possessions.

The massacre that took place at the village of Deir Yasin on 9 April 1948 in which 250 men, women, and children were killed, served its intended purpose which was to create a general exodus of Palestinians, thereby emptying the land of its people. Menachem Begin, the leader of the Irgun Zvei Leumi terrorist group which organized and carried out the massacre, later wrote: 'The Arabs began to flee in terror... the Jewish forces proceeded through Haifa like a knife through butter... shouting "Deir Yasin".'[5] Later he was reported to have declared: 'The massacre was not only justified, but there would not have been a state of Israel without the victory at Deir Yasin.'[6]

The Arab flight now became a rout, and Chaim Weizmann, first president of Israel, described the situation as 'a miraculous clearing of the land; the miraculous simplification of Israel's task'.[7]

The Arab states were alarmed at what was happening in Palestine and the territories of the neighbouring Arab countries were receiving an influx of fleeing Palestinians. On 14 May 1948, the Secretary-General of the League of Arab States contacted the Secretary-General of the United Nations and informed him that:

> The Arab states were compelled to intervene for the sole purpose of restoring peace and security and of establishing law and order in Palestine [and] to prevent the spread of disorder and lawlessness into the neighbouring Arab lands....[8]

B. The Armistice (1949)

Fighting broke out between the Arab states and the newly created state of Israel. The UN Security Council called for a truce and General Armistice Agreements were concluded between the parties.[9] As a result, the situation of territory was altered to approximately as shown in Table 12.1 (see Map M).

Table 12.1: Palestine at the General Armistice Agreements
Israeli-occupied territory	20,526,000 dunums (or 77.94 %)
The West Bank	5,450,000 dunums (or 20.74 %)
The Gaza Strip	347,000 dunums (or 1.32 %)
	26,323,000

The General Armistice Agreements also provided for the establishment of 'demilitarized zones' in the northern and southern regions of the country and of a 'no-man's land' in the central sector, as shown in Table 12.2.

Table 12.2: Demilitarized Zones under the General Armistice Agreements
1. *In the Israeli-Syrian Sector:*
 a) The northern sector of El-Abisiya-Khan Ed-Duweir area in the extreme north-easterly tip of Palestine — 4,000 dunums
 b) The central sector from Mazari' Ed-Daraja to 'Arab Esh-Shamalina on the shores of Lake Tiberias, and including Jisr Banat Ya'qub — 28,000 dunums
 c) The southern sector, running along the eastern shores of Lake Tiberias from the Arab village of Nuqeib to Samakh, and including the Hot Springs of El-Himma — 36,000 dunums
 68,000 dunums

2. *The Israeli-Egyptian Sector:*
In the El-Auja area, south of Beersheba on the road where it meets with the Sinai Peninsula Province — 260,000 dunums

3. *The Israeli-Jordan Sector:*
Four no-man's land areas:

a) In the Latrun-Bab El-Wad area on the main road between Jerusalem and Jaffa	64,000 dunums
b) In the city of Jerusalem between Israeli and Jordanian lines	900 dunums
	64,900 dunums

c) The site of ex-Palestine Government House on Jabal El-Mukabbir to the east of the City and the ex-Arab College (included in area under (b) above)

d) The Hebrew University area on Mount Scopus (area included in (b) above)

In regard to the City of Jerusalem which was designed to become an 'International Zone' under United Nations jurisdiction, the city was divided as shown in Table 12.3 (see Map N).

Table 12.3: Plan for Jerusalem in the General Armistice Agreement

a) The western (or new city) section under Israeli occupation	16,000 dunums
b) The eastern sector as part of Jordan	2,000 dunums
c) No-man's land including UN headquarters	900 dunums
	18,900 dunums

C. UN Resolutions on Palestine

No problem has occupied the attention of the United Nations and the world more than the Palestine conflict. In summary, resolutions adopted between 1948 and 1984 by the General Assembly and the Security Council,[10] which remain unimplemented, deal with the following subjects:

1. Repatriation of the 1948 refugees and payment of compensation to those who do not wish to return and for damage or losses sustained.

2. The resolution on Israel's admission into the membership of the United Nations Organization prescribed in the preamble that Israel will abide by the United Nations resolutions dealing with territory and the repatriation of those refugees who wished to return and for the payment of compensation to those who did not wish to return and for losses sustained.

3. The Palestine Conciliation Commission was established to protect and safeguard the property of the refugees pending their return, and to identify and evaluate such property.

Part Three: Palestine After the Mandate

4. In Resolution 242 the Security Council called for Israeli withdrawal from territories occupied in 1967, the termination of all claims or states of belligerency, freedom of navigation, the achievement of a just settlement of the refugee problem, and guarantee of the territorial inviolability and political independence of all states in the area.

5. The United Nations confirmed the principle of the inadmissibility of the acquisition of territory by force of arms and called upon Israel to withdraw completely and unconditionally from all the Palestine and other Arab territories occupied since 1967, including Jerusalem, with all property and services intact.

6. Israel was called upon to rescind all measures taken to change the status of Jerusalem.

7. Israel was called upon to take immediate steps for the return of those who fled from the territories occupied in 1967.

8. Israel was called upon to show respect for the inalienable rights of the civilian population affected by the 1967 war in accordance with the Geneva Conventions.

9. The United Nations considered Israeli policies and practices of annexation of the occupied Palestinian territory, including Jerusalem, as in violation of international law and the relevant resolutions of the United Nations.

10. Israel was condemned for violation of human rights in the occupied territories and called upon to desist from repressive practices.

11. The United Nations called for the recognition of the fundamental inalienable rights of the Palestinian Arab people, including the right of self-determination and the right to establish its own independent Arab state in Palestine.

12. The United Nations confirmed the legitimacy of struggle for self-determination for all peoples, including the people of Palestine.

13. The United Nations strongly called on Israel to rescind all measures to annex and/or settle its own citizens in occupied territories contrary to the provisions of the Geneva Convention.

14. The United Nations urgently called for the achievement of a comprehensive, just, and lasting peace, based on the resolutions of the United Nations and under its auspices, in which all parties concerned, including the Palestine Liberation Organization (PLO), would participate on an equal footing.

15. The United Nations adopted a resolution which 'determines that Zionism is a form of racism and racial discrimination'.

13

Israeli Seizure of Arab Property

A. Immovable Property

During 1948, the Israeli authorities enacted measures to legalize the seizure and confiscation of the patrimony and wealth of an entire nation. This outright plunder was described by British historian Arnold Toynbee as 'robbery'.[1]

The three pieces of legislation promulgated were: the Abandoned Areas Ordinance, the Absentee Property Regulations, and the Emergency (Cultivation of Waste Lands) Regulations.

According to these the Israeli authorities empowered themselves to declare a conquered, surrendered, or deserted area to be an 'abandoned area', and conferred emergency powers on the minister of agriculture and on the newly created custodian of absentee property.

The crucial provision in these three regulations was the definition of an 'absentee'. Any person was declared to be an absentee who was, on or after 29 November 1947 (the date of the Partition Resolution): a citizen or subject of any of the Arab states; in any of these states for any length of time; in any part of Palestine outside of the Israeli-occupied area; or in any place other than his habitual residence even if such place as well as his habitual abode were within Israeli-occupied territory.

The effect of this provision was, according to Don Peretz who conducted an extensive study into the property question of the refugees, that:

> Every Arab in Palestine who had left his town or village after 29 November 1947 was liable to be classified as an absentee under the regulations. All Arabs who held property in the new city of Acre, regardless of the fact that they may never have travelled farther than a few meters to the Old City, were classified as absentees. The 30,000 Arabs who fled one place to another within Israel, but who never left the country, were also liable to have their property declared 'absentee' [and] any individual who may have

gone to Beirut or Bethlehem for a one-day visit during the latter days of the mandate, was automatically an absentee.[2]

This writer who left his home in Katamon Quarter of Jerusalem to the safety of the Old City found himself declared an 'absentee' and his property confiscated.

In 1950, the Israelis went a step further by amending the Absentee Property Regulations and enacting a new Development Authority (Transfer of Property) Law which empowered the former to sell to the latter Arab property, and for the Development Authority 'to buy, rent, take on lease, take in exchange, or otherwise acquire property'. But its power 'to sell or otherwise transfer the right of ownership of property' was limited by the following conditions:

a) Such transfer of ownership can be made only to the State, the Jewish National Fund, certain government-approved institutions, or local authorities.

b) 'The right of ownership of land so acquired may not be re-transferred except with the consent of the Development Authority to one of the bodies' in the afore-mentioned categories.

c) Transactions of this nature, involving the transfer or re-transfer of ownership, must be 'effected by decision of the government in each individual case'.

Don Peretz commented that the Development Authority Law was based upon 'a sort of legal fiction'.[3]

The Israeli-enacted laws and regulations are in direct conflict with the provisions of the United Nations Resolution in accordance with which the state of Israel came into existence. The General Assembly, in recommending the creation of a Jewish state on Palestine soil, resolved that Arab rights, including property rights, should be protected; and that 'no expropriation of land owned by an Arab in the Jewish state shall be allowed except for public purposes'. The Resolution stipulated that 'in all cases of expropriation, full compensation as fixed by the Supreme Court shall be paid previous to dispossession'. The Resolution went on to prescribe that the provisions just quoted should, among others, be embodied in the 'fundamental laws of the state, and no law, regulation, or official action shall conflict or interfere with these stipulations, nor shall any law, regulation, or official action prevail over them'. The Resolution further resolved that the aforementioned provision, with others, 'shall be under the guarantee of the United Nations, and no modifications shall be made in them without the assent of the General Assembly of the United Nations'.[4]

Despite these United Nations stipulations and guarantees, the Israeli authorities wasted no time after the establishment of their state to enact laws and regulations and to take official action against the Palestinian Arabs which deviated basically from the terms of the Partition Resolution, the provisions of the United Nations Charter, and more specifically went against the Universal Declaration of Human Rights, to which the state of Israel is a signatory. This Declaration explicitly decrees in section 13(2) that 'Everyone has the right to leave any country, including his own, and to return to his country'; and in section 17(2) that 'No one shall be arbitrarily deprived of his property.'

B. Looting of Arab Movable Property

The general impression is that the only loss suffered by the Palestinian Arabs in their exodus from the country in 1948 was their immovable property which is anyway claimed by the Zionists as part of the ancestral homeland of the Jews. Those who support the Zionist fiction consequently believe that what happened in 1948 was the return of the land to its legitimate rightful owners of four thousand years ago.

While this claim is historically and legally false, little, if anything, is known about the extent, nature, and value of the personal possessions, household effects, goods, and all other movable assets found in the homes, shops, and factories of the Palestinians which were looted by the Israelis.

Henry Cattan, a Palestinian international lawyer and author, describes 'the looting which occurred in Palestine at the hands of the Israelis [as] reminiscent of days gone by prior to the advent of civilization'; and he points out that 'the testimony about the large-scale looting is unanimous',[5] as can be seen from the following quotes:

1. *Count Folke Bernadotte, UN Mediator:*
   Most of the refugees left practically all their possessions behind....
   Moreover, while those who had fled in the early days of the conflict had been able to take with them some personal effects and assets, many of the late-comers were deprived of everything except the clothes in which they stood, and apart from their homes (many of which were destroyed) lost all furniture and assets, and even their tools of trade.[6]

2. *Ralph Bunche, Acting UN Mediator:*
   The bulk of the refugees left their homes on foot at short notice taking little or nothing with them.[7]

3. *Director of the UN Disaster Relief Project:*
   While a few were able to carry personal effects and some money, flight was generally disorderly and with almost no possessions.[8]

4. *Edwin Samuel (son of Sir Herbert Samuel):*
   The next stage in this tragedy was widespread Jewish looting of Arab property.[9]

5. *George Kirk:*
   It was apparently at Jaffa that Jewish troops first succumbed to the temptation to indulge in wholesale looting... and within a few days, Jewish troops were looting the newly captured Arab suburbs of Jerusalem. See Kimche, *Seven Fallen Pillars,* p. 224; Levin, *Jerusalem Embattled,* pp. 116, 135-136 and 226.

   Ben Gurion himself afterwards admitted that the extent to which respectable Jews of all classes became involved was 'a shameful and distressful spectacle (Israel, *Government Handbook,* 5712, London, Seymour Press, 1951-2).'[10]

6. *S.G. Thicknesse* (1949):
   While it is comparatively simple to describe, or investigate, the present state of Arab immovable property, it is quite impossible to give any documented account of the fate of Arab movable property. It is very unlikely that the Government of Israel has assessed the value and extent of the immense amount of Arab property destroyed and looted (systematically as well as unsystematically) by Jewish groups and individuals both during and since the Palestine war.... The total value of such movable property must run into many million pounds.[11]

7. *The Israeli Custodian of Absentee Property:*
   ... the Arabs abandoned great quantities of property in hundreds of thousands of dwellings, shops, storehouses, and workshops. They also left produce in fields and fruit in orchards, groves, and vineyards, placing 'the fighting and victorious community before serious material temptation'.[12]

Henry Cattan comments on the latter statement:

'Temptation' is often an excuse pleaded as a mitigating circumstance by common thieves in criminal prosecutions, but this is the first time that 'temptation' has been put forward by a government as an excuse for the massive plunder of a nation on such a large scale.[13]

14

The Palestine Conciliation Commission

A. Appointment, Tasks, and Responsibilities

On 14 May 1948, the General Assembly recommended the appointment of a mediator between the disputing parties, and Count Folke Bernadotte of Sweden was selected.[1]

In his Report on the question of Palestinian losses and property left behind by the refugees, the UN Mediator stated:

> There have been numerous reports from reliable sources of large-scale looting, pillaging, and plundering, and of instances of destruction of villages without apparent military necessity.
>
> The liability of the Provisional Government of Israel to restore private property to its Arab owners and to indemnify those owners for property wantonly destroyed is clear, irrespective of any indemnities which the Provisional Government may claim from the Arab States.

He then suggested the establishment of a Palestine Conciliation Commission to assess Arab losses.[2]

On 11 December 1948, the General Assembly adopted a further Resolution establishing the Palestine Conciliation Commission as recommended by the UN Mediator and entrusted it with the general task of facilitating a peaceful settlement between the parties. In paragraph 11 of the Resolution, the General Assembly, among other things, instructed the Commission 'to facilitate the repatriation, resettlement, and economic and social rehabilitation of the refugees, and the payment of compensation'.[3]

To guide the Palestine Conciliation Commission in its deliberations, the Secretariat of the United Nations provided its members with two Working Papers.

The first, dated October 1949, dealt with a legal interpretation of paragraph 11, sub-paragraph 1, of General Assembly Resolution No. 194(III) of 11 December 1948 entitled 'Compensation to Refugees for Loss of or Damage to Property to be made good under Principles of International Law or in Equity' (see Appendix I).[4]

The second, dated March 1950, dealt with the question of 'Historical Precedents for Restitution of Property or Payment of Compensation to Refugees' (see Appendix II).[5]

With reference to the first, the Secretariat pointed out that paragraph 11 dealt with two distinct matters: 1. the right of refugees to return to their homes; and 2. the payment of compensation which presents itself under two different aspects, namely: *a)* payment of compensation to refugees not choosing to return to their homes; and *b)* payment of compensation to refugees for loss of or damage to property which under principles of international law or in equity should be made good by the governments or authorities responsible.

As regards *a)*, the compensation claims for property of refugees not choosing to return to their homes was recognized to rest on general legal principles and thus should be considered in the light of the Assembly's decision that refugees should be given the choice either to return to their homes and live at peace with their neighbours, or to receive compensation for their property if they chose not to return.

As regards *b)*, the compensation claims for 'loss of or damage to property which, under principles of international law or in equity, should be made good by the governments or authorities responsible', it was opined that from the legislative history of paragraph 11 of the Resolution, the cases which the Assembly particularly had in mind were those of looting, pillaging, and plunder of private property and destruction of property and villages without military necessity.

The Secretariat pointed out that 'all such acts are violations of the laws and customs of war on land' laid down in the Hague Convention of 18 October 1907, the rules of which, as stated in the Nuremberg Judgement in 1939 'were recognized by all civilized nations and were regarded as being declaratory of the laws and customs of war'. Articles 28 and 47 of the Hague Regulations, annexed to the Convention, the UN Secretariat went on to say, provide *explicitly* that pillage is prohibited. Article 23(g) prohibits destruction or seizure of the enemy's property unless such destruction or seizure be imperatively demanded by the necessities of war. Article 46 protects private property, and Article 56, paragraph 1, provides that the property of municipalities, and of institutions dedicated to religion, charity, and education, the arts and sciences, even when state property, shall be treated as private property. In addition to these rules, Article 3 of the Convention makes the explicit provision – particularly important in this connection – that a belligerent party which violates the provisions of the regulation shall, if the case demands, be liable to pay compensation.

With regard to the second Working Paper, the Secretariat pointed out that its purpose was to furnish some background for the principle of *either* return of the refugees to their homes and reinstatement in the possession of their property *or* for the payment of adequate compensation for their property, and to recall similar historical situations where claims of restitution of property or payment of compensation were put forward.

Such historical background became important during World War II, the Secretariat went on to say, when the question arose as to whether, according to international law, the Allied nations would be able to protect the property interests of the refugees from the Axis countries at the end of the war. At the International Law Conference in London, held in 1943 under the auspices of the Institut de Droit International, the International Law Association, the Grotius Society, and the Allied University Professors' Association, a collection of precedents was presented showing that in similar circumstances in the past, states had in fact safeguarded the interests of foreign nationals against their own governments. Of these precedents, it would appear that the following three, because of their similarity with the Palestine situation, should be mentioned:

1. *Treaty of Nummeguen of 17 September 1678 (Article XXI)*
    All the subjects of the one part as well as the other, both ecclesiastic and secular, shall be re-established in the enjoyment of their honour, dignities, and benefices of which they were possessed of before the war as well as in all their effects, movables and immovables and rents upon land seized and occupied from the said time as well as on the occasion of the war as for having followed the contrary party. Likewise in their rights, actions, and successions fallen to them, thought since the war commenced without nevertheless, demanding or pretending anything of the fruits and revenues coming from the seizing of the said effects, immovables, rents, and benefices till the publication of this present Treaty.

2. *Treaty of London of 19 April 1859 (Article XVI)*
    The sequestrations which have been imposed in Belgium during the troubles, for political causes, on any property of hereditary estates whatsoever, shall be taken off without delay, and the enjoyment of the property and estates above mentioned shall be immediately restored to the lawful owners thereof.

3. *Peace Treaty with Turkey of 10 August 1920 (signed but not ratified), Article 144*

(on the compensation of Armenian refugees who had fled from Turkey)
> The Turkish Government recognizes the injustice of the Law of 1915 relating to Abandoned Properties (*Emwal-il-Metroukeh*), and of the supplementary provisions thereof, and declares them to be null and void, in the past as in the future.
>
> The Turkish Government solemnly undertakes to facilitate to the greatest possible extent the return to their homes and re-establishment in their businesses of the Turkish subjects of non-Turkish race who have been forcibly driven from their homes by fear of massacre or any other form of pressure since January 1, 1914. It recognizes that any immovable or movable property of the said Turkish subjects or of the communities to which they belong, which can be recovered, must be found. Such property shall be restored free of all charges or servitudes with which it may have been burdened and without compensation of any kind to the present owners or occupiers, subject to any action which they may be able to bring against the persons from whom they derived title.

The Secretariat then dealt with the question of indemnities to be claimed on behalf of Jewish sufferers during World War II. The Jewish claim, it pointed out, was presented in a book entitled *Indemnities and Reparations* by Nehemiah Robinson and published by the Institute of Jewish Affairs of the World Jewish Congress in 1944.

The author dealt with the compensation problem from all its aspects, and in the end discussed the case of those who remained in or would be willing to return to their former homeland. With respect to this category of victim, the author makes a strong case that the United Nations should intervene on their behalf. There was, in his opinion, nothing revolutionary in this suggestion, for many cases of such intervention were known. The minorities treaties forced upon a number of states after World War I were just this sort of intervention. To carry out these suggestions, the author argues for the establishment of internationally organized courts or similar bodies, empowered to make decisions and execute them, irrespective of the residence of the respondents and the location of the goods. Only internationally organized jurisdiction and execution would guarantee full impartiality and justice, and would shorten the delays inherent in the usual system of two or three court instances in every case, the author pointed out.[6]

After World War II was over, most of the former Axis and Axis-occupied countries enacted laws in favour of such persons who had been persecuted or forced to leave their countries. Suffice to quote two examples:

Firstly, in the US occupied zone of Germany, a General Claims Law was passed on 10 August 1949 which provided:

Those persons shall be entitled to restitution pursuant to this law who, under the National Socialist dictatorship (30 January 1935 to 8 May 1945), were persecuted because of political convictions or on racial, religious, or ideological grounds and have therefore suffered damage to life and limb, health, liberty, possessions, property, or economic advancement.

Secondly, in the British zone of occupation in Germany, Law No. 59 entitled 'Restitution of Identifiable Property to Victims of Nazi Oppression' was passed on 12 May 1949. Article 1 provided:

The purpose of this Law is to effect to the largest extent possible the speedy restitution of identifiable property (tangible and intangible) to persons whether natural or juristic who were unjustly deprived of such property between 30 January 1935 and 8 May 1945 for reasons of race, religion, nationality, political views, or political opposition to National Socialism.[7]

Finally, the Working Paper made reference to the partition of India into the states of India and Pakistan which, it stated, bore some similarity to the problem of the Palestinians. In that case, bloodshed, riots, massacres, and murder caused minority groups on both sides to flee, but they were not divested of their property as was the case of the Palestinians. The matter was amicably settled to the satisfaction of both parties.

The Palestine Conciliation Commission paid little attention, if any, to the guiding principles of the two Working Papers of the Secretariat, and in the absence of any progress, the General Assembly adopted yet another Resolution on 14 December 1950 in which it reiterated its directions to the Palestine Conciliation Commission instructing it 'to make such arrangements as it may consider necessary for the assessment and payment of compensation in pursuance of paragraph II of Resolution 194(III)...' and to take measures 'for the protection of the rights, property, and interests of the refugees'.[8]

Had the Commission taken the action expected of it under this Resolution, the need for the present comprehensive Study at this belated date might have been avoided.

B. The 'Global' Assessment of Palestinian Losses (1951)

The Commission recruited the services of Mr J.M. Berncastle, who, until the termination of the Mandate in 1948, held the post of Chief Land Valuer in the Department of Land Settlement. This writer served in the same department as Land Officer in charge of the assessment of urban property and the classification of rural lands for taxation purposes. Other duties performed by the latter were to maintain a record of land ownership between Arabs and Jews and the periodical publication of such material in a *Village Statistics*, the last of which appeared in 1945 and is extensively relied upon in this Study.

Mr Berncastle made a general survey of the situation in a matter of a few months and came up with a 'global' assessment of the losses in immovable property of those Palestinians who fled the country or were expelled in 1948. His findings were that the extent of the so-called 'abandoned' Arab land was 16,324 square kilometers (or 16,324,000 dunums) out of a total area of 26,320 square kilometers, and estimated its approximate value at a total of £P 100,383,784.

In regard to movable property, such as the contents of homes, business premises, motor vehicles, livestock, etc., Mr Berncastle estimated Arab losses at £P 20 million. In explaining how he arrived at this figure, he said that he was unable to make a valuation of all such property since some categories of movable property do not lend themselves to a global evaluation, and since he had no means of knowing what property the refugees took with them and what they left behind.[9] He, therefore, confined himself to an attempt to estimate the approximate value of the movable property which belonged to the refugees before their exodus.[10]

The question of evaluation of immovable property as well as that of the losses sustained by the refugees in movable property and from other causes is dealt with at length in Part Five of this Study.

The Arab states did not challenge the figures of the 'global' assessment because the whole principle of compensation was entirely unacceptable to the Palestinians who demanded repatriation to their homes and payment of compensation only for the losses sustained by them in movables and others. With nothing further for the Commission to do in the Middle East, its members retired to New York and established an office at UN headquarters to carry out the identification and valuation of Arab immovable property.

In December 1952, the writer was invited to take charge of the office as Land Specialist. In 1956, Frank E. Jarvis, an Englishman recruited in England, took over with the title of Land Expert.

C. Identification and Valuation of Individual Immovable Property (1964)

The duties of Mr Jarvis were confined merely to the identification and valuation of individually owned Arab immovable property. He was not required to deal with Arab losses in movable property or even to differentiate between refugees wishing to return to their homes and those who did not wish to return and were willing to accept compensation. In 1964, Mr Jarvis completed his limited assignment and his Report was published by the Palestine Conciliation Commission in April of that year.[11] Attached to his Report were two schedules:

one in respect of urban areas indicating the total areas of vacant sites, the net annual value of buildings, and the quinquennial year of assessment; the other dealt with rural lands.

Summarized, these two schedules arrived at the conclusions given in Table 14.1.

Table 14.1: Valuation of Arab Immovable Property

Urban Areas (see Appendix III)[12]
  Vacant sites   26,490 dunums
  Net annual value   £P 217,707

Rural Areas (see Appendix IV)
1. Total area by sub-district (excluding Beersheba sub-district)
  Settled land: (RP/1)   2,720,211
          (RP/3)   2,156,484
          Sub-total   4,876,695 dunums
  Non-settled land: (RP/1)   2,473,880
          (RP/3)   423,844
          Sub-total   2,977,724 dunums
    Total   7,874,419 dunums

2. Individual Arab-owned land (RP/1)[13]
  Settled land   2,720,211
  Non-settled land   2,473,880
  Sub-total   5,194,091 dunums

3. Non-individual Arab-owned (RP/3)
  Settled land   2,156,484
  Non-settled land   523,844
  Sub-total   2,680,528
    Total   7,874,419

4. In regard to the Beersheba sub-district, the Land Expert stated the position to be as follows:
  Cultivable land:
  Non-bedouin   64,000
  Bedouin   1,811,000
  Uncultivable land   10,580,000
    Total   12,455,000 dunums

5. Summarized, individual Arab-owned land was stated to be as follows:
  Israeli-occupied territory   5,194,091
  (excluding Beersheba sub-district)
  Beersheba sub-district   1,875,000
    Total   7,069,091 dunums

In regard to the valuation of Arab property listed in Form RP/1, the Land Expert goes into great detail in explaining the method he used, but he did not summarize his findings in his final Report. An examination of his records revealed very little of value. The question of valuation will be dealt with at length in Part Five.

D. Commentary on Assessment and Identification of Ownership

In both the 'global' and 'identification and valuation' instances the methods used were deficient and the results fell short of the facts. Neither complied with the directives of the General Assembly in Resolutions 194 (III) and 394 (V), while the guiding principles in the two Working Papers of the UN Secretariat (see Appendices I and II) were completely ignored.

There are many reasons — apart from the political implications involved — why the Palestinians cannot accept the declared findings of the Land Expert. These reasons make it imperative for the present Study to be undertaken. Some of them are as follows.

First, the Land Expert, an Englishman and a stranger to Palestine, lacked the local knowledge required to enable him to understand the Arab mentality, habits, customs, and dealings in matters pertaining to property. He applied principles which may be applicable in England, and logical and palatable to the English mentality, but were certainly foreign to Arab customs and practices; and although some of these principles were introduced into Palestine legislation by the British Mandatory government, they remained on paper and at no time did the Arab inhabitants buy or sell property on the basis of the net annual value as assessed for taxation purposes. Ironically, the same British formula of 16 2/3 per cent used by the Land Expert had been introduced earlier by the Israeli authorities into Israeli legislation dealing with the liquidation of seized Arab property because it appeared plausible to the Western mentality and practices, and would consequently show Israel in a favourable light.

Second, the Palestinians were not invited to participate in the work of identification of property and assessment of the losses sustained by them as a result of their flight, expulsion, and dispossession although they demanded in 1956 to be allowed to do so. It is only natural for people involved in so serious a tragedy to be invited to take part in any assessment of their losses in order to protect their interests. To place the whole operation in the hands of one individual with no knowledge of the Arabs and their way of life is, to say the least, questionable.

Third, the Land Expert was obliged to rely entirely on the Palestine government land registers in the case of settled land; the urban and rural property tax records in the case of non-settled land; and partly on the registers of deeds in the case of land sales. To compile a record of ownership on the basis of tax records is unrealistic and cannot be accepted as just or conclusive.

Fourth, the Commission was well aware that neither the land registration nor the land taxation documents contained any record of buildings existing on the land in rural areas. Notwithstanding, no action was taken either with the Israel authorities to permit inspection on the ground or by any other means, to obtain descriptions of these buildings. This omission has been carried into the work of the Land Expert and makes his findings obviously incomplete.

Fifth, the Palestine Conciliation Commission was requested by the UN General Assembly to safeguard the rights, property, and interests of the refugees pending final settlement, but took no measures to fulfil its obligations. A proposal put forward in 1961 for the appointment of a custodian of Arab property, while it was passed by a majority vote in the Special Political Committee, failed to obtain the two-thirds majority required in the General Assembly because of devious and unethical Israeli tactics. The matter was raised again and again in subsequent years, but each time the draft resolution failed to obtain the necessary votes due to United States opposition.

The appointment of a custodian would have meant the protection of the property rights of the refugees from abuse and seizure and the payment to them of the income derived therefrom; the refugees would not then have had to depend on international charity for their livelihood. On the other hand, the work of identification and valuation can be seen as a step towards the ultimate liquidation of the Palestine problem by means of possible payment of compensation. This the Palestinians utterly reject.

Sixth, the Land Expert had no authority to decide what is Arab-owned land and what is not. His responsibilities were to identify the position as it existed in 1948 without tampering with the figures in one way or another. The last *Village Statistics* published by the Palestine government in 1945 gave the total area of Arab-owned land in Palestine (excluding the Beersheba sub-district) as 12,766,524 dunums; J.M. Berncastle, first Land Specialist of the Palestine Conciliation Commission, estimated the area to be 16,324,000 dunums; and the UN Special Committee on Palestine (UNSCOP) quoted a figure of 22,374,547 dunums. But the Land Expert, who obviously had access to these three sources, placed individual Arab-owned land at only 7,069,091 dunums. He arrived at this figure by considering that land classified in the 'uncultivable' non-taxable category was outside the realm of Arab ownership.

The present criticism of the work of the Land Expert could have been avoided had the Palestine Conciliation Commission not turned down in 1953 the reasonable proposals put forward by the writer in his capacity as Land Specialist to the Commission. The proposals would have made it possible to bring the work of the Land Expert closer to reality for the record, if nothing else. The suggestions were:

1. to publish the schedules of identification of immovable property in the refugee camps and other conspicuous places in order to give property owners the opportunity to examine the entries and to submit, on a prescribed form, any objections, amendments, or additions they might have;

2. simultaneously, to ask the refugees to submit, on another prescribed form, particulars of the other losses sustained by them as a result of their flight, expulsion, and dispossession;

3. to establish a panel of land valuers whose duty would be to divide the country into zones of approximate equal capital value in order to assist the Land Specialist in the valuation of the capital values of lands and buildings belonging to those refugees who chose not to return to their homes. A plan of the division envisaged by the writer has been reproduced as Map O and has been used as a basis of price values in Part Five.

Consequently, the work of the Land Expert as it stands at present is regarded – admittedly through no fault of his – as incomplete and containing omissions which could have been avoided had the Palestine Conciliation Commission fulfilled its prescribed role by acting in the best interests of the refugees. Some of the more important reasons for the discrepancies are explained hereunder.

a) Settled Rural Land

Particulars regarding name of owner, area, share, and location, entered in the form of Identification of Immovable Property (RP/1), were extracted from the microfilms of the land registers prepared by the Palestine government and can be accepted as accurate; and in regard to the tax category, this was taken from the rural property tax distribution list prepared by the Official Valuer.

The tax category classification was based on data collected by the government surveyor in the field in advance of land settlement operations. The surveyor was required to provide a description of the land to enable the Official Valuer to alter the tax category to the smaller unit of parcel. As has already been pointed out, the land surveyor's lack of sufficient knowledge of the English language to differentiate between the meaning of the words 'cultivable' and 'cultivated' and 'uncultivable' and 'uncultivated', upset the existing system of classification of land still further.

In regard to 'fixtures' on the land, such as buildings and trees, at first these constituted a part of the land register and could be owned and registered separately from the land; but in 1937, this procedure – inherited from the Ottoman regime and still prevalent in certain Arab countries – was discontinued. While some of the earlier land registers contain reference to buildings and trees, these are considered inadequate for the assessment of property values. Buildings constructed after the completion of land settlement operations are not recorded anywhere.

As regards the common or communal lands of the village, these were mostly registered at land settlement in the name of 'The High Commissioner for the time being in trust for the Government of Palestine'.[14] But this did not mean that such lands were actually government-owned. They were held nominally by the government for the benefit of the inhabitants of the village as a whole and used by them for the grazing of flocks and firewood gathering. No interference was known to have existed in these practices for many centuries past.

b) Non-Settled Rural Land

Particulars of such lands were taken from the rural property tax distribution list. Unlike settled land where the tax distribution list was prepared by the Official Valuer block by block and parcel by parcel, and which gave accurate names of owners, shares, areas, and location, the village tax distribution committee was given by the Official Valuer a schedule showing, by fiscal block, the total area by tax category; and it was up to the committee to distribute the tax among the reputed owners.

For generations, the Arab farmer had been used to the tithe system whereby the amount of tax, not the area, was the criterion. Under the new arrangement, the tax distribution committee continued the age-old procedure of concentrating on distributing the amount of tax levied among the landowners paying little attention to the area of each holding.

Since buildings as such were not taxable, the tax on a built-up area was calculated on the basis of the area of the plot of land on which the building stood. Buildings in orange groves and fruit orchards, as well as others constructed in the vicinity of towns and cities, were not liable for the payment of tax as such and were therefore not included in the tax records. Buildings constructed on non-taxable land are not recorded either as land or as building.

The *wa'er* (common or communal land) of the village, being non-taxable, was not generally included in the tax distribution list; and where such land was included, this was done administratively by the revenue staff for the purpose of balancing the totals of the block and village. The Land Expert admitted that such land, even where a record had been kept of it, was not included as in individual Arab ownership.

c) Urban Areas

The Land Expert used the greater part of his report to explain the valuation system he adopted in both urban and rural areas. But valuation of 'abandoned' Arab property has never been agreed to by the refugees. Any comment therefore on the methods used for arriving at the net annual value does not imply acquiescence in the objectives of the valuation. The following comments are made merely for the record:

(i) The chairman of the assessment committee was usually a surveyor of the Department of Land Settlement which was responsible for the assessment of property under the Urban Property Tax Ordinance. His duties included responsibility for the compilation of a 'field valuation sheet' for each parcel in which he entered, merely for statistical purposes, a detailed description of the property as well as his own estimation of the capital value. Since such data varied from one area to another and had no effect on the assessment which was based on the rental, the practice was later discontinued, but the older figures continued to appear in the unrevised records.

(ii) With regard to the assessment of the net annual value itself, there was a constant tug-of-war between the two official and two non-official members of the committee – the former anxious to make the assessment correspond to reality to avoid criticism by their superior, the latter, on the other hand, trying to keep the assessment down to the bare minimum to appease the taxpayer. The outcome was that the basis of assessment differed considerably even for identical buildings.

(iii) The Arabs of Palestine never approved of the Mandate and felt that they were being colonized against their will by a foreign power which was introducing Zionism, a doctrine whose ultimate aim was to take the country over. Political co-operation with the government was rejected throughout the period of British administration; and in the case of assessment of property for taxation purposes, the attitude of the Arab members on the committee was to keep assessments down to the bare minimum.

(iv) The assessment of property leased to government usually followed the rent actually paid because the committee could find no way of avoiding an assessment which did not correspond to the actual rent. Such assessments can be regarded as representing 'the rental at which the property might be expected to let from year to year in the open market' but there were too few of them to be used as guidance.

(v) Other rented property was under-assessed even in cases where the committee had evidence of the actual rental. The non-official members of the committee – and in some cases the owners themselves – would present the illogical argument that the government was not a partner in the ownership of the property. The compromise between the official and non-official members was usually in favour of the owner.

(vi) The assessment of property occupied by the owner was mostly nominal on the grounds that he was not receiving any financial benefits from it. Such assessments were nowhere close to the market value or the assessment of rented property.[15]

(vii) In regard to vacant land, the net annual value was based on the supposed capital value which the land might be expected to get in the open market. Here again, the assessment came nowhere near the true capital value on the grounds that the owner was not benefiting from the vacant land and should not be penalized by higher taxes, even though the potential value of the land might have been increasing from year to year. The Arabs believed – and out of experience rightly so – that in placing high taxation on vacant land, the government was compelling them to sell their lands to the Jews.

(viii) The Land Expert, in his calculations, appears to have overlooked certain important factors; for example, during World War II and until 1948, the law stipulated that rents in Palestine should not exceed their pre-war levels. Meanwhile, the value of the currency depreciated and the costs of construction tripled and quadrupled. Naturally, this meant that the net annual value in the tax records did not represent a true picture of rental values.

(ix) Finally, it should be pointed out that in cases where buildings changed hands, it was not unusual for the buyer to arrive at the sale price he was willing to offer by calculating the market value of the land plus what he considered would be the building cost of the construction thereon. Prior to 1939, the cost per square metre of construction was between £P 2 and £P 4, depending on the quality of the material and the work. After the war, labour and costs of construction went up to between £P 20 and £P 25 per square metre. Hence, the net annual value which continued to be based on pre-war figures could in no way be linked with the actual value of the property.

d) Land Sales

The Land Expert stated that he relied on another source to arrive at his valuation of individual Arab property, the land sales which took place during the years 1946 and 1947.

Legally, the parties to a land sales transaction were required to notify the registrar of lands at the time of registration of the amount of the sale; the registrar, if he was not satisfied with the price declared, had the authority to make his own assessment of the price on which to levy his land registration fee.

In practice, however, except in the case of land purchased by the government, and this usually took place through a case in the courts, the parties to the transaction invariably colluded to quote a far lower figure than the amount which actually changed hands in order to pay a lower registration fee. It was not uncommon for the registrar to overlook what was going on.

Despite the passage of forty years since the problem first arose, the Palestinians remain adamant in their refusal to part with their rights and interests in their homeland. There is, therefore, no useful purpose served in attempting to confine Palestinian losses in 1948 to a monetary assessment of their individual immovable property. Much more is at stake. A record of all types of losses suffered by the Palestinians with a corresponding monetary valuation is essential in order to inform future Palestinian generations and the rest of the world, and in the hope that some day justice will prevail. This is done in Part Five of this Study.

E. Blocked Bank Accounts

The Palestine Conciliation Commission did, however, succeed in its endeavours for some settlement with the parties in one respect. This was in the release of the blocked accounts in banks in Israeli-occupied territory and the transfer of safe deposits and safe custody items.[16]

In 1952, the Israeli government agreed to a gradual release of blocked accounts. By 1953, the Israelis had turned over for payment by the banks a total of £P 740,408. By 31 July 1965, a total of £P 2,801,009 of the blocked accounts of refugees and absentee owners had been released under the 1954 release scheme. Under the extended release scheme, as of 31 July 1965, £P 46,391 had been paid to owners of blocked accounts.

As regards figures covering the status of the release scheme for safe custody items and the contents of safe deposit lockers as of 31 July 1965, the position was reported to be as shown in Table 14.2.

This matter will be discussed further in Part Five.

Table 14.2: Results of Israeli Release Scheme

	total	released	balance
Boxes and parcels	60	48	12
Shares, bonds, etc.	800	274	526
Palestine government bearer bonds	434	323*	102
Safe deposit lockers	178	143	35

* To this figure should be added some 275 Palestine government bearer bonds released under the extended release scheme.

Part Four

Examination and Revision of United Nations Documents

15

Identification of Arab Land Ownership

A. General Remarks

The difference between the work of identification of Arab immovable property carried out by the Land Expert of the Palestine Conciliation Commission and the present Study is that, whereas the former – as pointed out earlier – dealt with property of *individual* Arabs and ignored all other factors, this Study covers, in addition to individual land ownership, what the Palestinians believe is the extent of their legitimate property rights and holdings in the total lands of a village, including the communal or common lands registered or recorded as public or state domain, in the name of the *mukhtar* (headman) or the High Commission, regardless of category of land tenure or system of taxation. It should be noted also that lands acquired and buildings constructed from general revenues by the Mandatory government, such as the *Tegart* police fortresses, harbours, post offices, telephone exchanges, hospitals, schools, railway buildings and tracks, etc., belong to the people of the country, and the share of the Palestinians in them must not be ignored.[1]

The lands of a village during the Ottoman regime and British administration periods were those which fell within boundaries which the villagers had established – and the government of the period had accepted – as the territory comprising that village; and all lands within these confines were deemed by the indigenous inhabitants to belong to them and to their descendants individually and collectively, with the government exercising certain controls as guardian over specific categories of land on behalf and for the sole benefit of the villagers, but with no rights of absolute ownership or authority of disposal. Hence, the inhabitants did not question these controls, and in fact welcomed any improvements which the government might carry out in the marginal lands of the village.

It should be emphasized that there is a great difference between nations where the government is of the people, by the people, and for the people, and countries where the inhabitants live under colonial rule or mandate. In regard to the first, both the government and the people form one indivisible unit in the knowledge that the government is of the people and is working in the best interests of its own country and its inhabitants as a whole. But, in the case of Palestine, both the Ottoman Turks and the British Mandatory government were foreign colonial powers of different stock, aspirations, and ambitions to the Palestinian inhabitants; they were imposed upon the country against the will of the majority by force of arms; and their presence and interests were principally concerned with domination and exploitation. Therefore, both foreign powers were constantly opposed, sometimes to the extent of open rebellion; and, to put it mildly, they were there in what might be described as a form of compulsory trusteeship pending the attainment of independence by the colonized in one way or another.

Furthermore, the legislation affecting land enacted by the Mandatory power was not in the best interests of the indigenous inhabitants but was designed to serve the policy of the Jewish national home as defined in the Balfour Declaration and the Mandate. The Arab inhabitants had no say in the administration of their homeland, and any protests against the passage of laws detrimental to Arab interests were ignored.

It is therefore ludicrous to assume that the Ottoman Turks and the British Mandatory actually held certain lands in Palestine in the sense that the Turkish and British governments held land in their own countries; that the Israeli government could be regarded as the successor of the British Mandatory; and that automatically Israel became the legitimate owner of land registered or recorded as state domain, public, or in the name of the High Commissioner to the exclusion of the inhabitants of the villages concerned.

The argument about Israel's so-called succession is even less convincing because the Israelis failed to act towards the Palestinians as a trustee or guardian. Instead of protecting the rights and interests of their Muslim and Christian wards, they expelled and dispossessed them of their individual homes and lands in a manner which has been described as 'robbery with a legal coating'.

In regard to land recorded as state domain, the above arguments are reinforced by a statement made by Sir John Hope Simpson who visited Palestine as far back as 1930 to advise the government on Jewish immigration, land settlement, and development. He confirmed the fact that the lands of a village belonged to its inhabitants and that government was duty-bound to develop such lands as are not privately owned for the benefit of the village as a whole. He pointed out:

> It is clear, however, that of the land which remains with the government at the present time, the area is exceedingly small, with the exception of tracts

Part Four: Examination and Revision of UN Documents

which, until developed, are required in their entirety for the maintenance of the Arabs already in occupation. It cannot be argued that the Arabs should be dispossessed in order that the land should be made available for Jewish settlement. That would amount to a distinct breach of the provisions of Article 6 of the Mandate.[2]

The Hope Simpson statement disposes of any doubt that the lands within the boundaries of a village — whether registered or recorded in the names of individuals, the *mukhtar*, or government — belong to the village individually and collectively, and that no outside element is entitled to claim or acquire property rights in them. This fact was not disputed by the Palestine government for, in its reply to the Jewish Agency's demand for the allocation of state domain for Jewish settlement, it stated:

> The question of the availability of state domain has been examined by government in some detail; and it has been shown that, although there are large areas of state domain, it cannot be assumed that government is in possession of extensive tracts of land which are lying idle. In fact, in respect both of land to which government has a settled title and land claimed by government as state domain but still subject to settlement of title, there is very little that is not already put to some useful purpose.

After this statement, the government gave an analysis of land (settled and non-settled) which it claimed to be, at the end of 1943, state domain occupied under the specified circumstances [see Table 15.1].

With regard to the communal or common lands of the village classified in the *matruka* category and used by the villagers for cattle-grazing and woodcutting purposes, the government regarded these as 'assigned for the inhabitants generally of some village or group of villages' and stated that 'the control of government over these lands was limited to that necessary to enable the public to benefit from them in the way intended'.[3] It should be pointed out that no part of such land could be sold. Thus, any land transaction which took place between Arab and Jew was confined to the individual parcel being sold and in no way transferred to the purchaser any rights which the seller might have in the common lands of the village.

However, even if it were to be admitted that the Mandatory government was the physical owner of any property in the country, logic decrees that on the termination of the Mandate, the property and assets of the departing foreign authority should be divided between the legal inhabitants in proportion to either their numbers or holdings, and not taken over lock, stock, and barrel by the minority group to the exclusion of the majority.

Table 15.1: The Occupation of State Domain

Government land used for public purposes:	
Forests, railways, roads, etc.	839,553 dunums
Earmarked for communal or public use	4,713
Unoccupied, including 'paper' claims	84,699
Available and offered for short-term lease	20,082
Uncultivable sand, marsh, or rocks	167,429
Arabs:	
Occupied under tenures derived from the Turkish regime	181,691
Occupied under long-term lease	1,222
Occupied under short-term lease	62,522
Leased to other than Arabs or Jews	3,249
Jews:	
Leased for long periods	175,088
Leased for short periods	2,432
Total	1,542,680[4]

One more point to remember is that even if the Zionist religious and historical claim to Palestine as their sole 'homeland' were to be admitted, the Israelis still would not have the right to dispossess, forcibly and without compensation, the indigenous Arab inhabitants of their property in order to settle in their place aliens, whose only connection with Palestine is through religion. Sovereignty over a country is one thing, title to property is another, and the former cannot superimpose itself on the latter. The principle of property ownership, of inheritance, and of holding, is generally the same throughout the world, and to make an exception of Palestine is a travesty of justice which cannot, and should not, be tolerated by the civilized world.

With regard to the Beersheba sub-district, which constitutes about one-half the territory of Palestine, the *Village Statistics* shows a figure of 1,936,380 dunums (or 15.39 per cent) as in Arab ownership; 65,231 dunums (or 0.52 per cent) in Jewish ownership; public lands as 2,279 dunums (or 0.02 per cent); and the bulk of the area, 10,573,110 dunums (or 84.07 per cent), as 'uncultivable' land. The fact that the ownership of the last was not described as either state domain, public, or government, is significant, and should now be explained.

The population of the Beersheba sub-district outside the limits of the town and its vicinity consisted entirely of nomads whose system of existence relied on the tribe, sub-tribe, and clan. The individual as such had no separate personality where land was concerned; he was regarded merely as a member of the larger

Part Four: Examination and Revision of UN Documents

group for cultivation purposes. Furthermore, according to tradition and custom, the bedouins had a god-given right to the land, to roam over and cultivate it as they wished, and this practice was not interfered with by either the Turkish regime during four hundred years of occupation or the Palestine administration during the thirty years of British Mandate. The bedouins saw no reason why they should limit themselves to any particular area or locality or have it registered under a special name or mode. In fact, the Palestine government was reluctant to extend the application of the land (Settlement of Title) Ordinance and the Rural Property Tax Ordinance to the Beersheba sub-district because it was aware of the stiff resistance, if not hostility, it would meet from the bedouin population. The bedouins continued to cultivate the land without interference or interruption, according to practices established by their ancestors from one generation to another, and if this limitless period of possession did not give them the right of ownership, it is not clear what would.

With regard to land classified as 'uncultivable', in which the government presumed that it might have some title, it should be noted that the whole area was traditionally recognized as belonging to the bedouins for grazing their flocks without any restrictions or hindrance, while certain nomad tribes from Jordan and the Sinai Peninsula exercised for centuries customary rights over pasturage during certain periods of the year. All these rights could not, and were not, ignored in law or in practice. This situation was recognized by the Palestine government in 1946 when it stated that 'it is not safe to assume that all the empty lands south of Beersheba or east of Hebron, for instance, are *mewat* (dead land).'[5]

The greatest difficulty encountered in this Study – also experienced by the Land Expert – has been to obtain information about the number and description of Arab buildings which existed outside the limits of towns and in and outside the built-up areas of villages. As already stated, the identification of property carried out by the Land Expert was based on the land registration and land taxation records of the Palestine government; because legislation did not require registration or taxation of buildings as such in rural areas, details thereof were obviously excluded from both the government records and the UN identification forms.

The number of such buildings constructed between the end of World War II, when building restrictions were lifted, and 1948 is considerable. But since these buildings were scattered, it was not normally government policy at the time to extend the limits of urban and village built-up areas to include new constructions, as much agricultural land which lay in between them would have been included.

The situation was not unknown to the government. In fact, a year before the British intention of terminating the Mandate over Palestine was announced, consideration was being given to the extension of the limits of urban and village built-up areas, the taxation of buildings constructed outside the boundaries of such areas with an assessed net annual value above a certain amount, and a general revision of the classification of rural lands to meet the considerable development and changes which had taken place after World War II. These proposals were dropped due to the impending departure of the British Mandatory from the country.

This Study must therefore be considered as inadequate regarding details of property and land of high potential value as building sites outside the limits of urban areas and within and outside village built-up areas (category 4) in rural areas.

To give a more accurate picture of the situation as it existed in 1948, in the writer's considered opinion – as the officer in charge of the assessment of property in urban areas and the Official Valuer under the Rural Property Tax Ordinance during the period of the Mandate – it would not be unreasonable or unrealistic to assume an increase of 25 per cent in the total area of both classifications. This approach conforms with the principles used during the period of the Mandate when consideration was being given to enlarging urban or village built-up areas to include developments and land with high potential as building sites.

Since value rather than area is involved in this Study, the matter will be dealt with in its appropriate place in Part Five.

Another problem of some magnitude encountered in this Study is connected with land planted as orange groves (categories 1 and 2) which contains buildings, artesian wells, water-pumping facilities, water canals or pipings, and property fencing forming a part of the establishment of an orange grove. In almost all cases, the capital value of these additions is greater than the value of the fallow land. There is no record of the extent or value of these extras either in the land and taxation records of the Palestine government and consequently none exists in the identification schedules of the Land Expert of the Palestine Conciliation Commission. Hence it will be necessary to assess the value of an orange grove on a basis which will take into account the situation as it was presumed to have existed on the ground in 1948.

B. Examination of the Work of the Land Expert

An extensive examination of the statistical data of the Land Expert of the Palestine Conciliation Commission relating to Arab-owned land in the territory occupied by Israel under the terms of the General Armistice Agreements of 1949 revealed the following:

1. As stated earlier, identification was confined to property indi-

Part Four: Examination and Revision of UN Documents

vidually owned by Arabs and entered on form RP/1. All other property was considered non Arab-owned and entered on form RP/3, but no indication was given as to what property was owned by Jews, and what was owned by non-Jews, what land was in communal or common ownership, public, or uncultivable, in order to define the extent of the holdings of each category. These were all lumped together according to tax category as outside Arab ownership.

This approach conflicted with Palestine government's record of land ownership by Arabs and Jews, as set out in its publication entitled *Village Statistics, 1945*.

The result was a considerable reduction in the extent of Arab-owned land in Palestine, reinforcing the Jewish-Zionist allegations that the country was always empty of inhabitants except for a few roaming nomads, joined after the immigration of Jews began in 1920 by strangers from the surrounding Arab countries who wished to participate in the economic blessings which the Jewish newcomers had brought with them.

2. In the case of the lands of villages divided by the armistice demarcation line, those falling on the Israeli side were roughly estimated; in others, the line was ignored giving the impression that all the lands of that village fell into Israeli-held territory.

3. The UN documents contained much striking out of figures, amendments, and more amendments, making it impossible in many instances to be sure of the final figure intended.

4. No distinction was made between villages whose inhabitants fled and villages some of whose inhabitants remained in their homes in 1948. A list of the latter was attempted but their properties were dealt with together with those who fled.

The writer, as the former Official Land Valuer of the Palestine government with responsibility to maintain a record of land ownership between Arabs and Jews, was obliged to examine personally the extracted information village by village in an attempt to reconstruct the position as he knows it existed in May 1948. Since the *Village Statistics* of the Palestine government is the more accurate and authoritative source, adjustments on that basis have been made to the findings of the Land Expert where the figures of the two sources were found to conflict. The approximate results appear in Appendices V, VI, VII, and VIII.

C. Revised Identification of Ownership Basis of Immovable Property

To meet the arguments and comments in the preceding pages, the system adopted in conducting the Revised Study was as follows:

1. To consider an Arab village or a Jewish settlement as a distinct independent entity and all the respective inhabitants – whether Arab or Jewish – as the owners of all the lands thereof and held in individual and collective ownership.

2. Where a wholly Arab town or village, or a wholly Jewish town or settlement, contained land registered or recorded as state domain, public, or government, these lands were entered as part of the Arab village or Jewish settlement as the case may be.

3. In the case of a mixed urban area with a significant Arab or Jewish ownership, land registered or recorded as state domain, public, or government, was divided between the two communities in proportion to their numbers.

4. In the case of an Arab village containing Jewish holdings, land classified as common or communal land and state domain was considered to belong to the original inhabitants.

5. Land held under government lease by the two communities was entered as Arab or Jewish as the case may be.

6. Roads, waterbeds (*wadis*), cemeteries, etc. (category 16B), have been included in the respective Arab village or Jewish settlement.

D. Conclusion

Guided by the principles enumerated above, the Revised Survey reviews the situation as it existed in Palestine prior to the date of the adoption of the UN Partition Resolution of November 1947 as it was altered in 1949 by the terms of the General Armistice Agreements concluded between the neighbouring Arab states and the Israelis.

Excluded from the Revised Survey are: (1) the territory of the West Bank (5,450,000 dunums); (2) the territory of the Gaza Strip (347,000 dunums) (see Appendix V); (3) Jewish settlements and Jewish-owned land in Arab towns and villages (1,615,000 dunums) (see Appendix VI); the three areas total 7,412,000 dunums.

The remaining land area of about 19,000,000 dunums (out of Palestine's total land area of 26,323,000 dunums) was dealt with by the Land Expert of the Palestine Conciliation Commission and is covered by this Revised Survey. As stated earlier, both surveys include the lands of villages some of whose inhabitants remained in their homes in 1948. The number of these, after having been joined by certain members of their families under the United Nations reunion scheme when hostilities ceased, was estimated to be in the neighbourhood of 170,000 persons (see Appendix VII).

The conclusions of the Revised Survey are approximately as shown in Table 15.2.

Table 15.2: Land Ownership in Palestine according to the Revised Survey

Urban Areas (Appendix VIII 'A')

1. Population

	1944	1948
	300,000	330,000

2. Total areas

in towns	109,628
Arab lands in Jewish settlements	2,293
	111,921

Rural areas (excluding Beersheba s/d)	Arab villages (App.VIII [B]) (dunums)	Jewish settlements (App. VIII [C]) (dunums)	total (dunums)
1. Citrus & banana groves (Cats. 1-3)	131,217	1,632	132,849
2. Village built-up areas (Cat. 4)	21,085	75	21,160
3. First-grade land (Cats. 5-8)	470,784	888	471,672
4. Second-grade land (Cats. 9-13)	2,926,471	11,212	2,937,683
5. Third-grade land (Cats. 14-15)	443,901	640	444,541
6. Uncultivable land (Cat. 16A)	2,376,622	1,324	2,377,946
7. Roads etc. (Cat. 16B)	83,161	—	83,161
	6,453,241	15,771	6,469,012
Beersheba s/d (Appendix VIII [B]):			12,450,000
		Total	18,919,012
Grand Total:		Urban	112,000
		Rural	18,919,000
			19,031,000

The Land Expert of the Palestine Conciliation Commission quotes in Appendix IV a figure of 5,194,091 dunums as individually owned Arab land (RP/1) in the territory occupied by Israel, excluding the Beersheba sub-district, as against the figure of 6,469,012 dunums in Table 15.2. The difference of

1,275,000 dunums may not be so great, but to consider the lands of the Beersheba sub-district of 12,450,000 dunums as non-Arab is unrealistic and unacceptable for the reasons explained.

In conclusion, apart from the political considerations involved, the Revised Survey shows that the Arab indigenous inhabitants of Palestine still own about 92 per cent of the total territory of Palestine which they regard as their homeland, against a Jewish land ownership of roughly 8 per cent (see Appendix VI).

Part Five

An Economic Assessment of Total Palestinian Losses in 1948

Written by Dr Atef Kubursi

16
Palestinian Losses: an Overview

A. Introduction

The decision of the United Nations in 1947 to partition Palestine without taking appropriate and effective measures to safeguard the lives, rights, and interests of the indigenous inhabitants of the country resulted in one of the great tragedies in the annals of the modern civilized world.

Four decades have now gone by and the situation has worsened. The Palestinian Arabs, who now number over four million, are scattered throughout the world, but about half of them are living either in refugee camps on the charity of the United Nations and international philanthropic institutions or under the rule of an unsympathetic and alien people.

A homeland is much too precious to be assigned a monetary value. No financial award, however large, could compensate fully for its loss. However, the Arab wealth in Palestine which was confiscated by the Zionists was substantial, and an accurate assessment would serve at least to indicate the magnitude of the calamity that has befallen the Arabs of Palestine. Not all aspects of the calamity can readily be measured in monetary terms. None the less, major psychological and human suffering may be assigned monetary values indirectly, just as the Jews were compensated by the Federal Republic of Germany (under the terms of the *Wiedergutmachung* programme, *Wiedergutmachung* meaning 'to make something good again') for the crimes of the Nazis. The following message is a quote from the *Wiedergutmachung* document:

> ...After the war, the occupation powers in Germany enacted laws in their individual zones which restored property confiscated by the Nazis to the original owners (mainly Jews). These laws were restricted to real property. They did not encompass personal damage to the victims of Nazi persecution – physical and psychological suffering, or unjust deprivation of freedom, or injury to a person's professional or economic potential. Nor

did these laws provide for assistance to the widows and orphans of those who had died as a result of Hitler's policies.[1]

The parallel with the Palestinian situation is evident. It is easy to see that if for 'victims of Nazi persecution' 'victims of Zionist persecution' was substituted a similar situation should apply to the Palestinians.

An attempt will be made here to assess both the physical and psychological Palestinian losses. Although this is not the first such attempt, it is the most comprehensive and precise assessment, based on valuation methods, data, and procedures that were not available to previous studies.

B. The Theoretical Basis for Compensation[2]

Economics is predicated on the fundmental postulate that human beings when unimpeded would seek to arrange their economic affairs in such a way as to obtain the greatest possible satisfaction. Any arrangement that does not produce this outcome is inadequate and will soon be displaced by one yielding a higher level of satisfaction (or 'utility'). That is, individuals will take advantage of any exchange of opportunities to achieve the greatest possible satisfaction where their willingness to trade is matched exactly by their opportunity to do so. Circumstances outside the objective conditions of the market that preclude such an outcome imply lower levels of utility – loss of welfare, as it is usually called. The size of this loss is indicated by the difference between the levels of satisfaction attainable in the two circumstances. Alternatively, it is equal to that monetary compensation that would permit the higher level of utility to be realized.

This conception of economic loss also suggests that social losses are the sum total of individual losses. This is true, however, only if all goods are *private* goods (those goods any individual's consumption of which reduces what is available to others in the market). In the case of *public* goods (those goods of which one individual's consumption does not diminish their availability to other members of the society), special adjustments would have to be made.

Essential to this analysis is the specification of each individual utility function and the determination of the effect on utility of the forced or imposed situations that lead to loss of welfare. Individual utility indices differ not only with respect to the arguments that define them, they also differ with respect to their nature. Typically all things that contribute to utility are included as arguments of those indices. This would make the list too long for any useful analysis. Alternatively, we may group these arguments under the following headings: private goods, public goods, individual psychological needs, and social psychological needs. Private goods include all the commodities and services desired and purchased by consumers; public goods include education, health services, etc.; individual

Part Five: An Economic Assessment of Total Palestinian Losses

psychological needs cover a wide spectrum comprising tranquillity, safety, absence of pain, family cohesiveness, etc.; and social psychological needs include national identity, cultural activities, etc.

The indices are predicated on two main assumptions:

1. that individuals shall be considered better off if they are in a position of their own choosing. Since we define utility as that which individuals attempt to maximize, it follows that they will choose rather more than less utility. An increase in utility can then be regarded as synonymous with being better off.

2. that individuals' utility depends entirely on the volume of commodities and services they consume and on the needs they satisfy. They will always be assumed to choose to consume more, or at least not less, of a commodity and to satisfy more of their needs rather than less.

This manner of defining the welfare function severely limits the form which social value judgements can take. If the welfare of society is held to depend upon the utility levels of the members of society, and upon nothing else, then the only further social value judgements to be made concern the welfare significance of each individual's utility index. In a totally egalitarian society each person's utility would count equally, though some form of interpersonal comparability of utility indices in cardinal terms would be necessary to give substance to this judgement. Alternatively, it might be held that some members of society are more deserving than others, and their utility indices would be weighted more heavily in the welfare function.

Whichever form is specified for the social welfare function, it is clear that individual losses are translated into social losses and the social welfare function can be used to assign valuation of these losses. The concept of compensation as developed by Hicks and Kaldor is a case in point.[3] The concept underlying the compensation principle is that if a change in a situation would result in some persons being better off and others worse off, those who gain could compensate the losers in such a way that on balance everybody would be better off.

Consider the representation of an individual's utility map in Figure 1. The numéraire (or money) is measured on the vertical axis and the commodity X on the horizontal. Consider first an individual who receives income OM_2 and purchases OX_1 of X at price P_2, and attains equilibrium at point A on U_I. If price is reduced to P_1, he will purchase OX_4 of X, and be in equilibrium at point B on U_{II}. The rise in his utility level from U_I to U_{II} is the increase in his satisfaction; the problem is to express this in money. Seen differently, the individual is maximizing his utility at point B and a forced situation (a more binding budget constraint) is imposed on him which forces him to point A on U_I. His loss of satisfaction is the difference between U_I and U_{II} and the challenge is to assign a dollar value to this loss. This can be done easily along the following lines developed by Hicks.

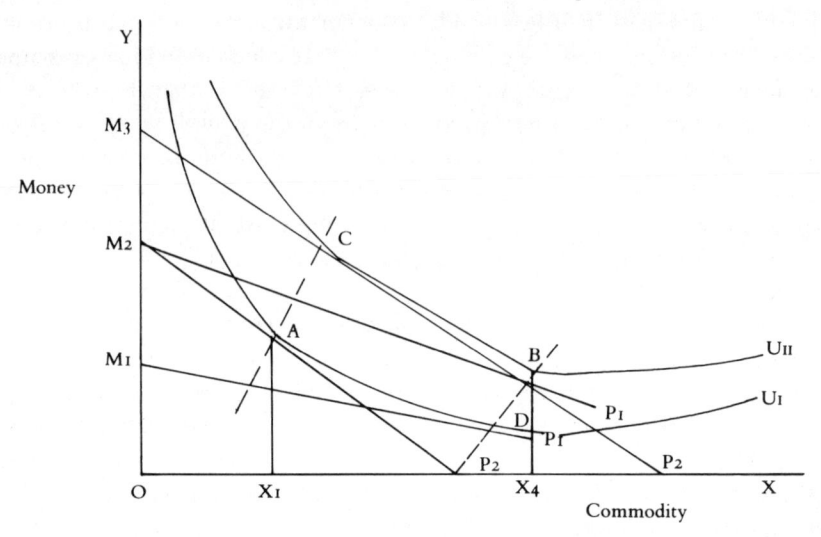

Figure 1: The Principle of Compensation

Construct a line with slope P_1 tangent to U_I (at D) to intersect the ordinate at M_1. If the individual income is reduced by M_1M_2 at the same time as the price is reduced, he will be just as well off at D as he was at A. The amount M_1M_2 is therefore a monetary measure of how much better off he is if the price falls and there is no change in his money income. Alternatively, M_1M_2 represents the financial compensation to be paid to the individual to take him back to his original utility level before the new imposed situation. M_1M_2 is called the 'compensating variation' for the price fall or for the forced situation.

Compensation is therefore synonymous with indemnification in the legal meaning of the undoing of damage done and losses suffered.

Total indemnification means, in essence, a return to a situation which existed before the loss was incurred. If it is done by way of restitution, the old situation is restored in specie. If it is done wholly or partially by way of compensation, the consequences of the damage are liquidated although the old situation is not restored in the true sense of the word.[4]

It is clear, however, that such a return to the old situation is possible only by way of total restitution or total indemnification and only when changes in the general financial, economic, social, and demographic situations are taken into account.

Part Five: An Economic Assessment of Total Palestinian Losses

C. Previous Valuations of Palestinian Losses and their Deficiencies
A list of Arab losses in Palestine should include the following items:
1. *Immovable property (real estate)*
This includes all types of land (rural and urban) whether privately or collectively owned, publicly recorded premises (airports, harbours, railways, buildings, schools, etc.), churches and mosques, etc.
2. *Movable property*
This includes a wide spectrum of commodities and assets ranging from consumer durables (appliances and furniture) to the tools and implements of industry, to human skills and education.
3. *Lost opportunities*
The income forgone due to loss of jobs and complementary inputs over a finite horizon constitutes a legitimate grievance that should be included in a comprehensive assessment of losses.
4. *Psychological damage*
Of special concern to human welfare are security, safety, identity, and self-realization. Any denial of these psychological 'commodities' would diminish the individual's equilibrium and happiness. In technical economic jargon it would force individuals to lower levels of utility.

As stated before, there is no financial compensation that could make up for the loss of Palestine and/or for the death of the countless Palestinians who resisted eviction by the Zionists in 1948. However, the United Nations Palestine Conciliation Commission attempted to assess these losses; but it considered only a very small sub-set of these losses, and assigned the meagre sum of about £P 120 million in 1951.[5] It is desirable and necessary, therefore, to re-examine the methodology used by the UN Land Specialist in 1951 and the work of the UN Land Expert in 1964,[6] and to re-evaluate these losses, adding to them the major components identified by broader considerations. We are emboldened to use this approach by a number of considerations: a) the economic theoretic justification along the lines of the Hicks-Kaldor compensation principle noted above; b) the settlement of Jewish claims by the Federal Republic of Germany, which included compensation for psychological damage and for denial of social needs.

Several other attempts have been made to identify and assess Palestinian losses. The UN Land Specialist's evaluation was indeed a major contribution to this literature. However, it was, as noted above, restricted to a small sub-set of the losses and assigned exceptionally low values to them.[7] There is also the study of the Arab Higher Committee (AHC) which was first published in Cairo in 1955 under the title *Palestinian Refugees: Victims of Imperialism and Zionism* and then in Beirut under the title *Statement* in 1961. The AHC assessments were substantially higher than those of the UN study and included several additional

121

non-real estate assets (e.g. factories, jewellery, livestock, public transport facilities, etc.). Nevertheless, these estimates failed to include lost opportunities of income generation, the depletion of human capital stock, innumerable public and private assets (schools, airports), and private and social psychological damage. While it represented an improvement on the UN Land Specialist's study, it fell short of computing the full range of losses and used below-market indices in the evaluation of real-estate losses.[8]

A third assessment was carried out by the Arab League Expert Group and produced similar results to those of the AHC.[9] Finally, Professor Yusif Sayigh attempted to redress some of the omissions in the preceding assessments in his book *The Israeli Economy* (1964). His coverage was more extensive, his indices more realistic and generally in conformity with economic principles, and his analysis was more perceptive and original than all the preceding attempts. Again Professor Sayigh's estimates, although more extensive than preceding studies, did not cover the full range of lost assets and missed opportunities, and disregarded psychological damage, etc. Besides, some of the figures used by Professor Sayigh were pure estimates which need confirmation by collation with the results of hard surveys, particularly those relating to real estate.

D. Plan of Part Five

A brief outline of Part Five of this Study is outlined here to set the tone for the development of our conclusions. The next chapter provides a detailed review of all past attempts at evaluating Palestinian losses. Chapter 18 presents a general overview of the Federal Republic of Germany's repatriation and compensation schemes for the victims of Nazi persecution as well as a reworking of the present value of these schemes in terms of today's prices. Chapter 19 examines the typology of Palestinian losses excluding land. Chapter 20 is devoted exclusively to the evaluation of rural and urban lands and housing. This is our major contribution and it was, therefore, felt necessary to devote a full chapter to the subject.

Finally, Chapter 21 concludes with an overall estimate of the losses and an analysis of their significance and the way they differ or relate to earlier estimates.

E. A Synopsis of the Results

Full compensation for Palestinian material losses would amount to a sizeable total of £P743 million in 1948 prices. Translating this total into 1984 prices in United States dollars brings it to $92,000 million.

The inclusion of human capital losses raises the total compensation to $147,000 million. Indeed, the inclusion of compensation for psychological damage and pain, following the FRG compensation schemes to Jews, would raise this total to a staggering $170,000 million.

17

Alternative Assessments of Palestinian Losses: an Analytical Review

A. Introduction

The question of Palestinian losses in 1948 has engaged the interest and passions of many scholars and institutions. Several attempts were made at assigning a monetary figure to these losses. The results differed markedly from one study to the other, the differences invariably being related to which areas of the spectrum of losses were covered and what prices were used to express physical property in monetary terms. Common to all the early attempts is the total acceptance of the principle of fairness of the Palestinian claims and the absence of 'hard' data to substantiate the calculations.

In this chapter, we intend to present these early attempts in a critical manner, realizing, however, the constraints and difficulties under which those estimates were made. We begin with the UN assessment.

B. The UN Palestine Conciliation Commission Estimates of the Value of 'Abandoned' Property

1. A Historical and Analytical Review

On 10 August 1951 the governments of Egypt, Jordan, Lebanon, Syria, and Israel were invited to send their representatives to a conference to be held in Paris, beginning on 10 September 1951. In its invitation the Palestine Conciliation Commission (PCC) pointed out that, during the period following the adoption by the UN General Assembly of Resolution 394 (V) on 14 December 1950, it had continued to seek solutions to problems arising out of the Palestine situation. Pursuant to the General Assembly's directive, the PCC had undertaken to carry out the obligation imposed upon it under paragraph 2 of that Resolution by creating its Refugee Office for the purpose of making certain practical arrangements for the solution of refugee problems.

Palestinian Rights and Losses in 1948

During the Paris Conference, the PCC submitted three concrete proposals on the question of compensation in particular and the refugee problem in general. The two relevant ones include:

1. that the government of Israel agree to the repatriation of a specified number of Arab refugees who could be integrated into the Israeli economy and who wish to return and live at peace with their neighbours;
2. that the government of Israel accept the obligation to pay, as compensation for property abandoned by those refugees not repatriated, a global sum based upon the evaluation reached by the PCC's Refugee Office; that a payment plan, taking into consideration the government of Israel's ability to pay, be set up by a special committee of economic and financial experts to be established by a United Nations trustee through whom payment of individual claims for compensation would be made.

Before making its proposal relating to payment of compensation, the PCC had undertaken to estimate the value of property abandoned by Arab refugees. The Commission's Refugee Office prepared this evaluation in accordance with General Assembly Resolution 394 (V).

The Office estimated that the extent of the land abandoned by Arab refugees was 16,324 square kilometers, of which 4,754 square kilometers were cultivable. The demilitarized areas and the Jerusalem no man's land were not included in this estimate. The term 'land' denoted immovable property; buildings and trees were regarded as integral parts of the soil on which they stood and valued together with it. The Office estimated the total value of this abandoned land at roughly £P100 million, made up as shown in Table 17.1.

Table 17.1: UN Refugee Office Estimate of the Value of Abandoned Land

Type of land	Palestine pounds
Rural lands	69,500,000
Urban lands, excluding Jerusalem	21,500,000
Jerusalem lands	9,000,000
Total	100,000,000

This estimate of immovable property was based on the value of the land for its existing use, as measured by the revenue which it would produce. In estimating the revenue, however, the Refugee Office used the Urban and Rural Property tax assessments of 29 November 1947, which was adopted as the date of valuation. No account was taken of *potential development value and no value was placed on uncultivable land adjacent to urban areas.*

Part Five: An Economic Assessment of Total Palestinian Losses

In approaching the problem of making a global valuation of Arab refugee movable property, the Commission's Refugee Office concluded that it was unable to make a valuation of *all* such property, since some categories of movable property did not lend themselves to global evaluation and since the Office had no means of knowing what property the refugees took with them and what they left behind. It confined itself to a feeble attempt to estimate a first-order magnitude of movable property which belonged to the refugees before their exodus. Although the Office took into account a long list of movable property, such as industrial equipment, commercial stocks, motor vehicles, agricultural implements, livestock, and household effects, it came up with very unrealistically low figures. The first method used was the percentages adopted at the time of the Turkish-Greek exchange of populations in the case of predominantly rural and predominantly urban populations. This calculation gave a total of £P 21,570,000. The second method involved the use of a percentage of national income of the Arab population of Palestine under the Mandate. It was considered that this should be 40 per cent, which gave a valuation of £P 18,600,000. Finally, the aggregate value of the various categories of movable property owned by Arabs under the Mandate was used. The proportion of this total representing the refugee property gave a figure of £P 19 million. An average approximate figure of £P 20 million was ultimately used by the Commission.

Thus, the Refugee Office arrived at the total sum of £P 120 million as representing the global value of total Arab movable and immovable property lost by the Palestinians who had to leave their country. This the PCC considered to constitute a debt by the government of Israel to the refugees.

The valuations made by the Refugee Office suffer from a number of deficiencies that were recognized by the Commission itself and that explain their subsequent moves to conduct a comprehensive identification and evaluation of immovable properties. The Commission's first Land Specialist John Berncastle made his evaluation at short notice without any fieldwork and on the basis of many assumptions that were known to be weak and inapplicable.

The Commission continued its attempt to come up with more defensible assessments. In 1952, it set up at UN Headquarters in New York, an office for the identification and valuation of Arab refugee property, and in May 1954 it established a sub-office in Jerusalem to speed up the programme.

The Commission subsequently dispatched its Land Specialist to Jerusalem to recruit the necessary staff and to set up and take charge of an organization designed to complete the identification project by the middle of 1957. The Office set up by the Land Specialist in Jerusalem began its operations late in December 1955. By the end of August 1957, the bulk of the identification process had been completed by Frank Jarvis, the newly appointed official with the title of Land Expert.

As regards the valuation tasks, the Land Expert made use of the sale prices realized for rural land in certain sub-districts and urban property in a number of towns. This work was resumed at Headquarters in June 1959, by the Commission's Office.

2. *Identification of Immovable Property*

The technical details of the identification and valuation processes are of considerable importance to this Study as they bear directly on the methodology utilized in subsequent sections. We begin first with the identification process.

The identification work essentially involved preparing record forms for each parcel of land owned by an Arab individual including partnerships, companies, and co-operatives. Other similar forms were prepared for parcels of land owned by religious bodies. Lists were also prepared of land recorded as state domain or Jewish, and of other parcels not owned by Arab individuals.

Record forms were also prepared for parcels falling under the following categories: 1. parcels which were recorded as state domain but which were subject to transfer to Arabs upon their payment of the unimproved capital value of the land (*badl mithl*); 2. parcels which were recorded as state domain but which had been occupied by Arabs for many years and which the Mandatory government regarded as let to the occupiers under implied leases; 3. parcels which were recorded as state domain and which were let to Arabs under long-term leases; 4. parcels which were owned by non-Arabs but which were let to Arabs on long-term leases.

The identification was extended to cover the 'no man's land' in the Jerusalem-Ramle area and the 'demilitarized zones' in the northern region. The border villages, those whose lands were cut by the armistice lines, presented the Commission with a special problem. Where the Land (Settlement of Title) Ordinance had been applied to a village, those parts which fell within Israel were included. In villages where the Ordinance was not applied, all Arab-owned land was included in fiscal blocks cut by the line.

The Commission made no attempt to distinguish between properties belonging to Arabs who were refugees and those who were not, as it believed that to make such a distinction would have been outside its scope.

3. *Valuation*

Unlike most commodities, a unit of land (a dunum) can vary widely in value from one location to the next. For instance, figures from £P 2 to £P 100, 000 per dunum were quoted in official Palestine government correspondence in 1946. The Commission recognized these difficulties and attempted to assign to each parcel its market value as of 29 November 1947. This date was chosen because it was that of the UN General Assembly decision to partition Palestine and the beginning of the exodus of refugees. In the Commission's opinion, land values were reasonably stable in Palestine, at that time. The market value was deemed to be the sale value of comparable land as specified in official records of realized sales between 1 January 1946 and 29 November 1947.

Obviously, only a small proportion of properties were sold during this period of approximately two years and it was found necessary to devise some means for relating the values established for properties which were sold to similar properties in the same location which were not sold. For this purpose, the Commission used tax categories of land in rural areas and net annual values as assessed for urban property tax in urban areas as the most reliable guides to grouping different parcels of land into categories of equal values.

4. Valuation Difficulties with the PCC Approach
An investigation of this magnitude can hardly be without deficiencies. The Commission's study is, however, particularly deficient on two counts. First, the use of sale data to reflect market values: although theoretically correct, in practice these numbers understate by a substantial margin, as we shall show later, the true value of the land. Buyers and sellers have a strong incentive to understate the value of the sale to escape the payment of taxes and registration charges. A correction is needed to take account of this widespread practice. Perhaps more damaging is the fact that the Commission did not use the sale values provided in the records to make its final evaluations and consequently its estimates are measurably below the declared value and far below the true market value.[1]

Second, more than 450,000 record forms for properties owned by Arabs were prepared. Since no computerized account of these data was generated, it is difficult to believe that this massive body of data could have been processed without significant data management problems and errors. Furthermore, there were many difficulties encountered with respect to built-up areas in rural land, especially in that the procedure of registration under the Land Ordinance was discontinued at an early date in the case of 'built-up areas' of villages. There were consequently no data on whether any particular parcel in these areas comprised a building or was only a bare site. There were about 540 Arab villages where this difficulty was encountered. The most glaring difficulty in this regard was, however, the treatment of land in the Beersheba sub-district. The Beersheba sub-district contained about 12.5 million dunums, 2 million of which were regarded as cultivable and were liable to payment of tithe (the Rural Property Tax Ordinance did not apply to this sub-district). The Commission, however, was unable to find the tithe records. As a consequence only a few parcels were included in the valuation and a major chunk of this sub-district was omitted from the total valuation of Arab land lost to Israel.

C. The League of Arab States Estimates[2]

The estimates of the Land Specialist of the Refugee Office of 1951 were glaringly low and inaccurate. In response to this, the League of Arab States commissioned an expert group to re-evaluate the losses. A total of £1,900 million sterling in 1948 prices was tallied from losses of land, livestock, factories, machinery, money, jewellery, vehicles, etc. A summary of the categories is presented in Table 17.2.

Table 17.2: A Summary of Arab Losses in Palestine

description	value £ million sterling
Citrus plantations (including buildings, tools, machinery, fixtures, etc.)	100
Banana plantations	1
Olive groves, fruit plantations, and other trees	275
Good cultivable lands	30
Cultivable lands of medium grade and grazing lands	220
Property in Arab towns and villages (lands, buildings, establishments, cattle, poultry, factories, machinery, etc.)	1,100
Movable property (including furniture, fixtures, money, jewellery, foodstuffs, agricultural products, commodities, means of land and sea transportation, such as vehicles, boats, and fishing craft, etc.)	200
Securities and deposits in banks (blocked)	6
Insurance companies' funds (blocked)	1
Grand Total	1,933

Source: *Arab Property and Blocked Accounts in Occupied Palestine*, Cairo, League of Arab States, 1956, p. 20.

The valuation of losses by the League of Arab States followed a detailed methodology which involved identifying the land lost according to its category of use and scarcity value. First, Arab-owned land was defined as in Table 17.3.

Part Five: An Economic Assessment of Total Palestinian Losses

Table 17.3: A Schedule of Arab-Owned Land in the Occupied Section of Palestine (Area in Metric Dunums)

	Arabs	Jews	government	others	total
Town areas	36,225	74,564	32,182	12,834	155,805
Built up areas	19,635	41,607	343	1,102	62,687
Citrus plantations	132,449	139,728	1,156	4,815	278,148
Other fruit trees	373,719	90,076	17,250	6,021	487,066
Cultivable lands	4,990,950	939,106	140,109	57,589	6,128,024
Uncultivable lands and forests	1,928,989	190,685	11,164,019	22,600	13,306,293
Grand total	7,481,967	1,474,766	11,355,059	105,231	20,418,023
Percentage	36.64	7.23	55.61	0.52	100.00

Source: Ibid., p. 21.

The next step was to identify the amount and nature of land seized by Israel from the Palestinian refugees. The resulting amounts and categories are listed in Table 17.4.

Table 17.4: Palestinian Refugee Property by Area and Use

	dunums
Citrus plantations	120,800
Banana plantations	1,000
Olive groves and other trees	530,600
Cultivable lands	5,000,000

The revenues of these lands were then estimated at over £47.5 million sterling, made up as shown in Table 17.5.

Table 17.5: Revenue from Arab-owned Land

	value in £ sterling
Revenue of citrus plantations, olive and fruit trees	14,750,000
Rents of Arab cultivable lands exploited by Israelis	10,000,000
Rents of Arab buildings, homes, and commercial establishments, etc.	22,750,000
Total	47,500,000

The revenue figures were derived from official Mandatory government publications. In the case of citrus plantations, annual exports in the mid-1940s were around 8 million cases, the cost of each case being 42 shillings,[3] of which 12 shillings constituted the expenditure per case, leaving 30 shillings as the net revenue per case. This results in a net total revenue of around £12 million sterling. The remaining £2,750,000 sterling are derived from olive trees and other fruit trees: the 300,000 olive trees on Arab lands yielded a yearly output of 6,000 tons and the net revenue per ton of olive oil was estimated then at £250 sterling or a net income of £1.5 million sterling; the remaining amount of £1.25 million sterling was derived from the sale of other fruits.

The average rent per dunum of cultivable land was put at £2 sterling per year. Thus, the rent on the 5 million dunums of cultivable land is £10 million sterling.

The League of Arab States estimated that the number of Arabs expelled from their homes exceeded one million people. Of this number, 300,000 were city dwellers – Jaffa 85,000, Lydda and Ramle 45,000, Acre 15,000, Haifa 70,000, Safad 15,000, Beisan 7,000, Majdal 10,000, and about 50,000 inhabitants in Jerusalem, Tiberias, Samakh, and other towns. Assuming five people to each family, the 300,000 city dwellers comprise 60,000 families living in 60,000 homes, with an average rent of not less than £230 sterling per year. Thus, the total rental loss on these houses is approximately £14 million. Another 700,000 refugees fled their rural homes and villages. Those comprise 140,000 households, with an average rent of £50 per annum. The net result is a total of £7 million. At the same time, these one million refugees had no less than 10,000 shops and commercial premises, and given an average rent of at least £175 per year, the total rental revenue was £1,750,000 per year. The total rental income lost is then £22,750,000.

The League of Arab States study also gave a thorough account of the funds of Palestinians frozen in occupied Palestine and the manner in which these funds were expropriated and tampered with by the Israeli authorities.

The total value of Arab deposits, during the Mandate, at Barclay's and Ottoman Banks exceeded £6 million sterling, whereas deposits at other foreign banks were estimated at about £500,000. On 20 July 1948, the Israeli authorities ordered the freezing of credits belonging to refugees in all the banks in occupied Palestine. The frozen accounts included demand deposits, savings accounts, guarantee funds, financial instruments of all sorts, jewels, and other valuables in safety deposit boxes. The experts of the Palestine Conciliation Commission estimated that these funds amounted to £6 million sterling and were owned by about 10,000 Palestinians. They included the assets of the Arab Bank and the Arab National Bank.[4]

The Palestine Conciliation Commission called on Israel to release the funds

Part Five: An Economic Assessment of Total Palestinian Losses

and organized a committee of experts of all parties concerned to work out the details. As noted above, the Israeli authorities were reluctant to release the funds; when they finally gave way to international pressure, they released only £1 million sterling. Even then, the Israelis imposed a compulsory 10 per cent national loan on every account and the Israeli custodian charged exorbitant fees for administering the released funds.[5]

The League of Arab States study presented two specific examples:

a) An Arab refugee in Amman received from Barclay's Bank in Jaffa a statement dated 1 February 1953, of his account at the termination of the British Mandate in Palestine on 15 May 1948. The statement showed that the amount of the deposit was £832 sterling on 15 May 1948. This sum was then converted into Israeli pounds. About £83 sterling were deducted for the compulsory national loan (i.e. 10 per cent of the deposit), £231 sterling were deducted as expenditures incurred by the department of the Israeli custodian of the property of Arab absentees (i.e. 28 per cent of the deposit). The remainder, £518, was converted into Israeli pounds. The actual value received by the refugee amounted in 1953 to £52 sterling.

b) Another refugee residing in Lebanon received a statement of his account from Barclay's Bank of Haifa showing a balance of £3,420 as of 15 May 1948. Of this amount, £342 was deducted on 12 June 1952 for the compulsory national loan. Another £2,577 was paid to the Israeli custodian. The net amount received by the refugee was less than £500.[6]

Although the League of Arab States study revealed a more comprehensive picture of Arab losses and gave careful consideration to the economic processes substantiating the Arab claims, it suffered from a number of serious deficiencies. First, the land figures were sketchy and insufficiently detailed. There was no account of how the total dunum figures were obtained and the description of land use was not precisely related to tax categories of rural land or net annual values of urban property. Second, there was a weak relationship between the net revenue figures on rental incomes from property and their asset (capital) value. For instance, if the prevailing real interest rate at that time was 4 per cent, an asset with a net income per year of £47 million should have been valued at £1,175 million. The total asset values of these lands were put at £626 million only in the League's study. Third, the revenue and rental income figures, although admittedly ingeniously derived, were generally arbitrary and differ from the real figures.

D. Professor Yusif Sayigh's Estimates

The 1956 study of the League of Arab States contained a significant amount of economic analysis; however, the level and validity of this analysis were limited. A more thorough analysis was undertaken by Professor Yusif Sayigh in his book on the Israeli economy.[7] Although the assessment and valuation of Arab losses in Palestine were not the major focus of his study, Professor Sayigh provides a detailed enumeration and a tentative methodology for conducting such a valuation.

Professor Sayigh insists that the loss of Palestine is principally a moral loss whose dimensions and costs exceed by far the loss of property and money. He divides the losses into the following categories:

1. *Personal Property*
(i)   houses
(ii)   hotels, shops, restaurants, offices, etc.
(iii)   furniture and fixtures of commercial concerns
(iv)   transport vehicles
(v)   furniture and household effects
(vi)   livestock
(vii)   bank deposits and guarantees
(viii) land
(ix)   stocks and inventories
(x)   office furniture and fixtures

2. *Arab Share of Public Property*
(i)   government buildings
(ii)   roads, railway lines and stations, ports, and airports
(iii)   public infrastructure – schools, hospitals, and laboratories
(iv)   water network
(v)   furniture and fixtures
(vi)   forests, grazing land, and public land
(vii)   Negev land
(viii) natural resources

3. *Income Opportunities*
This category includes the loss of employment and income opportunities from a going concern with high growth potential. Special attention was directed to the losses of professionals and skilled workers.

4. *Transitional Costs*
This includes the economic costs of the exodus and the repercussions on the economies of the West Bank and the Gaza Strip resulting from their separation from the economy of Palestine.

Part Five: An Economic Assessment of Total Palestinian Losses

5. *Separation Costs*
This category includes the economic burdens shouldered by the neighbouring Arab states as a consequence of having to absorb huge numbers of refugees and the economic losses to these countries that followed the closure of the Palestinian market.

A number of methodological rules were then employed by Professor Sayigh to account for the losses. Below, we present a brief summary of some of them.

a) Housing
A total of 750,000 refugees was identified, with five persons to a household. This means 90,000 houses in rural areas and 60,000 houses in urban areas. The unit price in the rural areas was put at £250 and the corresponding price in the urban areas at £2,500 [see Table 17.6].[8]

Table 17.6: Estimate of the Value of Palestinian Dwellings

	value (£)
Rural housing	22,500,000
Urban housing	150,000,000
Religious buildings (1,500 units at £3,000 each)	4,500,000
Auxiliary structures (i.e. garages, walls, etc.)	4,000,000
Total	181,000,000

b) Factories, Warehouses, and Commercial Buildings
Estimates of the values of these properties are shown in Table 17.7.

Table 17.7: Estimate of the Value of Factories, Warehouses and Commercial Buildings

	value (£)
Factories: 1,500 units × £5,000	7,500,000
Workshops: 5,000 units × £1,000	5,000,000
Offices: 5,000 units × £3,000	15,000,000
Shops (one for every 150 persons):	
a) Rural areas: 2,000 × £400	800,000
b) Urban areas: 3,000 × £2,500	7,500,000
Hotels: 1,000 units × £15,000	15,000,000
Restaurants and clubs: 2,000 units × £2,000	4,000,000
Warehouses: 2,000 units × £2,500	5,000,000
Total	59,800,000

c) Capital Sotck of Factories, Warehouses, etc.
A capital-output ratio of 4 was used to derive the capital stock from net income of these concerns. A total value of £15 million was placed on this stock.

d) Commercial Vehicles
A total of 1,000 trucks, buses, and lorries was assumed to be in operation in Palestine in 1948 with a total value of £15 million.

e) Personal Effects
A modest sum of £25 per refugee from the rural areas, or £12.5 million in all, and £400 per refugee from the urban areas, or £50 million in all, was chosen to represent the loss of personal effects. Thus, a total of £62.5 million was assigned to these losses.

f) Livestock
Using the figures in *Survey of Palestine* for the years before the war and using post-war prices (300 per cent increase), the total derived was £10 million.[9]

g) Bank Deposits and Guarantees
Considering only the portion that was not released, the total is put at £2 million.

h) Land
Estimates of loss of land are shown in Table 17.8.

Table 17.8: Land Losses

	value (£)
Citrus plantations: 132,000 dunums × £600	79,200,000
Fruit trees and olive groves: 384,000 dunums × £300	115,200,000
Irrigated land: 41,000 dunums × £100	4,100,000
Cultivable land (grains): 4,400,000 dunums × £40	176,000,000
Marginal land: 1,000,000 dunums × £16	16,000,000
Built-up areas in villages: 20,000 dunums × £60	1,200,000
Urban lands: 29,250 dunums × £400	11,700,000
Total	403,400,000

i) Stocks
Only a gross estimate is given; a total value of £5 million was considered to represent these losses.

j) Capital Stock of Offices, Hotels, Restaurants and Cafés
A total value of £3 million was put on these losses.

The total cost of losses under the category of personal property adds up to £757 million in 1948 prices and are made up as shown in Table 17.9.

Part Five: An Economic Assessment of Total Palestinian Losses

Table 17.9: Estimate of Losses of Personal Property

type	value (in £million)
Houses	181.0
Factories, warehouses, etc.	59.8
Capital stock of factories, warehouses, etc.	15.0
Commercial vehicles	15.0
Personal effects	62.5
Livestock	10.0
Bank deposits and guarantees	2.0
Land	403.4
Stocks	5.0
Capital stock of hotels, restaurants, etc.	3.0
Total	756.7

To this, a number of other losses were added, particularly those pertaining to loss of income from employment. Professor Sayigh had estimated the Arab share of national income of Palestine in 1945 to have been £63 million and around £68 million in 1948. The share of the refugees is put at two-thirds of the total or £46 million.

Based on this figure and an assumed rate of growth of 4 per cent per annum, it was estimated that this income would have been £79.65 million in 1962. Net investment was put at £132.7 million. This figure was derived on the assumption of a capital-output ratio of 4, a rate of growth of 4 per cent per year and a depreciation rate of 10 per cent. Accordingly, the calculation of the 1962 asset losses was made as shown in Table 17.10.

Table 17.10: Palestinian Asset Losses in 1962 Figures

description	value (in £million)
Original value of lost assets in 1948	756.7
Price adjustment between 1948 and 1962	279.9
Net investment between 1948 and 1962	132.7
Total	1,169.3

The total income lost was calculated to have increased to £921 million between 1948 and 1962. Thus, a total of £2,090 million were lost in 1962 prices comprising £1,169 million in assets and £921 million in accumulated losses of income.

To avoid mixing stocks and flows and wealth and income, Professor Sayigh re-estimates the share of national income of the refugees. This includes the £46 million plus the implicit rent on owner-occupied homes and the value of farmers' consumption (both of these items are generally excluded from national accounting in developing economies for lack of reliable data). The value of the latter was put at 50 per cent of the value added in agriculture which represented then 40 per cent of GNP. A new total of £55.2 million was derived. This was compared to the value of productive assets (i.e. the total value of £757 million minus the asset values of houses, fixtures and furnitures, money, livestock, and unused land). A capital-income ratio of 8.8 resulted from dividing the corrected asset value by the part of national income of refugees. But since gross output to income in Palestine was estimated to be around 2, the implicit capital-output ratio of his calculations is the reasonable value of 4.

A number of deficiencies remain in this approach. It is true that it is more comprehensive in coverage and analysis than any of the previous studies on this subject; his data, however, are not based on a thorough and detailed enumeration of Arab holdings and the distinctions in terms of quality and type are therefore limited. A great deal of importance is attached to the capital-output ratio and despite a careful attempt to separate productive from 'non-productive' capital, Professor Sayigh may have confused income and wealth. What was perhaps needed is not a separation of productive from non-productive capital, as this is too arbitrary a distinction; rather, a separation of income from labour and income from property would have been more helpful. This distinction will be made in our Study.

Since Professor Sayigh's examination was peripheral to his study, there is no reason why he should have justified his methodology more thoroughly. The methods of evaluation of stocks and movable properties, fixtures and furnitures, transport vehicles, etc., require more careful and thorough examination than he was able or could have been expected to give at the time he undertook the study.

E. Concluding Remarks

It is clear from the preceding analysis that the UN figures grossly underestimate the true losses of the Palestinians: the Arab League estimates are generally inconsistent; and Professor Sayigh's estimates are not fully comprehensive. In Table 17.11 we present a summary of the valuations of losses of these three studies. It is clear from the data that the UN estimates are exceptionally low and aggregative and those of the Arab League are generally too high. Professor Sayigh's estimates are almost half-way between.

Part Five: An Economic Assessment of Total Palestinian Losses

Table 17.11: Previous Estimates of Palestinian Losses in 1948 (in £million)

	Refugee UN Office	AHC valuation	Professor Sayigh
Land and houses	100.00	1726.0	644.2
Movable property	20.00	207.0	112.5
Lost income	—	—	—
Total	120.00	1933.0	756.7

In the discussion to follow we shall attempt to rectify as many as possible of the weaknesses and deficiencies of previous studies. Chapters 19 and 20 are devoted to this task. In the next chapter, the discussion is focused on a review of the Federal Republic of Germany compensation schemes.

18

German Reparation Payments and Restitution of Property to Jews

A. Introduction

Under *Wiedergutmachung*,[1] which means literally 'to make something good again', the government of the Federal Republic of Germany (FRG) and the individual German states made substantial payments as reparations and indemnification to the victims of Nazi persecution, particularly to Jews inside and outside Germany and to the state of Israel. These payments reached the level of DM85,800 million in 1984 [see Table 18.1]. This figure, however large, substantially understates the real economic value of these payments inasmuch as most of them were made in the 1950s, 1960s, and 1970s when the purchasing power of the Deutsche Mark was substantially higher than it is now. A simple adjustment for the German inflation rate would raise this figure by a factor of 3.

The restitution payments had their origins in the laws of the occupying powers in their individual zones which also restored, where possible, property confiscated by the Nazis to the original owners. These laws were restricted to property. They did not cover personal damage to the victims for physical and *psychological* sufferings, unjust deprivation of freedom, or injury to a person's professional or economic potential. Nor did these laws provide for assistance to the widows and orphans of those who had died as a result of Hitler's policies. It is compensation for these damages that Jews demanded from the Federal Republic of Germany and were able to secure with the help of the Western occupying powers.

B. The Luxembourg Agreement and the Israeli-German Treaty

The terms of the treaty concluded on 26 May 1952 between Germany and the three Western occupying powers which was to effect the transition of the Federal Republic of Germany from occupied territory to sovereign state, compelled the new state to pay restitution. The Luxembourg Agreement of 10 September 1952 between the government of the FRG and Israel and various

Jewish organizations clarified and defined the final framework and mechanisms that were to regulate the restitution payments.

Among the many provisions of this agreement was the requirement that the government of the FRG pay DM3,000 million ($714.3 million at the prevailing exchange rate at that time) to Israel and about DM450 million to various Jewish organizations. The payment to Israel was in 'recognition' of its needs to settle Jews who had suffered under the Nazi regime. The payments to Israel in the early 1950s were mainly in goods produced in Germany given the latter's war-torn economy. The monetary payments, however, were made to the Jewish organizations representing claimants at the Conference on Jewish Material Claims Against Germany at the Hague and Luxembourg.

To guarantee the compensation promised in the Transitional Treaty of 26 May 1952 and the Luxembourg Agreement of 10 September 1952, several laws were enacted. The first was the Supplementary Federal Law for the Compensation of the Victims of National Socialist Persecution of 1 October 1953; it was followed on 29 June 1956 by the Federal Law for the Compensation of the Victims of National Socialism (*Bundesentsch Laedigungsgesetz*) which substantially increased the effectiveness of the 1953 law in favour of those receiving compensation. A Final Federal Compensation Law was put into effect on 4 September 1965, to broaden the coverage and to improve the assistance offered.

C. Restitution for Lost Property[2]

Claims for lost property as a result of Nazi persecution are handled in accordance with the provisions of the Federal Restitution Law (*Bundesruecker-stattungsgesetz*, or BRUEG) of 19 July 1957.

The original restitution statutes were issued by the occupying authorities of the three Western Zones and Berlin to expedite the restitution of existing property and to settle related legal questions. But these laws were applied differently in the different zones and the government of the FRG recognized the need to harmonize their terms and applications and to extend their coverage to properties no longer existent and which, therefore, could not be returned in their natural state.

The major principle adopted in these statutes was the use of *replacement value* as of 1 April 1956 as the basis of valuation of lost property.

As of 1 January 1984 more than 734,900 claims had been made on the basis of BRUEG and 734,700 of them had been settled. Furthermore, claimants who missed the 1959 deadline were able to make *hardship applications* for lost household goods, precious metals, and jewellery in areas outside the FRG up to 1966. The responsible government office in Berlin has reported that about 300,000 claims have been processed on the basis of this provision.

Part Five: An Economic Assessment of Total Palestinian Losses

The total value of payments of restitutions for lost property exceeded DM4,250 million, although initially the financial obligations under BRUEG were limited to DM1,500 million.

D. Indemnification for Persecution of Persons

A novel feature of the *Wiedergutmachung* compensation programme is the indemnification of persons for persecution for political, racial, religious, or ideological reasons, affecting people who suffered physical or *psychological* injury. Compensation under the BEG laws covered loss of freedom, income, professional and financial advancement, health, and tranquillity. It also provided compensation for artists and scholars whose work disagreed with Nazi tenets and who were presumed to have suffered as a result. Finally, it guaranteed assistance to the survivors of deceased victims.

Table 18.1: German Public Expenditures in Restitution for Nazi Damages as of 1 January 1984

		in million DM
I.	Expenditures thus far:	
	Compensation of Victims (BEG)	56,200
	Restitution for Lost Property (BRUEG)	3,912
	Israeli Agreement	3,450
	Global Agreements with 12 nations including Austria	1,000
	Other (Civil Service, etc.)	5,200
	Final Restitution in Special Cases	356
	Sub-Total	70,118
II.	Anticipated future expenditures:	
	Compensation of Victims (BEG)	13,800
	Restitution for Lost Property (BRUEG)	338
	Other (Civil Service, etc.)	1,400
	Final Restitution in Special Cases	184
	Sub-Total	15,722
III.	Total (in round figures):	
	Compensation of Victims (BEG)	70,000
	Restitution for Lost Property (BRUEG)	4,250
	Israeli Agreement	3,450
	Global Agreements with 12 nations including Austria	1,000
	Other (Civil Service, etc.)	6,600
	Final Restitution in Special Cases	540
	Total	85,840

Source: Federal Republic of Germany, *Focus on Restitution in Germany*, p. 6.

Of the 4,393,365 claims submitted under the various compensation schemes between 1 October 1953 and 31 December 1983, over 4,390,049 or 99.9 per cent of all claims had been settled by 1 January 1984. Up to this date, compensation payments equalling DM56,200 million had been made. Approximately 40 per cent of those receiving compensation live in Israel, 20 per cent in the Federal Republic of Germany, and 40 per cent in other countries. Jews, however, account for over 90 per cent of claimants.

In addition to these basic legal provisions, several other compensatory laws have been enacted to aid persons who suffered as a result of discrimination practised by the Nazi regime.

Mention must be made also of the lump-sum payments made to former concentration camp internees who were the object of 'medical experimentation' by the Nazis and those made to Palestinian prisoners of war who, on account of their Jewish background, did not receive the humane treatment which should be accorded to all prisoners of war under the provisions of international law. While BEG legislation was intended to aid persecuted Jews, a special fund was set up to assist those persecuted by the Nazis for having Jewish ancestry although they themselves were not Jews.

E. Jewish Classification of Damage[3]

The losses suffered by Jews under Nazi persecution covered every aspect of their lives, according to their claims for indemnification. However, a concise list of these damages was prepared in view of their realization that indemnification, and especially the measures designed to provide for and ensure it, depends largely on the specific damage.

Two large groups were considered to represent the details of Jewish claims: a) damage to property including rights and interests; b) damage to persons.

Damage to property included, *inter alia,* damage to: 1. immovable property; 2. appurtenances of immovables; 3. movable property; 4. enterprises (industrial, commercial, artisanal, professional); 5. capital or fortune; 6. income from whatever source; 7. securities, shares, accounts, claims, mortgages; 8. contracts (insurance, leases, employment contracts, pensions); 9. rights from patents, copyright, trademarks.

Damages to persons comprised: 1. loss of life; 2. loss of health; 3. forced labour; 4. deportation, enforced residence, imprisonment, segregation; 5. maltreatment; 6. degradation.

This list of losses will be adopted in this Study in our attempt to assign values to Palestinian losses in 1948.

F. Concluding Remarks

In total about DM70,000 million have been paid under all the compensation schemes. Another DM15,700 million are estimated to be required to fully settle all claims under these schemes. This will bring the total (rounded up) to DM85,800 million.

A summary of all public expenditures by the FRG on restitution programmes as of 1 January 1985 is presented in Table 18.1.

The value of a Deutsche Mark a year ago is certainly less than its value today because of interest rates. We could have started last year with less than one DM and got one DM today by putting the money in the bank for a year and earning interest on it. Performing a present value calculation on the yearly payments raises the value to DM347,307 million (using a 4 per cent interest rate) [see Table 18.2], and to DM517,703 million (using a 6 per cent interest rate) [see Table 18.3].

Two important aspects of these compensation schemes are of special significance to our Study. First, the compensation payments were not made in a single period and so the total figure of DM85,800 million understates the true purchasing power equivalent of this total. Assuming that this amount was spread evenly over the period 1953 to 1983, and using the rate of change of FRG prices on a yearly basis and augmenting to the present according to the scheme defined below, we obtained a total figure of DM163,360 million in consistent 1983 prices.[4]

Let K_t be the yearly payments; P_t the rate of change of prices in year t over the previous year x; then K_{tT} is the value of yearly payments at time t at the terminal year T.

$$K_0 (1+P_1)(1+P_2)(1+P_3) \ldots (1+P_N) = K_{0T}$$
$$K_1 (1+P_2)(1+P_3)(1+P_4) \ldots (1+P_N) = K_{1T}$$
$$K_2 (1+P_3)(1+P_4) \quad\quad \ldots (1+P_N) = K_{2T}$$

$$K_{N-1}(1+P_N) \quad\quad\quad\quad \ldots = K_{N-1\,T}$$

Therefore the final value (F_T) is

$$F_T = K_t [\sum_{\gamma=0}^{N-1} \pi_{j=1+\gamma}^{N}(1+P_j)]$$

Second, compensation payments for psychological injury and loss of professional potential introduce an important principle with significant consequences for Palestinian compensation claims. It is our considered opinion that the fundamental principles used by the FRG to compensate Jews should be relied upon in compensating the Palestinians for their losses.

Palestinian Rights and Losses in 1948

Table 18.2: Present Value of Compensation Payments in 1983 Prices (lower interest multiplier) (Billions of Deutsche Marks)

	price multiplier	interest multiplier	present value
1954	2.6907	3.2434	24.9706
1955	2.6853	3.1187	23.9620
1956	2.6404	2.9987	22.6551
1957	2.5760	2.8834	21.2525
1958	2.5206	2.7725	19.9956
1959	2.4663	2.6658	18.8123
1960	2.4443	2.5633	17.9274
1961	2.4058	2.4647	16.9664
1962	2.3563	2.3699	15.9782
1963	2.2855	2.2788	14.9020
1964	2.2189	2.1911	13.9113
1965	2.1797	2.1068	13.1399
1966	2.1060	2.0258	12.2074
1967	2.0728	1.9479	11.5528
1968	2.0382	1.8730	10.9230
1969	2.0021	1.8009	10.3169
1970	1.9382	1.7317	9.6035
1971	1.8406	1.6651	8.7691
1972	1.7430	1.6010	7.9847
1973	1.6305	1.5395	7.1821
1974	1.5238	1.4802	6.4539
1975	1.4389	1.4233	5.8600
1976	1.0475	1.3686	4.1019
1977	1.3317	1.3159	5.0142
1978	1.2954	1.2653	4.6899
1979	1.2444	1.2167	4.3320
1980	1.1795	1.1699	3.9482
1981	1.1138	1.1249	3.5848
1982	1.0587	1.0816	3.2764
1983	1.0190	1.0400	3.0323
Total	57.0939	58.3283	347.3066

KO = 2.8613
KO × Price Multiplier = 163.3628
KO × Price Multiplier × Interest Multiplier = 347.3066

Table 18.3: Present Value of Compensation Payments in 1983 Prices (higher interest multiplier) (Billions of Deutsche Marks)

	price multiplier	interest multiplier	present value
1954	2.6907	5.7435	44.2187
1955	2.6853	5.4184	41.6320
1956	2.6404	5.1117	38.6188
1957	2.5760	4.8223	35.5438
1958	2.5206	4.5494	32.8111
1959	2.4663	4.2919	30.2872
1960	2.4443	4.0489	28.3175
1961	2.4058	3.8197	26.2937
1962	2.3563	3.6035	24.2951
1963	2.2855	3.3996	22.2317
1964	2.2189	3.2071	20.3617
1965	2.1797	3.0256	18.8700
1966	2.1060	2.8543	17.1997
1967	2.0728	2.6928	15.9707
1968	2.0382	2.5404	14.8154
1969	2.0021	2.3966	13.7292
1970	1.9382	2.2609	12.5384
1971	1.8406	2.1329	11.2329
1972	1.7430	2.0122	10.0353
1973	1.6305	1.8983	8.8562
1974	1.5238	1.7908	7.8080
1975	1.4389	1.6895	6.9559
1976	1.0475	1.5938	4.7770
1977	1.3317	1.5036	5.7293
1978	1.2954	1.4185	5.2577
1979	1.2444	1.3382	4.7648
1980	1.1795	1.2625	4.2608
1981	1.1138	1.1910	3.7956
1982	1.0587	1.1236	3.4037
1983	1.0190	1.0600	3.0906
Total	57.0900	83.8015	517.7025

KO = 2.8613
KO × Price Multiplier = 163.3630
KO × Price Multiplier × Interest Multiplier = 517.7025

19

The Typology of Palestinian Losses: a Re-evaluation

A. Introduction

The Palestinian economy which Israel usurped was a viable economy with a significant flow of output and income that sustained a growing population of approximately 2 million people in 1948. In 1944, national income at market prices was estimated at £P123 million. In Tables 19.1 and 19.2 we present estimates of national income at different periods. It is clear from these tables that national income in Palestine was significant and growing fast. Although inflation in the 1940s was high, it does not account for the full increase in national income between 1939 and 1944, as is clear from the data in Table 19.3.

Given the prevailing real interest rate at the time (4 per cent), it is legitimate to claim that the total wealth in Palestine (physical and human) in 1944 was of the order of £P3,075 million. The Arab share of this wealth is roughly 51.2 per cent, given the estimate of Loftus[1] of Arab net domestic product of £P63 million in 1944. This translates into £P1,575 million.[2]

Since non-property income (labour income) then constituted about 50 per cent of total income,[3] the value of non-human wealth should be around £P787.5 million. The refugees represented 55 per cent of the Arab population of Palestine and, on the basis of this proportion, their share of non-human wealth would be £P433 million in 1944 prices. Indeed, this is a lower bound (minimum figure) because part of the human wealth was lost as refugees lost the complementary inputs. Most of the refugees were engaged in farming.[4] When they were deprived of their land, their human capital was lost too. Refugees who were not farmers lost their labour skills through unemployment. They were confined to camps by the sheer economic force of being excess labour in already labour-surplus economies.

If lost opportunity and deterioration of human capital, through lack of use or absence of complementary inputs, were to be valued, another £P300 million

147

would have to be added to the losses of the refugees, bringing the total to £P733 million in 1944 prices.

Since prices and quantities in 1948 were higher than in 1944, an upward adjustment of the 1944 figures is needed. If real growth is put at 4 per cent per year (a modest figure in historical perspective), and if prices are assumed to rise

Table 19.1: National Income of Palestine, 1939, 1942, and 1943 (£P million)

	1939	1942	1943
Agriculture, fisheries and forests	5.97	18.51	20.20
Manufacturing, mining, and private utilities	5.97	14.72	21.70
Contract building and construction	1.84	5.82	5.70
Housing	3.40	4.25	4.80
Transport and finance	4.59	9.33	11.00
Hotel, restaurant and domestic service	1.50	2.50	3.00
Other services	1.75	7.98	9.60
Government	3.47	5.81	7.20
Total	30.04	75.89	90.00

Source: Robert Nathan et al., *Palestine: Problems and Promise, an Economic Study*, Public Affairs Press 1946, Washington, D.C., p. 156.

Table 19.2: National Income of Palestine, 1944 (£P million)

Agriculture and livestock	28.257
Fisheries	.850
Manufacturing and handicrafts	28.233
Housing	6.149
Building and construction	5.655
War Department airline employment	3.914
Palestine troops	2.270
Transport and communications	8.247
Commerce and finance	19.700
Government and local authorities	7.501
Hotels, restaurants, and cafés	3.069
Domestic and other services	6.831
Overseas income	2.000
Total	123.023

Source: R. Loftus, *National Income of Palestine*, Government Printer, Jerusalem, 1944, p. 1.

Part Five: An Economic Assessment of Total Palestinian Losses

Table 19.3: Inflation and Real Rate of Growth of GNP in Palestine, 1939 to 1944

year	price	nominal national income	real national income in 1939 prices
1939	100	30.04	30.04
1940	131	—	—
1941	166	—	—
1942	211	75.89	35.97
1943	230	90.00	39.13
1944	248	123.02	49.61

Source: The price index is the cost of living index for Arabs and Jews from *Palestine Year Book,* p. 162. Nominal national income figures are from Tables 19.1 and 19.2 of this section. Real national income is calculated by dividing nominal NI by the price index.

at the modest rate of 6 per cent per year, the refugees' share of property wealth in 1948 would have totalled £P634 million and of total wealth £P1,073.2 million. In 1984, these values would have risen to £P19,600 million and £P33,200 million respectively (using an interest rate of 4 per cent and an average annual inflation rate of 6 per cent). The US dollar equivalents of these amounts are $79,000 million and $133,800 million, respectively.

Taking the lower of these figures as the working value of lost assets, a rough value of $79,000 million is required to compensate the Palestinian refugees for their loss of these assets and to put them in an economic position equivalent to that before they were driven out of their homeland in 1948.

It is useful to make a simple comparison of this value to the amount received by Jews and others from the FRG as compensation for Nazi persecution. Our figures showed a total present value of DM347,000 million. In US dollar equivalents this is approximately $116,000 million, slightly less than the compensation required to settle the overall Palestinian claims. The major difference between the two measures is due to the long period that has elapsed since the Palestinian losses. While the Germans dealt directly and promptly with their victims, the Israelis have shrugged off their responsibility.

The detailed enumeration of property losses by type of asset and by value is undertaken in the following sections. We begin with capital.

B. Ownership of Capital

There are few countries for which estimates of national wealth have been compiled and few of them claim that they are anything more than rough approximations. Palestine is numbered among those countries which have not attempted a complete enumeration of national wealth. Nevertheless, certain basic information is available and will be presented here.[5] Special care must be exercised to distinguish the shares of Arabs and Jews.

> The additional problem of separating the relative shares of the two broad groups of the population in the wealth of the country has involved additional difficulties which have been overcome only by the use of the methods of approximation which must further widen the margin of error that limits the value of all such estimates.[6]

The enumerated capital includes: rural and urban land; industrial capital; agricultural capital; livestock; commercial and private vehicles; commercial assets; financial assets; private and personal wealth; infrastructure; forestry; natural resources.

Rural and urban lands are the main capital. Their valuation was realized through a thorough and detailed analysis, and a complete chapter (chapter 20) is therefore devoted to this assessment. The remaining assets are assessed below.

a) Industrial Capital

The Palestine government's Census of Industry in 1943 covered a total of 3,470 establishments, of which 1,558 were Arab and non-Jewish interests. Of the five concessions which existed then, three were Jewish-owned: Palestine Electric Corporation, Palestine Potash Ltd, and Palestine Salt Co. The other two were Arab-owned: Jerusalem Electric and Public Service Corporation and Shukri Deeb and Son, Ltd.

The census did not cover the entire industrial sector but excluded, notably, small enterprises in printing and publishing, garages, laundries and small workshops which were predominantly Arab-owned. The findings of this census are presented in Table 19.4.

Net output in manufacturing, mining, and private utilities was estimated in 1943 [see Table 19.1] to exceed £P21.7 million. The difference of about £P6.9 million between the national accounts estimate and that of the census may be accounted for entirely by the exclusion of small businesses from the 1943 census. Using an average capital-output ratio for Arab establishments of 1.197, we obtain a value of £P8.3 million as additional Arab industrial capital in this sector. This brings the total accumulation of capital invested in the industrial sector to about £P28.7 million. The Arab share works out as follows: £P2.1 million of capital invested in the census-included establishments; £P8.3 million of capital invested in the census-excluded establishments; £P2.5 million in the Arab-owned concessions. This gives a total of £P12.9 million in 1943 prices.

The 1948 value of Arab capital in industry, assuming a 10 per cent nominal growth rate per year between 1943 and 1948, is estimated to be approximately

Part Five: An Economic Assessment of Total Palestinian Losses

£P20.7 million.[7] The share of the refugees is again put at 55 per cent of the total, resulting in an approximate value of £P11.4 million.

Table 19.4: Ownership of Industry in Palestine, 1943

item		Arab & other non-Jewish	Jewish	concessions	total
Establishments	No.	2,558	1,907	5	3,470
Capital invested	£P	2,064,587	12,039,929	6,293,681	20,452,197
Horse power		2,625	57,410	133,673	194,708
Gross output	£P	5,658,222	29,040,679	2,131,467	36,830,368
Net output	£P	1,724,793	11,487,843	1,631,474	14,844,110
Persons engaged	No.	8,804	37,773	3,400	49,977
Capital-output ratio		1.197	1.053	3.857	1.378

Source: *A Survey of Palestine*, p. 567.

b) Agricultural Capital

Three types of agricultural capital are to be distinguished here: first, agricultural implements of all sorts; second, the stock of livestock maintained by the farmer; third, rural fixtures and houses (a special section will be devoted to that category).

The *Survey of Palestine* values Arab agricultural capital at £P13.100 million in 1942 prices, divided thus:[8] Arab rural housing £P9 million; Arab agricultural implements £P1 million; Arab livestock (at pre-war prices) £P3.1000 million. This gives a total of £P13.100 million.

Translating these sums into 1948 prices, we get the following values: Arab rural housing £P15.9 million; Arab agricultural implements £P1.8 million; Arab livestock £P9.3 (assuming 300 per cent inflation). The total now becomes £P26.9 million.

However, a simple examination of the valuation of rural housing reveals that these figures seriously undervalue the premises. If the rental income of rural premises is used as a basis for valuation, a much higher capital value would have to be assigned to this item.

Annual rent on rural houses in 1948 averaged about £P30. If 10 per cent of this value is deducted for maintenance, a net value £P27 is left. Using the real rate of interest of 4 per cent as a basis of translating income into capital, an average value of £P675 is assigned to each house. Professor Sayigh estimates that 750,000 refugees had vacated 150,000 houses: 60,000 in urban areas and 90,000 in rural areas.[9]

Thus, total refugee losses in rural housing alone are valued at £P60.7 million, or five times more than the valuation of all Arab rural housing in the *Survey*. To point out the absurdity of the *Survey's* valuation we may look at the problem in a different manner and ask what implicit rental income could the *Survey* have assumed to reach the valuation of £P9 million. Using our 4 per cent real rate of interest, the implicit net rental income on rural property in the *Survey's* calculation is £P4 per year. Surely, this is a gross understatement of the average rental income from rural houses and fixtures.

Accepting the *Survey's* valuation of livestock and implements but adjusting the valuation of rural Arab houses and using the 55 per cent ratio of refugees to the total Arab population of Palestine, the following agricultural losses emerge: rural housing £P60.7 million; livestock £P5.1 million; agricultural implements £P1 million. These total £P66.8 million.

The distribution and valuation of Arab livestock in Palestine are presented in Table 19.5.

Table 19.5: Estimated Number and Value of Livestock in Arab and Jewish Ownership

	Arab (1943) number	*Jewish (1942)* number	total 1942-43 number
Cattle	214, 570	28,375	242,945
Buffaloes	4,972	—	4,972
Sheep over 1 year	224,942	19,120	244,062
Goats over 1 year	314,602	10,174	324,776
Camels over 1 year	29,736	—	29,736
Horses	16,869	2,152	19,021
Mules	7,328	2,534	9,862
Donkeys	105,414	2,322	107,736
Pigs	12,145	—	12,145
Fowls (excl. chickens)	1,202,122	669,506	1,871,628
Other poultry	16,394	74,259	90,653
Estimated total value at pre-war prices	£P 3,100,000	£P 1,440,000	£P 4,540,000

Source: *A Survey of Palestine*, p. 568.

c) *Commercial and Private Vehicles*

In 1945 the *Survey* estimated that a total of 9,673 vehicles were on the road in Palestine with a value of £P3.2 million. The Arab share was £P1.3 million. Details are provided in Table 19.6.

This valuation of Arab vehicles rises to £P1.730 million when expressed in 1948 prices. Of this total the refugees account for £P952,000. [See Table 19.6.]

Part Five: An Economic Assessment of Total Palestinian Losses

Table 19.6: Motor Vehicles, Number and Estimated Value in Arab (Including Other Non-Jewish) and Jewish Ownership, 1945

	number	value in £P'000 Jewish	value in £P'000 Arab and other	value in £P'000 total
Omnibuses	1,342	566	377	943
Commercial vehicles:				
Light	921	106	57	163
Heavy	3,111	717	386	1,103
Taxis	1,248	150	183	333
Private	3,051	343	281	624
Total	9,673	1,882	1,284	3,166

Source: *A Survey of Palestine*, p. 568.

d) Commercial Capital and Stocks

Commercial activity covers both internal and external trade and finance. Internal trade in Palestine was strongly influenced by the availability of transport facilities, marketing channels, patterns of production, and size of the market. In rural areas and farming communities where primitive agricultural production was prevalent, and where transport facilities were limited or non-existent, the economic system was self-sufficient and only small commercial establishments were in operation.

On the other hand, in the areas where citriculture, horticulture, and industrialization prevailed, a network of retail and wholesale markets developed and a significant proportion of the domestic labour force was absorbed in this activity.

In 1944, trading establishments numbered 14,000,[10] and about 7,447 persons paid taxes on £P6 million of income derived from such trade activities. The average rental income on these premises was valued at £P175 per year. Again, assuming repairs and maintenance expenses to average 10 per cent of rental income, and dividing net rental income by the real rate of interest, the average capital value of such premises is £P3,937 per unit. Thus, a total of £P55.1 million represents the capital value of these premises in 1944.

Given that the net output of commerce in the national accounts was then £P19.7 million, this results in a reasonable capital-output ratio of 2.8. Since commercial activity is very sensitive to market size and the latter to population, it is possible to argue that the proportion of the Arab refugee population to the total population of Palestine is as good an indicator as any of their share in the total value of commercial premises. Thus, a total of £P30.3 million is deemed to be their share. In addition, the *Survey* assigns a value of £P1.951 million to commodity stocks owned by Arabs. Therefore, the total value of commercial fixed and circulating capital owned by the Arab refugees is £P31.4 million in 1944 prices or £P45.9 million in 1948 prices.[11]

e) Hotels and Restaurants
Professor Sayigh estimates a total of £P19 million as the value of Arab hotels and restaurants in Palestine in 1948.[12] Since not all of these premises were vacated after the Israeli occupation, only the usual 55 per cent can be assigned to the refugees. Thus, a total of £P10.5 million can be added to the losses of the Palestinians who were forced to abandon their restaurants and hotels.

The details of Professor Sayigh's estimations are as follows: 1,000 hotels × £P15,000/ unit = £P15 million; 2,000 restaurants × £P2,000/unit = £P4 million. The total is £P19 million.

f) Financial Assets
Up to the end of the nineteenth century money-lenders supplied the credit needs of the bulk of the population. About the year 1900, a Jewish banking company was established to provide credit facilities to Jewish colonists. At the same time a number of credit co-operatives were formed to provide credit facilities to the Jewish settlers.

After World War I, large-scale Jewish immigration accompanied by the import of large amounts of capital created the conditions for the emergence of modern banking. By 1935, a total of 113 banks were operating in Palestine of which eighteen were classified as commercial banks; six of the total were foreign banks.[13]

Deposits totalled £P17.2 million on 20 June 1936 and by the same date in 1939 they had reached £P20.2 million.[14] Foreign banks accounted for about 64 per cent of the deposits in 1939.

From the outbreak of the war in September 1939 until about the end of 1941, war events dominated banking developments. Heavy withdrawals of deposits from local banks forced a number into liquidation. Thus, the total number of banks operating in Palestine was gradually reduced, so that by the end of the war the number of commercial banks had dropped to twenty-five, comprising five foreign and twenty local.[15]

By July 1941, total deposits held by banks and credit co-operatives began to rise and this trend was maintained throughout the period 1941 to 1945. On 31 October 1945, total deposits had reached the level of £P84.9 million. The distribution of these deposits was as follows: Arab deposits £P12.5 million; Jewish deposits £P67.5 million; other deposits (including government) £P4.9 million. This gives a total of £P84.9 million.

Several local banks developed rapidly during the war. Table 19.7 shows the paid-up capital, reserve funds, total deposits, and total advances and bills

Part Five: An Economic Assessment of Total Palestinian Losses

discounted at the Arab Bank Ltd and the Arab National Bank Ltd at the end of each year, commencing with the figures for the month of August 1939.

Table 19.7: The Arab Bank and the Arab National Bank Paid-Up Capital, Reserve Funds, Total Deposits, and Advances, 1939-45

	paid-up capital	reserve funds	total deposits	total advances and bills discounted
31.8.39	209,494	32,205	376,180	456,186
31.12.39	209,506	34,309	299,223	462,617
31.12.40	209,790	37,848	245,619	412,064
31.12.41	209,818	38,577	532,515	499,790
31.12.42	213,634	40,859	1,330,953	992,377
31.12.43	480,508	148,971	3,430,197	2,392,268
31.12.44	1,120,000	559,731	5,067,421	3,311,176
31.10.45	1,415,752	977,877	6,970,728	5,256,214

Source: *A Survey of Palestine,* p. 559.

Total deposits in these two banks increased from £P376,180 in August 1939 to £P6,970,728 at 31 October 1945. This is generally explained by the fact that Arab farmers had enjoyed rising prices for their products and had accumulated substantial amounts in cash some of which had been deposited with banks and the remainder hoarded.

If we were to assume that the deposits at these two banks grew at half the rate of growth they had achieved between 1943 and 1945, total deposits in 1948 would have reached £P12.4 million.[16]

Deposits at other banks, particularly foreign banks, have been assumed to have totalled £P6.5 million; of which 6 million were deposited at Barclay's and the Ottoman banks and the remainder spread over a number of smaller foreign banks.

On 20 July 1948, the Israeli authorities ordered that all credits belonging to refugees in all the banks in occupied Palestine should be frozen. The frozen accounts included demand deposits, savings accounts, guarantee funds, financial instruments of all sorts, jewels, and other valuables in safety deposit boxes. The experts of the Palestine Conciliation Commission estimated these funds to amount to £P6 million owned by about 10,000 Palestinians including the assets of the Arab Bank and the Arab National Bank. Indeed, such an estimate is far below the actual deposits and paid-up capital in 1945.

Total Arab deposits were already over £P12.5 million in 1945. The outbreak of war in 1948 must surely have resulted in some withdrawals, but many refugees were forced to leave at short notice and many felt that their departure was temporary. Besides, the total value of deposits is only one item of many financial instruments left behind.

Even when a liberal allowance for withdrawals of 50 per cent of deposits by the refugees is entertained, the total remaining deposits would exceed £P9 million. If the customary 2:1 ratio of deposits to other financial instruments and liquid wealth (jewellery and gold) is accepted, then another £P4.5 million would have to be added to the £P9 million, giving a total of £P13.5 million: a more realistic assessment of financial losses sustained by the refugees.[17]

The Palestine Conciliation Commission called on Israel to release the funds and organize a committee of experts from both sides to work out the details of their release. Israel was reluctant to unblock the funds. Moreover, when they finally succumbed to international pressure they released only £1 million sterling. Even then, the Israelis had imposed a compulsory 10 per cent national loan on every account and the Israeli custodian charged exorbitant fees for administering the released funds.[18] The net outcome of all this is to reduce our estimates by £P1 million.

According to the *Survey of Palestine* over £P39.3 million of Palestine's foreign assets in 1945 were held by the Arab population.[19] These assets included £P29.2 million of net currency reserves and about £P9.3 million in net banking reserves. Indeed, a portion of these assets have not been recovered and could legitimately be added to other monetary losses. If only a third of these assets were lost, this would raise the net monetary losses to £P26.5 million.

The Arab Bank did liquidate and pay back all its depositors and the above figure must be adjusted in consequence. On 31 October 1945 the Arab Bank total deposits were about £P3.8 million.[20] Deducting this amount in its entirety would leave a net monetary loss of £P22.7 million. The share of the refugees is again assessed at 55 per cent; this puts their share of the monetary losses at £P12.5 million.

g) Private and Personal Wealth
This wealth category includes all personal movable properties, whether physical or financial. We have already estimated the financial losses. Therefore, we shall now restrict ourselves to an assessment of personal effects and household furniture and fixtures. The UN Palestine Conciliation Commission Refugee Office concluded that it was unable to make such aggregate evaluation of Arab refugee movable properties, since some categories of movable property did not lend themselves to global evaluation and since there was no means of knowing what properties the refugees took with them and what they left behind.[21]

None the less, the Office adopted two methods. The first involved the use of the percentages adopted at the time of the Turkish-Greek exchange of

Part Five: An Economic Assessment of Total Palestinian Losses

populations, whereas the second stipulated the use of 40 per cent of the Arab share in national income at the time.

The Office took into account a long list of movable property such as: industrial equipment, commercial stocks, motor vehicles, agricultural implements, livestock, and household effects. It is clear, however, that the Office grossly underestimated these losses. This is evident on account of the fact that consumer expenditure studies show that in most countries an average of 16 to 20 per cent of total consumer expenditure generally goes on clothing, household equipment and furniture. In Table 19.8 we present data on different country groupings classified by per capita income level and the average share of total consumption allocated to clothing and household durables. The corresponding expenditures on these two items were 21.8 per cent in Greece, 14.6 per cent in Korea and 22.2 per cent in Israel.[22]

Table 19.8: Consumer Expenditures on Clothing and Household Durables

per capita income (US dollars)	clothing	household durables
100–500	0.074	0.074
500–1000	0.138	0.092
1000–1500	0.109	0.093

Source: Constantino Lluch, Allan Powell, and Ross Williamson, *Patterns in Household Demand and Saving*, Oxford: Oxford University Press, 1977, p. 52.

The major flaw in the UN Office's estimation procedure lies in its failure to distinguish between stocks and flows. Indeed, only 20 per cent or so is allocated yearly to expenditure on personal and household effects; but if household and personal items last for more than one year, as in fact they do, then they need to be accumulated as a stock.

An easy alternative to accumulating these flows over time is to use the concept of permanent consumption out of permanent income and to convert permanent income into wealth. Thus, we begin by postulating a standard marginal propensity to consume of 80 per cent out of permanent income and a 20 per cent share of total consumption allocated to personal and household effects. Let:

$$\text{Permanent income} = \sum_{i=0}^{\infty} \lambda i \, \gamma_{t-i}$$

where λ is the weight of current income in the formation of permanent income. It is generally less than one ($\lambda < 1$).

$$\text{Permanent consumption} = (.8) \left(\sum_{i=0}^{\infty} \lambda i \, \gamma_{t-i} \right)$$

Permanent consumption expenditures on clothing and household effects =

$$(.2)(.8)\sum_{i=0}^{\infty} \lambda\, i\gamma_{t-i}$$

The stocks of household effects and clothing are then =

$$\frac{(.2)(.8)\sum_{i=0}^{\infty} \lambda\, i\gamma_{t-i}}{r + d}$$

where r is the real rate of interest and d is the depreciation rate of this stock.

Assuming a constant real income of £P123 million, a real rate of interest of 4 per cent, and a depreciation rate of 10 per cent, our estimate of the stock of clothing and household effects in 1948 is £P196.8 million. The share of the refugees is 55 per cent or £P108.2 million, half of which they could have taken with them. Thus, a low estimate of £P54 million is assigned to these losses in 1948.

h) Infrastructure

Palestine enjoyed an efficient transportation system with all types of facilities: roads, railways, water and air transport. Development of these means was systematic and deliberate and served to avoid duplication and promote complementarity. By the early 1940s, Palestine had a number of communications facilities which helped to mobilize factors of production and trade, and relayed information that was instrumental in accelerating economic growth. The total contribution of these facilities to national output reached £P8.3 million in 1944. Given the high capital-output ratio (usually 4 and higher) of this sector, a total of £P33.2 million could easily be assigned to these facilities. It may be necessary to deduct the capital value of vehicles from this to avoid double counting. This would reduce the capital valuation of £P30 million. Since the development of this infrastructure involved substantial time-lags, it may not be legitimate to impute only one-half of this value to the Arabs since they had paid more for it over the years than Jews who had come in large numbers only in the late 1930s to mid-1940s, and much of this infrastructure was built in the early 1930s. Nevertheless, only the lower proportion of 50 per cent will be used here: this results in a total valuation of £P15 million. The share of the refugees is again 55 per cent or £P8.3 million. Converting this value to 1948 prices results in a total of £P12.1 million.

i) Natural Resources, Water and Forestry

Although Palestine was not rich in natural resources, there were many that were or could have been developed. Palestine had chemicals from the Dead Sea

Part Five: An Economic Assessment of Total Palestinian Losses

(potassium, chlorine, and bromine); limestone, clay, and sand for cement and brick production; phosphates; sand for glass manufacture; kaolin for pottery and ceramics; oil products; salt for food industries and tanning; water and a temperate climate for agriculture and tourism.

It is admittedly difficult to assign an accurate value to these resources in the absence of detailed information on prices, volumes, and cost of production. Therefore, our estimates of property losses undervalue the total losses actually suffered by the Palestinians inasmuch as we neglect to assign values to the loss of natural resources. If anything, the loss of water alone could be worth a substantial amount.

C. Concluding Remarks

Palestinian losses in non-human wealth were staggering. We have managed to include at best a small sub-set of them. If losses in human wealth and the cost of psychological damage, pain, and suffering were included, substantial new values would be added. Clearly, the largest Palestinian loss is that of land. This is the subject of the next chapter.

Excluding urban and rural land losses, a total of £P214.2 million has been identified as the cost to the Palestinian refugees of non-land losses in 1948. Agricultural capital accounted for the largest item of these losses with a total value of £P66.8 million. Private and personal property losses added another £P54 million. The smallest losses are associated with commercial and private vehicles. No estimate of losses in natural resources was made, for lack of any reliable data on volume and prices.

Indeed, the estimation of these refugee losses is generally sensitive to two factors. First, the proportion of refugees to the total Arab population of Palestine is assumed to be 55 per cent. Any higher proportion would raise the magnitude of the losses. Since there is good reason to believe that the refugees were principally the well-to-do people of Palestine, it is conceivable that the value of their share of property would be higher than their share in the total population. Secondly, the net product of Palestine in 1944 was assumed to be roughly divided between the Arabs and Jews. There are also strong grounds that suggest that the Arab share in the net domestic product of Palestine should be higher, since the Palestinians owned most of the resources of the country and their numbers were very much greater than those of the Jews. Besides, the national accounting estimates would most likely understate their contributions, given the inevitable difficulties accounting procedures have in measuring non-market activities in traditional sectors.

As will be argued later, the summation of property losses would result in a capital valuation greater than that derived from capitalizing the Arab share of net domestic product. This discrepancy may be a strong indicator of a measurable underestimation of the Arab share in the net domestic product of Palestine in 1944.

Table 19.9: Alternative Valuations of Palestinian Physical and Human Losses (in £P million)

	low (50%)	average (60%)	high (68.61%)
Physical Losses			
1944 prices	512.5	615.0	703.0
1948 prices	750.3	900.0	1,029.6
1984 prices	23,200.0	27,830.0	31,800.0
1984 prices (billion US$)	92.8	111.3	127.2
Physical and Human Losses			
1944 prices	812.5	915.0	1,003.0
1948 prices	1,189.5	1,340.0	1,468.5
1984 prices	36,700.0	41,430.0	45,400.0
1984 prices (billion US$)	146.8	165.7	181.6

20

Valuation of Palestinian Urban and Rural Real Estate Losses

A. Introduction

The purpose of this chapter is to identify and value rural and urban land and buildings vacated by Palestinian refugees in 1948. This is not the first time that such a valuation has been attempted. It is, however, the first systematic appraisal of these losses.

This chapter makes extensive use of a hitherto neglected set of United Nations records relating to real estate holdings in Palestine in 1946 and 1947. These records identify urban and rural properties by sub-district, village or town block and parcel number, by tax category of net annual value, by type of ownership, and by ethnic background of the owner. We also draw on a second rich but neglected source of data relating to all property sales as registered in the official records of the government of Palestine between 1 January 1946 and 19 November 1947. Drawing on these two sources, records of sales, ownership, prices, and nature of property were coded for computer analysis. The results are the focus of this chapter.

In general, the basis for land appraisals is the selling price of the property. But when the recorded prices do not accurately reflect market prices, indirect tests are needed. First, the present values of the net streams of expected incomes of these representative farms were used as proxies for their capital values. Second, location and land fertility indicators were compared to sale values to determine the consistency of the two series.

The selling price of a unit of land in Palestine may understate its true value inasmuch as sellers and buyers have equal and common incentives to report lower values as they would both save on taxes and registration fees. However, it is equally true that only prime parcels of land would generally be sold. Since the prices realized on the sales are generally used to estimate the values of comparable but unsold land, this procedure may overestimate the overall value of the land.

The use of the selling price as depicted in the realized sales therefore rests on the assumption that these two opposing forces (one to underestimate and the other to overestimate) would cancel each other out.

B. A Methodological Note

The literature on land appraisal identifies six theoretical models for this purpose. A brief description of these models and their applicability to our problem is presented here.

a) Replacement Costs Less Depreciation Adjusted by Sales for the Local Area (RCLD)
This is the traditional model which has been used by many assessing jurisdictions throughout the United States.[1] It has only recently been computerized to a point where it can easily and rapidly assess values for properties. The problem with this method, as far as it concerns our task, is that it includes many features which must be combined together in order to arrive at the valuation of a property. These features include types of foundation, interior construction, plumbing – a long list of materials priced per unit. In other words, the data requirements for this method are too extensive and are, therefore, difficult to use in estimating Palestinian land and housing losses in 1948.

b) Multiple Regression Analysis (MRA)
This model uses the hedonic price function to determine values of various components of the property.[2] This analysis features the use of factors or variables considered by the model builder to be important in determining market value. This method proved very valuable to our task. Using MRA we were able to identify the importance of location, tax category, and area as the major determinants of the variance in rural land sale values, while the size of town, net annual value, and the number of floors were singled out as the main determinants of the variance in urban areas.

c) Adaptive Estimation Procedure
This method is similar to MRA with the exception that the coefficients of the regressions are now determined by an iterative feedback method.[3] This method is regarded as superior to MRA because it avoids some of the latter's regressivity problems. In our assessment of values, we have attempted to take into account differential fertility factors, based on a geological map of Palestine.

d) Comparable Sales Selection (CSS)
This method initially selects several parcels of land which were sold within a specified period of time and which are considered to be similar (even identical) to the property to be valued. Coefficients from a multiple regression equation are then used to make a final estimate of value.

This is a very simple method, and one that is suitable to apply to our problem.

Sale values were identified by tax category, location, and time; it was therefore possible for us to use these averages (as simple, weighted, or regression coefficients) to evaluate the total area of land with similar characteristics (as identified by the tax category) and in the same location (generally a village).

This method works particularly well when the number of sales are large (these numbers should at least exceed the number of parameters in the regression equation).

e) Averaging Procedure Model (APM)

The mean sale price per dunum or per square metre for various types of property is used to construct tables to appraise property with similar characteristics. Models of this type are particularly used in Pennsylvania, in the United States. This method requires a good deal of subjective intervention, which has the advantage of drawing on the views and experiences of experts and practitioners in the field.

In many instances, we were faced with the problem of lack of data for a particular village or even for a whole sub-district for a given tax category. Invariably, we had recourse to land specialists with first-hand experience and knowledge to guide our selection of applicable norms from neighbouring villages or sub-districts.

f) Trending Model (TM)

The current sale values are adjusted by a correction factor derived from the discrepancy of true sale to actual sale for each stratum within any given market area.[4]

Again, this method requires subjective intervention and the adjustment of actual data to fit more closely to model builders' knowledge and experience. Adjustments of this kind are particularly necessary in our case given the alleged tendency to under-report the correct sale values of property by both sellers and buyers and the tendency to use out-dated prices.

The procedures or models which can most easily be applied to the problem of appraising Palestinian losses in rural and urban land and buildings appear to be the trending model and the comparable sales selection analysis. As indicated above, recourse was also made to multiple regression analysis on the raw data to determine the pattern and extent of influence of several variables on the sale values realized on some properties.

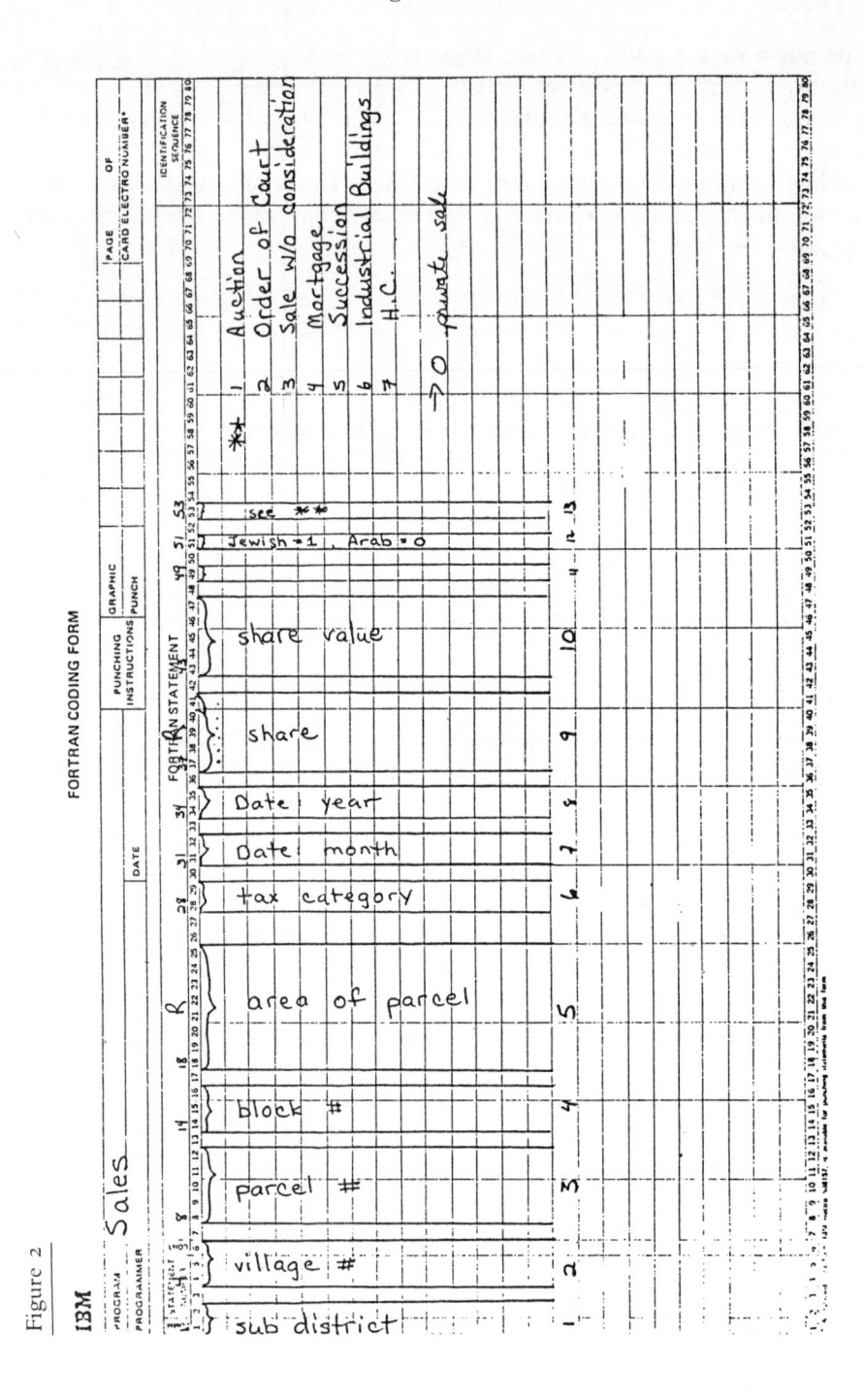

Palestinian Rights and Losses in 1948

Figure 2

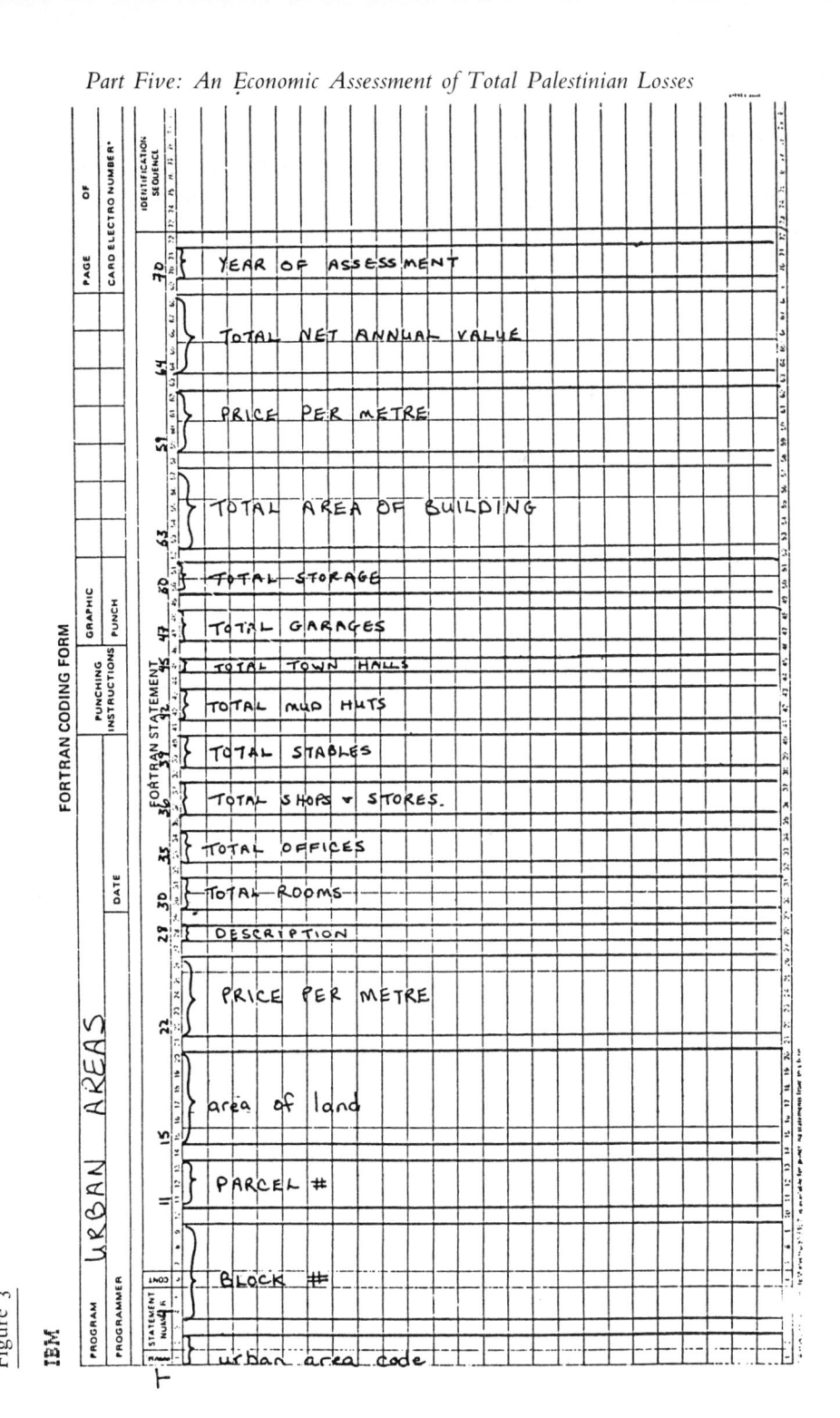

Part Five: An Economic Assessment of Total Palestinian Losses

Figure 3

FORTRAN CODING FORM — IBM

PROGRAM: URBAN AREAS

- YEAR OF ASSESSMENT
- TOTAL NET ANNUAL VALUE
- PRICE PER METRE
- TOTAL AREA OF BUILDING
- TOTAL STORAGE
- TOTAL GARAGES
- TOTAL TOWN HALLS
- TOTAL MUD HUTS
- TOTAL STABLES
- TOTAL SHOPS & STORES
- TOTAL OFFICES
- TOTAL ROOMS
- DESCRIPTION
- PRICE PER METRE
- area of land
- PARCEL #
- BLOCK #
- urban area code

C. A Note on the Data

Three types of data were collected, computer-coded, and processed. These include data on sales of rural land and urban property and data on ownership patterns.

Over 4,000 recorded sales were identified and coded by sub-district, village, parcel number, block number, area of parcel, tax category, date of sale by month, day, and year, share sold, value realized, private or public ownership, Jewish or Arab sale, and by type of sale. The details of these codes are presented in Figure 2.

More than one million records on urban areas were coded and stored. The following codes were used: urban area code, block number, parcel number, area of land, assessed price per metre, description of land, total number of rooms, total number of offices, shops, stables, huts, town halls, garages, storage rooms, area of buildings, price per metre of built-up area, net annual value, and finally the year of assessment. The details of these codes are presented in Figure 3. Similar codes were used for the rural areas.

Some gaps in the data, particularly the sales data, emerged in the course of their coding and processing. Complete data for all villages and tax categories only existed for very few sub-districts. The gaps are primarily the result of the absence of any recorded sales of particular grades of land in some villages or the total absence of any sale records for any tax category for an entire village.

Extensive coverage is noted for Acre, Beisan, Tiberias, Haifa, Tulkaram, Jaffa, Ramle, Nazareth, Safad, and Jerusalem. Few records existed for Gaza, Nablus, Ramallah, Hebron, and Jenin.

When gaps were identified, the following rules were used. First, Gaza was considered similar to Ramle, Hebron to Jerusalem, Jenin to Haifa and Tulkaram, Ramallah and Nablus to Jerusalem. Second, when no sales were recorded under a particular tax category in a given village, the average for the sub-district for the same tax category was used. Third, when a zero appears under a given tax category in a sub-district, the average for all sub-districts for the same tax category was used.

Urban land data proved to be more complicated, given their sheer magnitude. However, fewer gaps were encountered. The most glaring gap was the identification of a zero entry under a building area when an office or rooms were noted. This gap is significant inasmuch as it understates the areas of buildings and their values. To correct this gap, an average room size for the town was established and used to fill in the missing data.

Prices per metre of buildings provided another source of difficulty. They ranged from a low of about £P1.7 to a high of £P4.5. But these prices were apparently representative of cost before World War II. A major adjustment took place between 1940 and 1948 and so these prices had to be adjusted upward. The scale of the adjustment will be discussed in the latter part of this chapter.

D. Valuation of Rural Land

The consequence of using several methods and norms is naturally a multiplicity of values. However, these values are not substantially different from one another and indeed some procedures dominate over others.

Simple averages are seen to result in very high valuations which are not internally consistent. They are also generally sensitive to extreme values and when they are assigned equal weights they tend to generate extreme values. The weighted averages suffer from the same difficulty of being sensitive to extreme values but the weighting scheme infuses a proportionality criterion that moderates this sensitivity. Although we shall present the results of using both simple and weighted averages, we have opted to use the lower but more realistic and defensible estimates generated by using weighted averages.

Differential grades of land result in differential values and these are expressed in the calculations of sale values when these are classified by tax category and by village. To assess the geographical factor, the same calculations were conducted at the village level in each sub-district. Valuations by village and tax category were conducted, again using simple and weighted averages.

We shall present only four tables on rural land values in the text below; the rest of the results are in Appendix X. In Table 20.1, we present the results of using simple and weighted averages for each sub-district independent of tax category and village to assign values to rural losses. In the case of data gaps we used the corresponding averages of the remaining numbers.

Two valuations emerged. Using the simple average, a total of £P633.6 million was estimated, whereas using weighted averages a total of £P391.1 million resulted. Both valuations exclude the 12.5 million dunums in Beersheeba which should add another £P25 million to each of these totals.

Alternatively, when the minimun values are assigned to the sub-district with no recorded sales, the simple averages result in a valuation of £P510 million, whereas the weighted averages result in a valuation of £P329 million [see Table 20.2].

The results of differentiating sale values by tax categories are presented in Table 20.3 for the weighted averages and in Table 20.4 for the simple averages. It is clear from these results that the total value of Arab rural land in Palestine in 1946/7 prices was of the order of £P304.4 million using weighted prices and £P436.9 million using simple averages of prices. Again a value of £P25 million should be added to these totals to include the valuation of the rural land in Beersheeba sub-district.

Table 20.1: Valuation of Palestinian Rural Land Losses: Global Averages (Average)

sub-district	total area (dunums)	simple average	valuation simple average (£P)	weighted average	valuation weighted average (£P)
Acre	772,878	127.475	98,522,623	52.138	40,296,313
Beisan	238,775	15.733	3,756,647	16.871	4,028,373
Tiberias	264,661	85.628	22,662,392	21.667	5,734,410
Haifa	611,244	56.449	34,504,113	40.227	24,588,512
Tulkaram	351,379	39.910	14,023,536	37.430	13,152,116
Jerusalem	281,878	238.119	67,120,507	195.489	55,104,048
Jaffa	166,905	553.941	92,455,523	341.987	57,079,340
Ramle	657,105	44.924	29,519,785	47.678	31,329,452
Gaza	775,134	44.924	34,822,120	47.678	36,956,839
Hebron	1,161,491	119.406	138,688,994	69.085	80,241,606
Jenin	255,676	48.180	12,318,470	38.829	9,927,643
Nablus	23,414	119.406	2,795,772	69.085	1,617,556
Nazareth	360,787	71.039	25,629,948	31.167	11,244,648
Ramallah	6,240	119.406	745,093	69.085	431,090
Safad	525,674	106.552	56,011,616	36.903	19,398,948
Total	6,453,241		633,577,139		391,130,896

Source: Appendix X.

Table 20.2: Valuation of Palestinian Rural Land Losses: Global Averages (Minimum)

sub-district	total area (dunums)	simple average	valuation simple average (£P)	weighted average	valuation weighted average (£P)
Acre	772,878	127.475	98,522,623	52.138	40,296,313
Beisan	238,775	15.733	3,756,647	16.871	4,028,373
Tiberias	264,661	85.628	22,662,392	21.667	5,734,410
Haifa	611,244	56.449	34,504,113	40.227	24,588,512
Tulkaram	351,379	39.910	14,023,536	37.430	13,152,116
Jerusalem	281,878	238.119	67,120,507	195.489	55,104,048
Jaffa	166,905	553.941	92,455,523	341.987	57,079,340
Ramle	657,105	44.924	29,519,785	47.678	31,329,452
Gaza	775,134	44.924	34,822,120	47.678	36,956,839
Hebron	1,161,491	15.733	18,273,738	16.871	19,595,515
Jenin	255,676	48.180	12,318,470	38.829	9,927,643
Nablus	23,414	15.773	369,309	16.871	395,018
Nazareth	360,787	71.039	25,629,948	31.167	11,244,648
Ramallah	6,240	15.773	98,424	16.871	105,275
Safad	525,674	106.552	56,011,616	36.903	19,398,948
Total	6,453,241		510,088,749		328,936,451

Source: Appendix X.

Table 20.3: Valuation of Palestinian Rural Losses by Tax Category (Weighted Averages) (£P)

TABLE: WEIGHTED AVERAGE

	TAX 1-3	TAX 4	TAX 5-8	TAX 9-13	TAX 14-15	TAX 16	TOTAL
• Sub-district: Acre							
Areas by categories	8,858.000	3,424.000	86,435.000	216,680.000	55,696.000	401,785.000	772,878.000
Weighted average	105.696	102.740	67.864	27.715	14.703	72.674	55.866
Valuation by weighted average	936,255.168	351,781.760	5,865,824.840	6,005,286.200	818,898.288	29,199,323.090	43,177,369.346
• Sub-district: Beisan							
Areas by categories	722.000	467.000	13,385.000	149,458.000	9,455.000	65,288.000	238,775.000
Weighted average	164.162	299.651	22.490	21.347	19.456	68.270	35.142
Valuation by weighted average	118,524.964	139,937.017	301,028.650	3,190,479.926	183,956.480	4,457,211.760	8,391,138.797
• Sub-district: Tiberias							
Areas by categories	411.000	1,382.000	21,262.000	158,257.000	13,690.000	69,659.000	264,661.000
Weighted average	24.926	500.353	32.180	11.527	19.524	68.270	31.108
Valuation by weighted average	10,244.586	691,487.846	684,211.160	1,824,228.439	267,283.560	4,755,619.930	8,233,075.521
• Sub-district: Haifa							
Areas by categories	126.000	2,400.000	34,056.000	311,786.000	37,392.000	225,484.000	611,244.000
Weighted average	77.006	207.926	55.381	34.601	7.290	39.931	36.744
Valuation by weighted average	9,702.756	499,022.400	1,886,055.336	10,788,107.386	272,587.680	9,003,801.604	22,459,277.162
• Sub-district: Tulkaram							
Areas by categories	15,979.000	999.000	18,516.000	270,734.000	1,855.000	43,296.000	351,379.000
Weighted average	63.410	70.000	26.327	34.740	18.782	68.270	39.748
Valuation by weighted average	1,013,228.390	69,930.000	487,470.732	9,405,299.160	34,840.610	2,955,817.920	13,966,586.812
• Sub-district: Jerusalem							
Areas by categories	31.000	2,433.000	32,458.000	71,520.000	23,077.000	152,359.000	281,878.000
Weighted average	164.162	299.651	78.270	31.472	19.456	31.314	38.121
Valuation by weighted average	5,089.022	729,050.883	2,540,487.660	2,250,877.440	448,986.112	4,770,969.726	10,745,460.843
• Sub-district: Jaffa							
Areas by categories	45,308.000	756.000	18,624.000	85,300.000	35.000	16,882.000	166,905.000
Weighted average	279.976	1,344.924	440.693	343.522	439.358	250.234	332.235
Valuation by weighted average	12,685,152.608	1,016,762.544	8,207,466.432	29,302,426.600	15,377.530	4,224,450.388	55,451,636.102

Part Five: An Economic Assessment of Total Palestinian Losses

● Sub-district: Ramlé							
Areas by categories	40,543.000	1,580.000	67,438.000	351,665.000	16,527.000	179,352.000	657,105.000
Weighted average	125.983	286.357	53.196	39.369	24.066	26.055	42.707
Valuation by weighted average	5,107,728.769	452,444.060	3,587,431.848	13,844,699.385	397,738.782	4,673,016.360	28,063,059.204
● Sub-district: Gaza							
Areas by categories	18,940.000	2,560.000	56,078.000	530,958.000	85,384.000	81,214.000	775,134.000
Weighted average	125.983	286.357	53.196	39.369	24.066	26.055	40.221
Valuation by weighted average	2,386,118.020	733,073.920	2,983,125.288	20,903,285.502	2,054,851.344	2,116,030.770	31,176,664.614
● Sub-district: Hebron							
Areas by categories	8.000	1,246.000	10,154.000	246,803.000	100,155.000	803,125.000	1,161,491.000
Weighted average	164.162	299.651	78.270	31.472	19.456	31.314	31.024
Valuation by weighted average	1,313.298	373,365.146	794,753.580	7,767,384.016	1,948,615.680	25,149,056.250	36,034,487.968
● Sub-district: Jenin							
Areas by categories	4.000	282.000	8,361.000	156,523.000	7,464.000	83,042.000	255,676.000
Weighted average	70.494	207.596	47.556	34.629	7.546	39.931	36.174
Valuation by weighted average	281.976	58,542.072	397,615.716	5,420,234.967	56,323.344	3,315,950.102	9,248,948.177
● Sub-district: Nablus							
Areas by categories	.000	.000	5,647.000	540.000	13,729.000	3,498.000	23,414.000
Weighted average	164.162	299.651	78.270	31.472	19.456	31.314	35.689
Valuation by weighted average	.000	.000	441,990.690	16,994.880	267,111.424	109,536.372	835,633.366
● Sub-district: Nazareth							
Areas by categories	59.000	1066.000	19,639.000	208,751.000	6,379.000	124,893.000	360,787.000
Weighted average	76.058	242.110	51.898	29.058	8.691	39.931	34.342
Valuation by weighted average	4,487.422	258,089.260	1,019,224.822	6,065,886.558	55,439.889	4,987,102.383	12,390,230.334
● Sub-district: Ramallah							
Areas by categories	.000	.000	.000	1,001.000	196.000	5,043.000	6,240.000
Weighted average	164.162	299.651	78.270	31.472	19.456	31.314	30.967
Valuation by weighted average	.000	.000	.000	31,503.472	3,813.376	157,916.502	193,233.350
● Sub-district: Safad							
Areas by categories	228.000	2,490.000	78,731.000	166,495.000	72,867.000	204,863.000	525,674.000
Weighted average	52.683	498.260	51.961	14.529	19.524	72.674	45.795
Valuation by weighted average	12,011.724	1,240,667.400	4,090,941.491	2,419,005.855	1,422,655.308	14,888,213.662	24,073,495.440
Total land	131,217.000	21,085.000	470,784.000	2,926,471.000	443,901.000	2,459,783.000	6,453,241.000
Total valuation	22,290,138.701	6,614,154.308	33,287,628.245	119,235,699.786	8,248,475.407	114,764,016.819	304,440,117.266

Source: Appendix X.

Table 20.4: Valuation of Palestinian Rural Losses by Tax Category (Simple Averages)
(£P)

	TAX 1–3	TAX 4	TAX 5–8	TAX 9–13	TAX 14–15	TAX 16	TOTAL
			TABLE: SIMPLE AVERAGE				
• Sub-district: Acre							
Areas by categories	8,858.000	3,424.000	86,435.000	216,680.000	55,696.000	401,785.000	772,878.000
Simple average	105.690	102.740	118.406	59.915	71.493	72.674	74.638
Valuation by simple average	936,255.168	351,781.760	10,234,422.610	12,982,382.200	3,981,874.128	29,199,323.090	57,686,038.956
• Sub-district: Beisan							
Areas by categories	722.000	467.000	13,385.000	149,458.000	9,455.000	65,288.000	238,775.000
Simple average	259.608	384.187	22.495	16.949	44.659	84.380	38.247
Valuation by simple average	187,436.976	179,415.329	301,095.575	2,533,163.642	422,250.845	5,509,001.440	9,132,363.807
• Sub-district: Tiberias							
Areas by categories	411.000	1,382.000	21,262.000	158,257.000	13,690.000	69,659.000	264,661.000
Simple average	24.926	463.430	32.529	34.536	15.199	84.380	48.718
Valuation by simple average	10,244.588	640,460.260	691,631.598	5,465,563.752	208,074.310	5,877,826.420	12,893,800.926
• Sub-district: Haifa							
Areas by categories	126.000	2,400.000	34,056.000	311,786.000	37,392.000	225,484.000	611,244.000
Simple average	64.296	232.940	42.354	39.093	17.155	58.439	45.836
Valuation by simple average	8,101.296	559,056.000	1,442,407.824	12,188,650.098	641,459.760	13,177,059.476	28,016,734.454
• Sub-district: Tulkaram							
Areas by categories	15,979.000	999.000	18,516.000	270,734.000	1,855.000	43,296.000	351,379.000
Simple average	73.261	70.000	33.529	39.321	18.782	84.380	46.090
Valuation by simple average	1,170,637.519	69,930.000	620,822.964	10,645,531.614	34,840.610	3,653,317.480	16,195,079.187
• Sub-district: Jerusalem							
Areas by categories	31.000	2,433.000	32,458.000	71,520.000	23,077.000	152,359.000	281,878.000
Simple average	259.608	384.187	91.314	32.115	44.659	37.158	45.748
Valuation by simple average	8,047.848	934,726.971	2,963,869.812	2,296,864.800	1,030,595.743	5,661,355.722	12,895,460.896
• Sub-district: Jaffa							
Areas by categories	45,308.000	756.000	18,624.000	85,300.000	35.000	16,882.000	166,905.000
Simple average	576.008	2,184.939	408.100	495.016	439.358	221.911	487.323
Valuation by simple average	26,097,770.464	1,651,813.884	7,600,454.400	42,224,864.800	15,377.530	3,746,301.502	81,336,582.580

Part Five: An Economic Assessment of Total Palestinian Losses

• Sub-district: Ramle							
Areas by categories	40,543.000	1,580.000	67,438.000	351,665.000	16,527.000	179,352.000	657,105.000
Simple average	136.571	233.048	69.073	54.683	24.615	25.598	52.946
Valuation by simple average	5,536,998.052	368,215.840	4,658,144.974	19,230,097.195	406,812.105	4,591,052.496	34,791,320.663
• Sub-district: Gaza							
Areas by categories	18,940.000	2,560.000	56,078.000	530,958.000	85,384.000	81,214.000	775,134.000
Simple average	136.571	233.048	69.073	54.683	24.615	25.598	51.955
Valuation by simple average	2,586,654.740	596,602.880	3,873,475.694	29,034,376.314	2,101,727.160	2,078,915.972	40,271,752.760
• Sub-district: Hebron							
Areas by categories	8.000	1,246.000	10,154.000	246,803.000	100,155.000	803,125.000	1,161,491.000
Simple average	259.608	384.187	91.314	32.115	44.659	37.158	37.580
Valuation by simple average	2,076.864	478,697.002	927,202.356	7,926,078.345	4,472,822.145	29,842,518.750	43,649,395.462
• Sub-district: Jenin							
Areas by categories	4.000	282.000	8,361.000	156,523.000	7,464.000	83,042.000	255,676.000
Simple average	220.169	774.554	312.802	34.629	39.006	189.926	95.112
Valuation by simple average	880.676	218,424.228	2,615,337.522	5,420,234.967	291,140.784	15,771,834.892	24,317,853.069
• Sub-district: Nablus							
Areas by categories	.000	.000	5,647.000	540.000	13,729.000	3,498.000	23,414.000
Simple average	259.608	384.187	91.314	32.115	44.659	37.158	54.501
Valuation by simple average	.000	.000	515,650.158	17,342.100	613,123.411	129,978.684	1,276,094.353
• Sub-district: Nazareth							
Areas by categories	59.000	1,066.000	19,639.000	208,751.000	6,376.000	124,893.000	360,787.000
Simple average	134.824	242.110	302.920	29.058	49.509	189.926	100.661
Valuation by simple average	7,954.616	258,089.260	5,949,045.880	6,065,886.558	315,817.911	23,720,427.918	36,317,222.143
• Sub-district: Ramallah							
Areas by categories	.000	.000	.000	1,001.000	196.000	5,043.000	6,240.000
Simple average	259.608	384.187	91.314	32.115	44.659	37.158	36.585
Valuation by simple average	.000	.000	.000	32,147.115	8,753.164	187,387.794	228,288.073
• Sub-district: Safad							
Areas by categories	228.000	2,490.000	78,731.000	166,495.000	72,867.000	204,863.000	525,674.000
Simple average	32.656	489.115	374.410	14.529	15.199	18.169	72.196
Valuation by simple average	7,445.568	1,217,896.350	29,477,673.710	2,419,005.855	1,107,505.533	3,722,155.847	37,951,682.863
Total land	131,217.000	21,085.000	470,784.000	2,926,471.000	443,901.000	2,459,783.000	6,453,241.000
Total valuation	22,290,138.701	6,614,154.308	33,287,628.245	119,235,699.786	8,248,479.407	114,764,016.819	436,959,670.192

Source: Appendix X.

The robustness of the results for the weighted prices under the different valuation schemes is another argument for their adoption. Several other criteria based on a priori expectations are used to substantiate this adoption. First, the grade differentials of land appear to be preserved under this weighting scheme. In other words, it is to be expected that the value of citrus, banana, and fruit lands should dominate lower grades of land in tax categories 9-13, 14-15, and 16. This dominance is preserved.

Second, it is to be expected, for instance, that land near Acre, Jaffa, Haifa, and Jerusalem, which is uncultivable and capable of being used for building, should have higher values than comparable land in Nazareth, Tulkaram, Beisan, and Tiberias. Again this expectation is fulfilled.

Another independent confirmation of the sale values may be obtained through a capitalization of the streams of net real incomes of farm lands. Since farming income is sensitive to location, climatic conditions, and type of crops, three representative farms located in different areas, and which were studied in detail in the *Survey of Palestine* are singled out for analysis here.[5]

Farm A is in the hills around Jerusalem and comprises 95 dunums of which only 30 dunums are used for plantation crops. The gross income of the farm is £P177.050, whereas net income is only £P100.400. The gross income from plantation crops is £P83.300. The details of production and income on the 30 dunums devoted to plantation crops are in Table 20.5.

Table 20.5: Income from Farm A: Plantation Crops

crop	area (dunums)	yield (kgs)		value per kg (£P)	gross value (£P)
Olives	10	700		40	28.000
Figs	10	2,000	dried	9	18.000
Table grapes	5	2,500		5	12.500
Apricots	3	2,100		8	16.800
Almonds	2	160		50	8.000
Total	30				83.300

Source *A Survey of Palestine*, p. 281.

A total of 45 dunums are devoted to the production of annual crops. The gross income from this production is £P51.650. Given an annual cost of 450 mils per dunum, a net income of £P31.400 is identified. In addition to plantation crops and annual crops the farm derives a total of £P11.350 in net income from livestock.

The total annual net income of this farm is estimated to exceed £P100.400. It is derived as shown in Table 20.6.

Part Five: An Economic Assessment of Total Palestinian Losses

Table 20.6: Net Farm Income: Farm A

details	gross income (£P)	expenditures (£P)	net income (£P)
Plantation crops	83.300	25.650	57.650
Annual crops	51.650	20.250	31.400
Livestock	42.100	30.750	11.350
Total	177.050	76.650	100.400

Source: *A Survey of Palestine*, p. 284.

Net income per dunum devoted to plantation crops is £P1.922 which when capitalized using a discount rate of 4 per cent yields an average value of £P48. This is almost exactly equal to the average dunum price used in valuing tax categories 5-13 in the Jerusalem area. The net income per dunum in the production of annual crops is about 698 mils which yields a capitalized value of £P17.444. The corresponding value used in Table 20.3 for the same category of land in Jerusalem sub-district is £P19.456.

These figures are close enough to lend a measure of reliability to the estimates used in our tables, particularly those corresponding to the weighted averages.

A similar analysis was carried out using information on Farm B located in Jenin sub-district. The area of this farm is 135 dunums of which 10 dunums are devoted to plantation crops and 120 dunums to annual crops in a three-course rotation.

The details of income generated are presented in Table 20.7.

Table 20.7: Net Farm Income: Farm B

details	gross income (£P)	expenditures (£P)	net income (£P)
Plantation crops	28.000	7.000	21.000
Annual crops	137.500	66.000	71.500
Livestock	42.100	30.750	11.350
Total	207.600	103.750	103.850

Source: *A Survey of Palestine*, p. 286.

The net capitalized value for tax categories 9-13 in Jenin using the net stream of income of Farm B is £P39.450. This is slightly higher than the value of £P34.629 shown in Table 20.3 but close enough to make the number credible. We would in general prefer our estimates to be on the low side.

The value of £P304.4 million is chosen to represent a low estimate of Palestinian losses of rural land, exclusive of the losses in the Beersheeba sub-district. If the latter were included this estimate of the total loss would rise to

£P329.4 million in 1946/7 prices. Applying the standard inflation adjustment raises this value to £P398.6 million in 1948 prices.

A third independent check uses the geographical details of each sub-district. The valuation of rural property village by village allowing for locational differences and grade differences results in a total valuation of £P329.4 million in 1946 prices (see Appendix X). The inclusion of locational details in addition to the fertility differences resulted in the same total value for rural losses. This is another confirmation of the reliability of our estimates. This value rises to about £P398.6 million in 1948 prices.

In Appendix X we show two valuations of rural losses based on village details. Valuation 1 is based on the weighted average price in each village, whereas valuation 2 is based on the weighted average of all villages in a given sub-district. Fortunately, the two valuations are marginally different from one another.

Table 20.8: Valuation of Arab Urban Lands and Buildings in Palestine in 1947

urban area	land area (dunums)	building area (dunums)	value of land (£P)	value of building (£P)	total value of buildings and land (£P)
Acre	1,749	266	146,273	514,493	660,765
Beisan	590	72	85,709	125,712	211,421
Nazareth	4,585	310	212,469	715,217	927,686
Safad	1,053	191	104,215	371,240	475,455
Tiberias	611	127	283,040	364,928	647,968
Haifa	15,421	1,490	6,724,481	5,963,818	12,688,299
Jerusalem	10,798	1,043	4,902,832	11,754,215	16,657,047
Jaffa	9,683	1,035	3,504,084	4,500,730	8,004,814
Ramle	1,569	81	271,980	139,487	411,467
Lydda	3,210	167	556,453	287,570	844,023
Beersheba	3,256	169	90,680	290,802	381,482
Tel Aviv	1,970	190	752,225	511,239	1,263,464
Majdal	1,146	282	331,480	779,486	1,110,966
Shafa 'Amr	304	45	8,466	33,220	41,686
Total	55,675	5,468	17,974,387	26,352,157	44,326,544

Source: Appendix XI public lands are allocated according to population shares of land owned by Arabs and Jews and using the old vector of prices per metre of buildings.

Part Five: An Economic Assessment of Total Palestinian Losses

E. Valuation of Urban Property

Extensive information on urban land holdings and buildings in Palestine in 1947 was collected by the UN Land Expert. As noted above, these data formed the basis of our estimates of Arab urban property losses in 1947. Thirteen urban areas (or towns) are the focus of this section. More than 55,675 dunums of land and 5,468 dunums of buildings were identified to belong to Palestinians before 1948. These were lost following Israel's creation.[6] The major losses, as is clear in Tables 20.8 to 20.11, are concentrated in Haifa, Jerusalem, Jaffa, and Nazareth. The proportion of built-up areas on Arab urban lands varied from town to town, and those used were calculated from the UN data which are presented in Appendix XI. The highest proportions are in Majdal (24.7 per cent), in Tiberias (21 per cent), and in Safad (18.2 per cent). The overall effective average ratio of built-up area to land area is 9.8 per cent.

Table 20.9: Valuation of Arab Urban Lands and Buildings in Palestine in 1947

urban area	land area (dunums)	building area (dunums)	value of land (£P)	value of building (£P)	total value of buildings and land (£P)
Acre	1,479	266	146,273	514,493	660,766
Beisan	587	71	85,273	123,966	209,239
Nazareth	4,585	310	212,469	715,217	927,686
Safad	1,049	191	103,820	371,240	475,455
Tiberias	673	139	311,761	399,347	711,108
Haifa	16,490	1,593	7,190,629	6,372,000	13,562,629
Jerusalem	10,636	1,027	4,829,276	11,629,748	16,459,024
Jaffa	9,613	1,028	3,478,752	4,554,040	8,032,792
Ramle	1,569	81	271,986	139,487	411,467
Lydda	3,210	167	556,453	287,570	844,023
Beersheba	3,341	173	93,047	297,560	390,607
Tel Aviv	1,648	179	705,640	481,510	1,187,150
Majdal	1,146	282	331,480	779,486	1,110,906
Shafa 'Amr	304	45	8,466	33,220	41,686
Total	56,530	5,552	18,325,325	26,698,884	45,024,209

Source: Appendix XI; public lands are allocated according to population shares of land owned by Arabs and Jews and using the new vector of prices per meter of buildings.

Palestinian Rights and Losses in 1948

The average price per dunum of land in the various urban areas was taken directly from UN statistics (see Appendix XI). These prices are considered, by experts familiar with market prices at the time, to be somewhat on the low side. However, the discrepancies between market prices and these weighted averages are not considered to be substantial and so no adjustment was made to them. The fact that they are regarded as low has the advantage of refuting any charge that Arab claims are being exaggerated. In Tables 20.8-20.11, the weighted average price per dunum of land in each urban area is the same.

However, the average prices per square metre of buildings were found to understate grossly the true cost of replacement at the time. Thus, in Tables 20.8 and 20.9 the valuation of Arab urban buildings was undertaken using the UN data, whereas in Tables 20.10 and 20.11, a new set of prices per square metre of buildings that reflect the market values in 1947 was adopted. The difference in price by town is presented in Table 20.12.

Table 20.10: Valuation of Arab Urban Lands and Buildings in Palestine in 1947

urban area	land area (dunums)	building area (dunums)	value of land (£P)	value of building (£P)	total value of buildings and land (£P)
Acre	1,749	266	146,273	2,660,000	2,806,273
Beisan	590	72	85,709	648,000	733,709
Nazareth	4,585	310	212,469	3,720,000	3,932,469
Safad	1,053	191	104,215	1,910,000	2,014,215
Tiberias	611	127	283,040	1,905,000	2,188,040
Haifa	15,422	1,490	6,724,481	29,800,000	36,524,481
Jerusalem	10,798	1,043	4,902,832	26,075,000	30,977,832
Jaffa	9,683	1,035	3,504,084	22,770,000	26,274,084
Ramle	1,569	81	271,980	810,000	1,081,980
Lydda	3,210	167	556,453	1,670,000	2,226,453
Beersheba	3,256	169	90,580	1,352,000	1,442,680
Tel Aviv	1,970	190	752,225	4,180,000	4,932,225
Majdal	1,146	282	331,480	2,538,000	2,869,480
Shafa 'Amr	304	45	8,466	405,000	413,466
Total	55,675	5,468	17,974,387	100,443,000	118,417,387

Source: Appendix XI; public lands are allocated according to population shares of land owned by Arabs and Jews and using the old vector of prices per metre of buildings.

Part Five: An Economic Assessment of Total Palestinian Losses

Naturally, major differences in the valuation of buildings emerge under the two price vectors. Since the higher prices are more in line with the market norms in 1947, we have opted to use the estimates of Tables 20.10 and 20.11.

According to our figures, Arab urban losses in 1947 are evaluated at £P118.4 million. Of this total, almost £P18 million represents the value of vacated urban lands, and the remaining £P100.4 million the value of vacated buildings. In 1948 prices, these estimated losses rise to £P130.3 million.[7]

A number of observations should be made here to justify and validate the figure of £P130.3 million.

First, the land owned by the Arabs in the urban areas of Palestine includes that of Muslims, Christians, and other non-Jews lumped together. It is generally presumed, mistakenly, that the Arabs of Palestine are only those who profess the religion of Islam. The principle adopted here is to include all non-Jews as one

Table 20.11: Valuation of Arab Urban Lands and Buildings in Palestine in 1947

urban area	land area (dunums)	building area (dunums)	value of land (£P)	value of building (£P)	total value of buildings and land (£P)
Acre	1,479	266	146,273	2,660,000	2,806,273
Beisan	587	71	85,273	640,800	726,073
Nazareth	4,585	310	212,469	3,720,000	3,932,469
Safad	1,049	191	103,820	1,910,000	2,013,820
Tiberias	673	139	311,761	2,087,646	2,399,407
Haifa	16,490	1,593	7,190,629	31,858,680	39,049,309
Jerusalem	10,636	1,027	4,829,276	25,685,940	30,515,216
Jaffa	9,613	1,028	3,478,752	22,607,853	26,086,605
Ramle	1,569	81	271,986	810,000	1,081,986
Lydda	3,210	167	556,453	1,670,000	2,226,453
Beersheba	3,341	173	93,047	1,387,183	1,480,230
Tel Aviv	1,848	179	705,640	3,927,370	4,633,010
Majdal	1,146	282	331,480	2,538,000	2,869,480
Shafa 'Amr	304	45	8,466	405,000	413,466
Total	56,530	5,552	18,325,325	101,908,472	120,233,797

Source: Appendix XI; public lands are allocated according to population shares of land owned by Arabs and Jews and using the new vector of prices per metre of buildings.

Palestinian Rights and Losses in 1948

group which is considered as representative of Palestinian refugees.

Second, the weighted prices of land were cross-classified against net annual values. The rank correlations were all higher than 0.72 (a perfect correlation coefficient is equal to one). This indicates that the vectors of weights and prices are consistent with a priori orderings of value as represented by net annual values.

Third, the old vector of per metre prices of urban buildings was scaled upward using two principles – the relationship of one price to another is generally preserved in the two vectors and the blow-up scalars were calculated on the basis of changes in construction workers' wages and prices of construction materials between 1939 and 1947.

Fourth, whenever more than one estimate was made, the lower estimate was always adopted.

Fifth, several Arab households remained in their premises and so the total figure may overstate the magnitude of Arab urban property losses. However, our findings indicate that the proportion of urban lands and buildings that remained in the hands of Palestinians who opted to stay in Palestine in 1948 is only a tiny fraction of their original holdings. A case in point is Jerusalem, where it is estimated that at most 1,000 dunums of urban lands could be claimed to have remained in Arab hands after 1948. But given our modest estimates of the buildings on Arab land, and the adoption of the lower estimates of Arab shares in public lands, any overestimation in this regard is balanced, if not cancelled, by this source of underestimation.

Table 20.12: Prices per Metre of Urban Buildings in Palestine

urban area	old price ($£P$)	new price ($£P$)
Acre	1.944	10
Beisan	1.746	9
Nazareth	2.307	12
Safad	1.943	10
Tiberias	2.873	15
Haifa	4.000	20
Jerusalem	11.324	25
Jaffa	4.430	22
Ramle-Lydda	1.722	10
Beersheba	1.720	8
Tel Aviv	2.690	22
Majdal	2.765	9
Shafa 'Amr	0.737	9

Part Five: An Economic Assessment of Total Palestinian Losses

In any case, even when the value of land owned by Arabs who remained in Palestine and retained ownership of their property is subtracted from the totals in Tables 20.8 to 20.11, the resulting figures are only marginally changed.

F. Concluding Remarks

A total of £P528.9 million represents the value of Arab real estate losses in Palestine. By any standards this is a modest figure, even in 1948 prices. In fact it is an underestimate. But low as it is, it is still many times (over six times) higher than the valuation of these losses by the UN Refugee Office. What is surprising about this discrepancy is the fact that we have used exactly the same UN data that should have formed the basis of their valuation. The only exception is the adjustment of building prices. But this exception can explain no more than one-tenth of the discrepancy. The UN estimate of Palestinian real estate losses in 1948 is thus shamefully unrepresentative of their true market value.

21

Palestinian Losses: a Final Balance Sheet

A. Introduction

A homeland is much too precious to be assigned a monetary value; and no people in history have been known willingly to trade their heritage for material benefits. No financial compensation – however attractive or substantial – could offset the effects of its loss. The loss of Palestine is principally a moral one, whose dimensions and costs stretch far beyond property and money.

The Palestinian wealth confiscated by the Zionists in Palestine was, however, considerable and the costs they imposed on the Palestinians exceeded their property losses. These costs must be assessed, despite the passage of time and despite the fact that no monetary value could ever equal or compensate the loss of a homeland. The principal reason for making the assessment is to document the scale and consequences of the calamity that has befallen the natives of the Holy Land. Its dimensions are not purely financial; they involve major psychological and human suffering that may only indirectly be assigned monetary values, like the Jewish claims against Germany under the *Wiedergutmachung*.

Palestinian property losses add up to a sizeable £P743 million in 1948 prices. When human capital losses are added, the total rises to £P1,182.2 million. When these sums are converted into 1984 prices, using the United States inflation rate between 1948 and 1984 and the prevailing rate of exchange of $4.03 to the British pound in 1948, the losses amount to a staggering $147,000 million for the all-inclusive wealth losses and $92,000 million for the restrictive physical property valuation.

It is legitimate to consider the appropriateness of using United States dollars and inflation rates. It is legitimate to ask whether it would be more appropriate to use British pounds and British inflation rates instead, given the close association between Britain and Palestine then. The 1984 value of the Palestinian losses using British inflation rates between 1948 and 1984 amounts to £48,900 million for the all-inclusive wealth valuation and £30,600 million for the valuation exclusive of human wealth.

The valuation in British pounds is significantly lower than in US dollars. But either valuation is indicative of major losses incurred by the Palestinians. The dollar valuation is perhaps more valid given the international standing of the dollar and its unequivocal dominance of the world financial markets. Most Arab economies of the area have broken their strong links with Britain and established new links with other trading partners using the dollar as the dominant international currency. The British pound has suffered major losses over the years and it is inconceivable that Palestine would have maintained its earlier ties to the British economy and the British pound, had it remained Arab and independent.

B. Distribution of Losses by Item

The losses of major items are presented in Table 21.1. The largest losses are those of rural land, accounting for 53.6 per cent of the total property losses. Urban and rural land losses together account for about 72 per cent of these losses.

Table 21.1: The Distribution of Palestinian Losses in 1948 Prices

items	value (£P million)
Industrial capital	11.400
Agricultural capital	66.800
Commercial and private vehicles	0.950
Commercial capital and stocks	45.900
Hotels and restaurants	10.500
Financial assets	12.500
Private and personal wealth	54.000
Infrastructure	12.100
Rural land	398.600
Urban property	130.259
Total	743.050

Agricultural capital losses and losses of personal and household effects contribute £P66.8 million and £P54 million, respectively. Together they account for about 17 per cent of the total. The smallest losses are those of commercial and private vehicles.

Human capital losses are real and substantial. The loss of complementary inputs reduced the productive Palestinian farmers to the status of surplus

Part Five: An Economic Assessment of Total Palestinian Losses

agricultural workers in the basically surplus labour economies of Jordan, Syria, and Lebanon. Skilled Palestinian workers also had to compete with the indigenous workers in the host countries against several handicaps. A large number of them had to wait for months or years before they were able to find work, thereby wasting their potential and losing their proficiency.

The addition of human capital losses to property losses is justifiable and necessary. But the valuation procedure is not complete unless we add yet another sum to compensate for psychological suffering, dislocation, and loss of life and limb. The Jews were able to obtain enormous sums of money from the Federal Republic of Germany in compensation for these sufferings and losses. Merely on the basis of the proportion of the total compensation received by Jews from the FRG for these items, another $23,000 million at least would have to be added to the total compensation bill in 1984 prices.

It has not been possible to find out how many Palestinians lost their lives or were injured during the creation of the state of Israel, and attempts to make a fair estimate have failed. However, the number is not inconsiderable since it was Zionist policy to terrorize the Palestinians into leaving their homes and country. Thus, before 15 May 1948 when the Jewish state was due to come into existence, the Zionists carried out a few calculated 'massacres' of the Deir Yasin type. This is confirmed from the following quotes.

a) Sir John Bagot Glubb disclosed that a British officer of the Jordan Arab Legion under his command enquired of a Palestine government Jewish official 'whether the new Jewish state would not have many internal troubles in view of the fact that the Arab inhabitants of the Jewish state would be equal in number to the Jews'. The Jewish official is reported to have replied: 'Oh no! That will be fixed. A few calculated massacres will soon get rid of them.'[1]

b) Arieh Yitzhaqi, Jewish historian and researcher, accused Palmach (the striking force of Hagana, controlled by the Jewish Agency) of operations similar to those of ETZEL (the Irgun Zvei Leumi led by Menachem Begin) and LEHI (the Stern Gang led by Yitzak Shamir). He wrote:

> If we assemble the facts, we realize that, to a great extent, the battle followed the familiar pattern of the occupation of an Arab village in 1948. In the first months of the War of Independence, Hagana and Palmach troops carried out dozens of operations of this (Deir Yasin) kind, the method adopted being to raid an enemy village and blow up as many houses as possible in it. In the course of these operations, many old people, women and children were killed wherever there was resistance.[2]

Yitzhaqi then lists some of the Arab villages raided and the number of Arabs killed:

Palestinian Rights and Losses in 1948

1. *Balad Esh-Sheikh* – 60 killed, most of them non-combatants.
2. *Sa'sa* – 20 houses were blown up over their inhabitants and some 60 Arabs were killed, most of them women and children.
3. *Katamon Quarter of Jerusalem* – Arab women working as servants in the St Simon Monastery were killed. (*Note:* Other deaths known to the writer who lived in Katamon Quarter were 7 at Semiramis Hotel; and 14 buildings were blown up killing another 3 persons.)
4. *Lydda Town* – orders were given to fire on anyone seen in the streets... in a few hours, going from house to house and firing at every moving target. According to the commander (of Palmach) report, 250 Arabs were killed.

Arieh Yitzhaqi concludes: 'There were also the indiscriminate reprisal attacks on Arab civilian commmunications, in which many innocent citizens were killed.'[3]

Other large-scale massacres were:

5. *Deir Yasin* – 250 men, women, and children.
6. *Ed-Dawayima* – 200 persons mostly between the ages of 70 and 90.

No figures are available for people killed in the major cities of Jaffa, Haifa, and Jerusalem, or the smaller towns such as Acre, Nazareth, Ramle, and Lydda, whose inhabitants were expelled. The numbers were none the less very large and the value of $23,000 million is surely a low estimate for these losses in human life and psychological damage.

C. Relationship of Our Estimates to Previous Estimates

The United Nations estimate of £P120 million is a substantial undervaluation of Palestinian losses. The scale of underestimation is embarrassingly large: the UN estimate is 16.2 per cent of ours. Significantly, we used the United Nations data base, presumably the same that their assessors used to reach a different valuation. We were unable to find a vector of prices that is consistent with the UN estimate. The data in Appendices X and XI demonstrate clearly and unequivocally that had the UN Land Experts used their data base correctly, their valuation would have been much closer to ours.

A detailed presentation of the alternative estimates of Palestinian losses is presented in Table 21.2. It is clear that the alternative valuations result in different estimates. It is interesting, however, to note that some major similarities remain despite the significant differences in the procedures and data bases utilized. The focus of the discussion here is to compare our valuation of the losses with previous attempts. To do so we defined the losses in terms of their various components.

The Arab League study is highly aggregative and does not provide detailed estimates for most of our components. Rural land losses are, however, broken

Part Five: An Economic Assessment of Total Palestinian Losses

down in terms of grades of land and are, therefore, more comparable. The total value of these losses in the Arab Higher Committee study is slightly more than half of our estimate and that of Professor Sayigh. However, a very high value is assigned to urban property losses in the Arab League study. But these losses include cattle and poultry, factories, and machinery. If we were to aggregate our estimates to match those of the AHC, we would arrive at £P213 million, which is only a quarter of the League's estimates. On the other hand, Professor Sayigh's estimate of these same assets is £P286.7 million – a figure which is much closer to ours.

A total of £P200 million is the estimate assigned by the AHC to movable property losses. This is again significantly higher than either our estimate of £P67.5 million or Professor Sayigh's of £P79.5 million.

It is obvious that the degree of comparability of our estimates with those of Professor Sayigh is very high. While there are some glaring differences as regards the individual components of the losses, these are mainly the result of different definitions and data.

The unique credibility of our global figures derives principally from their consistency with the capitalization of national income and from the solid data base of most of our estimates.

Two other features of our calculations deserve notice. First, we took the step of valuing human capital losses along the same principles used for valuing any other capital item. Second, we included an aggregative figure for psychological damage, following the precedent set by the Federal Republic of Germany's *Wiedergutmachung* compensation scheme.

Table 21.2: Alternative Valuations of Palestinian Property Losses in 1948 (in £P million)

items	UN	AHC	Sayigh	this Study
1. Industrial capital			15.0	11.4
2. Agricultural capital			10.0	66.8
3. Commercial and private vehicles			15.0	0.95
4. Commercial capital and stocks			5.0	45.9
5. Private and personal property	20	200	62.5	54.0
6. Hotels and restaurants			3.0	10.5
7. Financial assets		7	2.0	12.5
8. Infrastructure				12.1
9. Rural land		220	390.5	398.6
10. Urban property	100	1100*	253.7	130.3
Total	120	1933	756.7	743.050

* This figure includes lands, buildings, establishments, cattle, poultry, factories, machinery, etc.

Although it is true that Professor Sayigh attempted to accumulate the income losses of the refugees over time, his procedures were excessively time-variant and non-addable. Our valuation depended on the shares of labour income in the national accounts of the time and the use of consistent capitalization procedures similar to those currently in use in the literature and courts.

D. The Capitalized Income Approach versus the Itemized Approach

When income is treated as the return on capital, a total valuation of £P 634 million can be assigned to the property losses of Palestinian refugees in 1948. On the other hand, a total estimate of £P743 million is derived from a detailed enumeration of refugee losses in 1948. The two estimates vary by a total of £P109 million or 14.7 per cent. This difference could arise from a combination of the following factors: *a)* the Palestinian share in net domestic product being estimated low; *b)* the share of labour income in net domestic product being estimated high; *c)* the real rate of interest being estimated high; *d)* the valuation of property losses being on the high side.

Factors *b)*, *c)* and *d)* are not likely to explain the discrepancy because only the low estimates of property losses were used, labour income share in total net domestic product at the time could not possibly have exceeded 50 per cent, given the nature of the Palestinian economy in 1948, and the real rate of interest is already low enough.

The first factor perhaps offers a better explanation of the difference between the two estimates of Palestinian property losses. There are strong grounds for believing that Loftus and others have exaggerated the share of Jews in net domestic product of Palestine in 1944/5. The financial and human capital that Jewish immigrants brought to Palestine in the 1930s and early 1940s was indeed substantial. However, the numbers of Jews in Palestine then and their share in total land ownership were so low that productivity differentials between them and Arab Palestinians could not possibly justify or explain the high share of net domestic product assigned to them. Furthermore, there is always the possibility that national income accounting procedures which lay heavy emphasis on organized market transactions could underestimate the products and income flows of traditional sectors. Consequently, the discrepancy could well be due to an underestimation of the Arab share in net domestic product which is derived primarily from traditional sector activities.

E. Concluding Remarks

Although this is not the first attempt at assessing Palestinian losses, it is based on new, more comprehensive, consistent, and precise identifications and valuations, using the most recent methods and procedures and the rich data sets of the United Nations.

Part Five: An Economic Assessment of Total Palestinian Losses

The basic premise of the valuation of Palestinian losses is that human beings when unimpeded would seek to attain the highest level of utility given their economic endowments and prices. Given the chance, individuals will take advantage of any exchange opportunity to move to their highest level of satisfaction where their willingness to trade is matched exactly by their ability to do so. Circumstances outside the objective conditions of the market that prevent the economic agents from reaching their preferred status result in loss of satisfaction and welfare. The size of these losses is generally identified as the difference between the maximun level of satisfaction possible and that which is realized under the forced circumstances. Compensation is a mechanism to reinstate the individual in the situation he or she had chosen before other circumstances intervened.

A homeland is too precious to be assigned a monetary value. This principle cannot be emphasized too strongly. Similarly, no financial compensation, however large, could make up for the loss of a homeland. Nor is there any compensation for the loss of human life, the dissolution of families, and the separation of loved ones. Our expression of these losses in financial terms does not mean that the figure we reached would compensate the Palestinians for the loss of Palestine. It is simply a historical and monetary valuation of the injustices perpetrated by the Zionists, no more and no less.

Maps

MAP A

Ottoman Administrative Districts (1914)

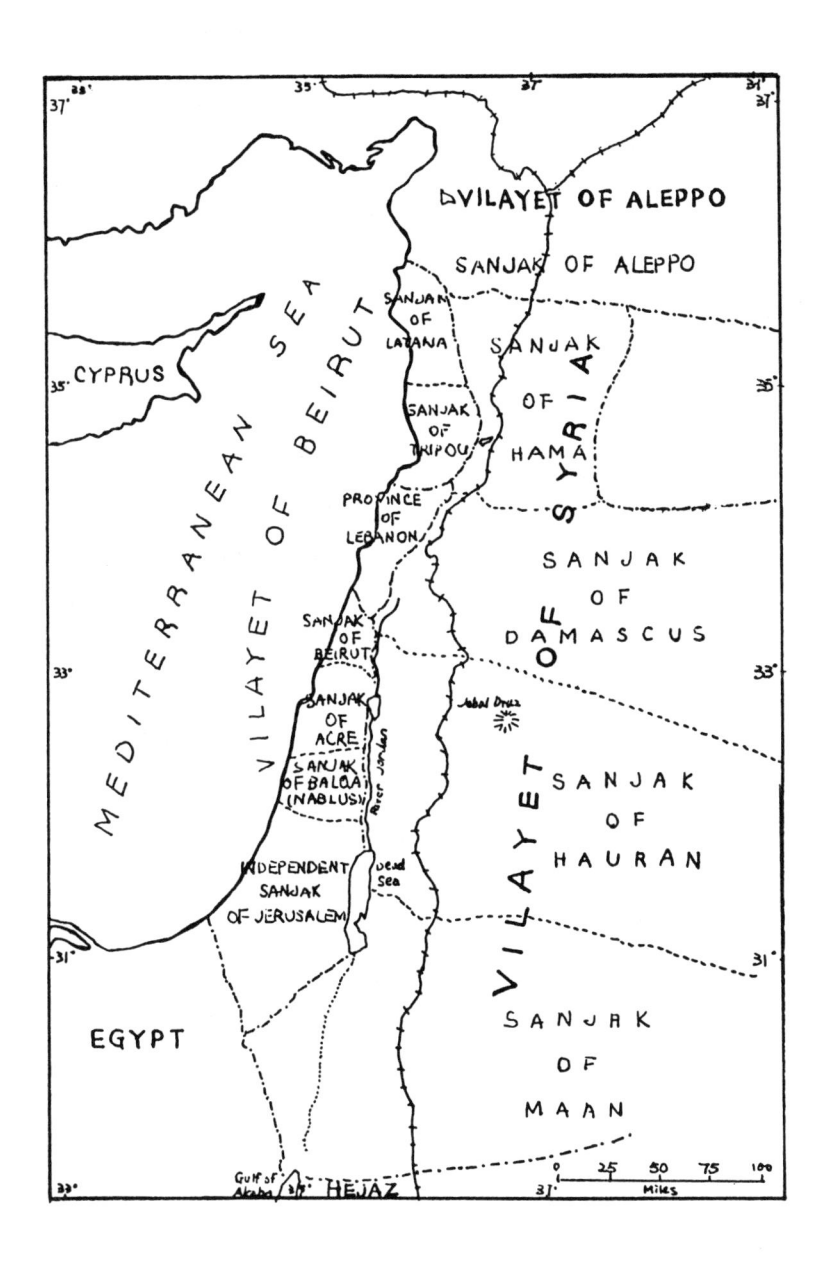

MAP B

The Eastern Arab World

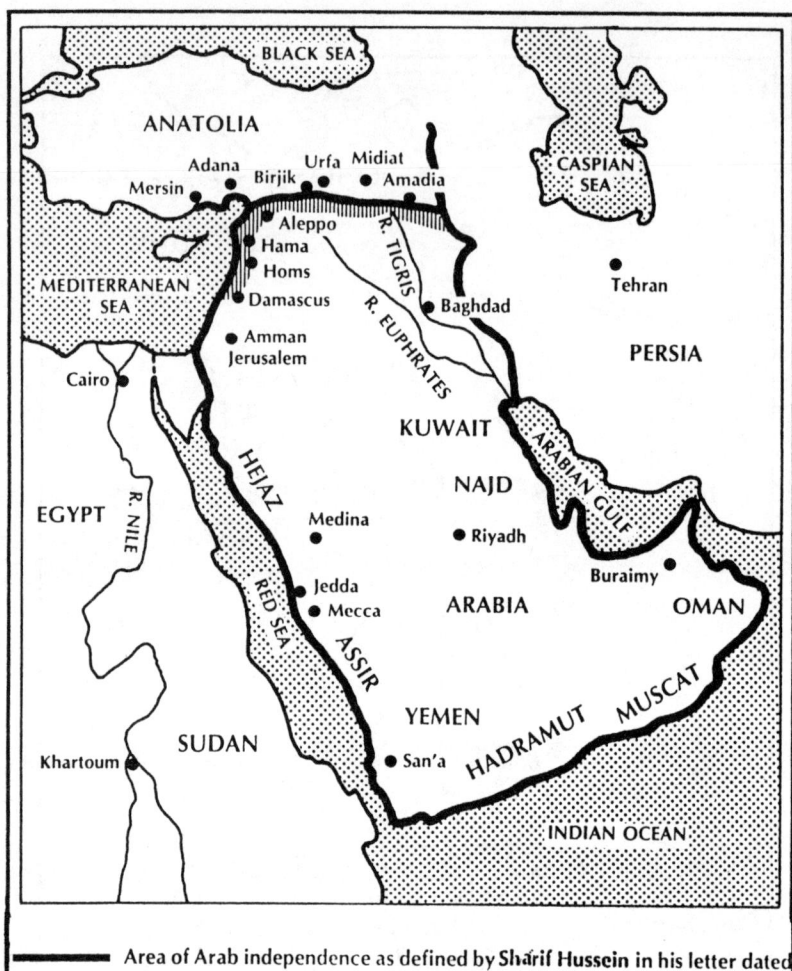

———— Area of Arab independence as defined by **Sharif Hussein** in his letter dated 14 July 1915 to Sir Henry McMahon, British High Commissioner in Egypt.

||||||||||||||||||| Area excluded from Arab independence as defined by Sir Henry McMahon in his letter to Sharif Hussein No. 4 dated 24 October 1915 and further explained by letter No. 6 dated 14 December 1915.

MAP C

Syria 1916

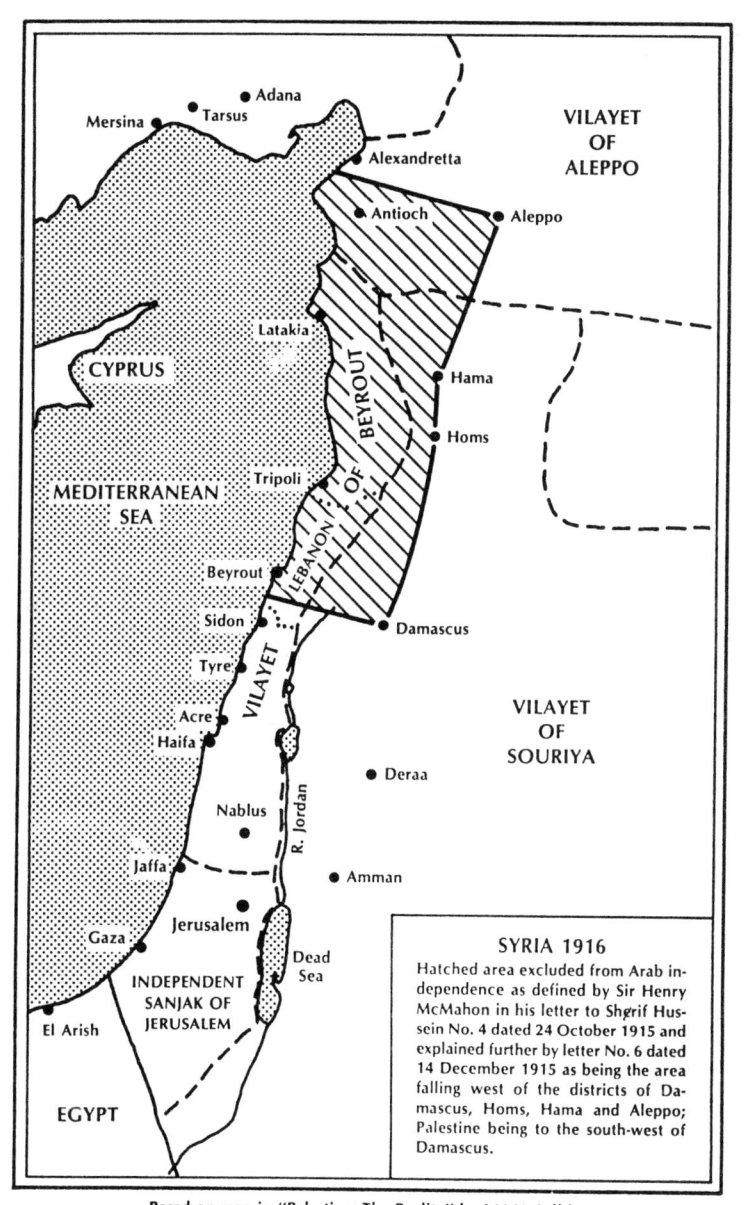

SYRIA 1916

Hatched area excluded from Arab independence as defined by Sir Henry McMahon in his letter to Sherif Hussein No. 4 dated 24 October 1915 and explained further by letter No. 6 dated 14 December 1915 as being the area falling west of the districts of Damascus, Homs, Hama and Aleppo; Palestine being to the south-west of Damascus.

Based on map in "Palestine: The Reality" by J.M.N. Jeffries

MAP D

Partition of Syria and Iraq
Under the Sykes-Picot Agreement (1916)

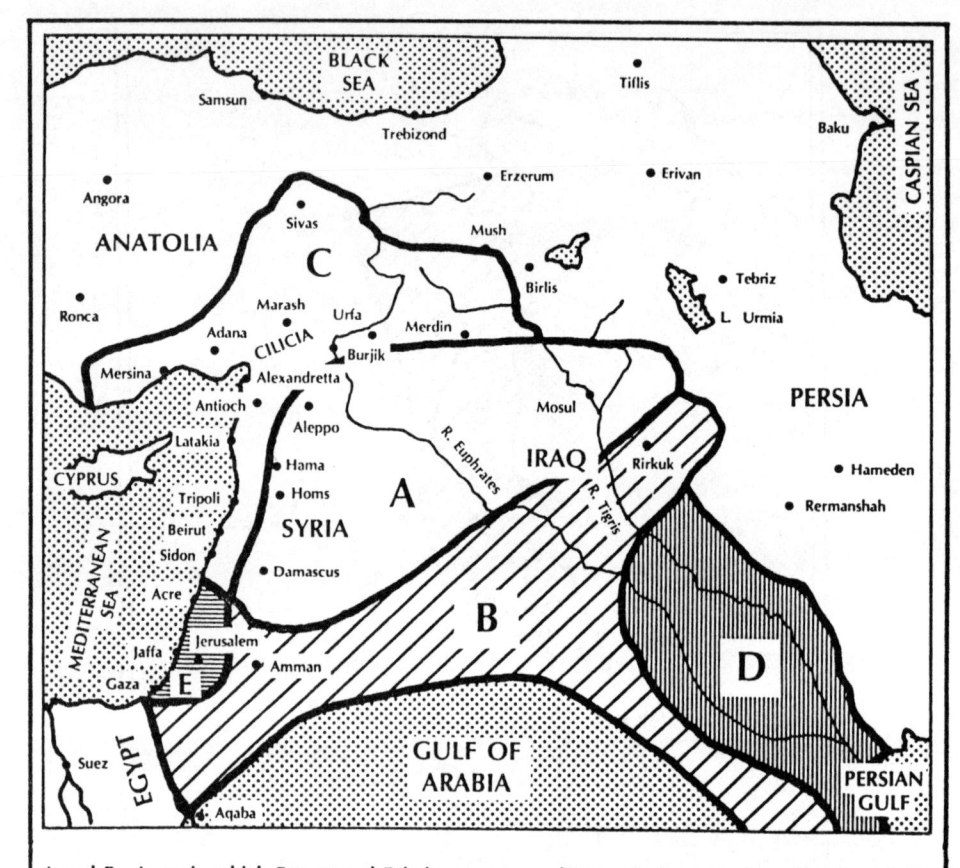

A and B - Areas in which France and Britain are prepared to recognize an independent Area State or a Confederation of Arab States.

In Zone A, France ⎱ To have priority and special privileges of administration
In Zone B, Britain ⎰ and control

In Zone C, France ⎱ To have direct and indirect control.
In Zone D, Britain ⎰

In Zone E, An international administration.

MAP E

Zionist Proposals for a "Zionist State"
As Submitted to the Paris Peace Conference 1919

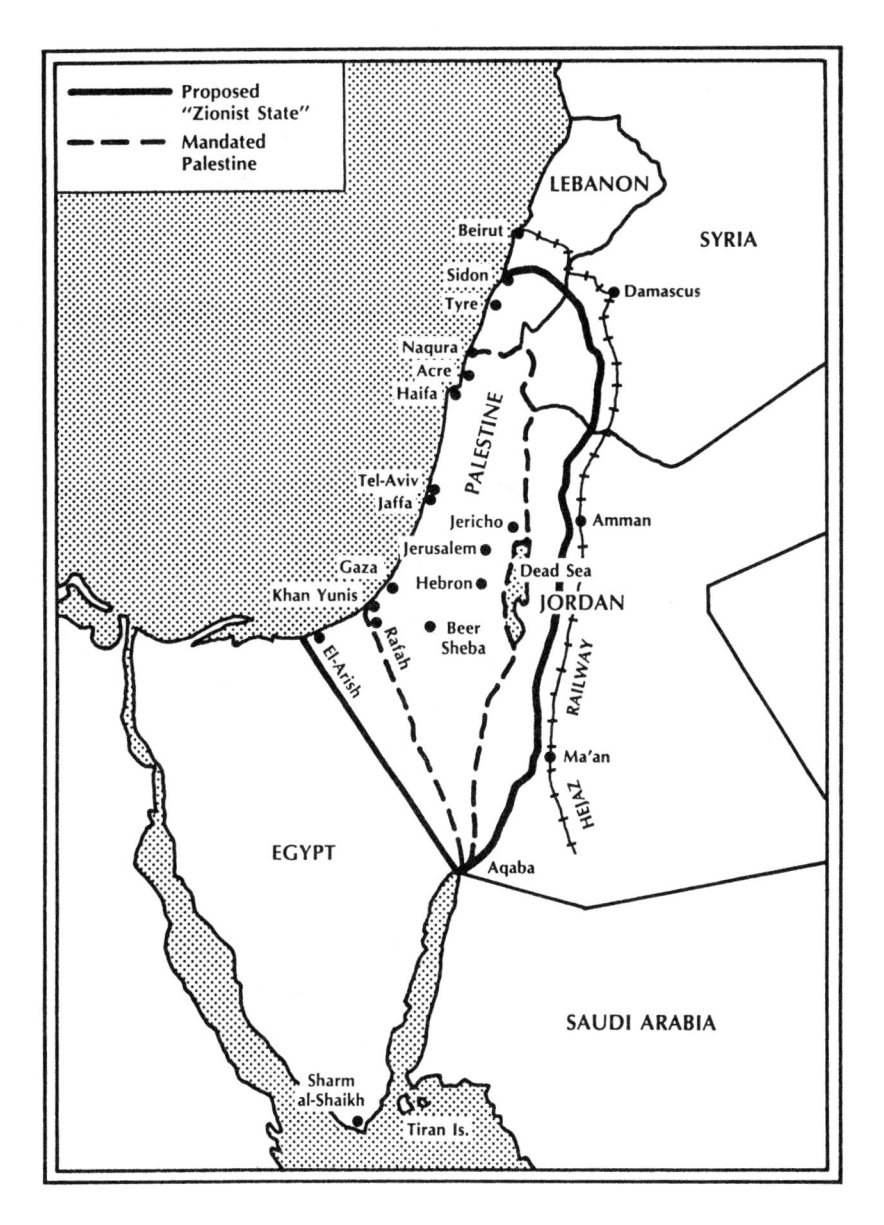

MAP F

British and French Mandates over the Eastern Arab World (1920)

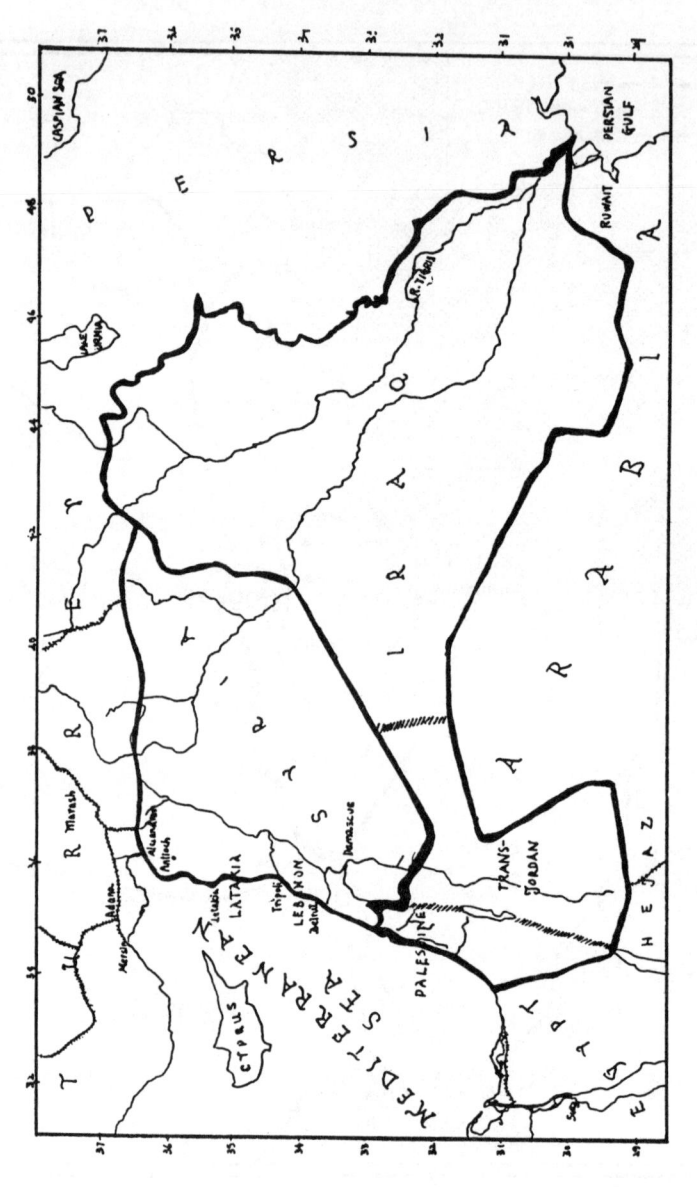

MAP G

Mandated Palestine 1920-1948
Area: 10,435 sq. miles

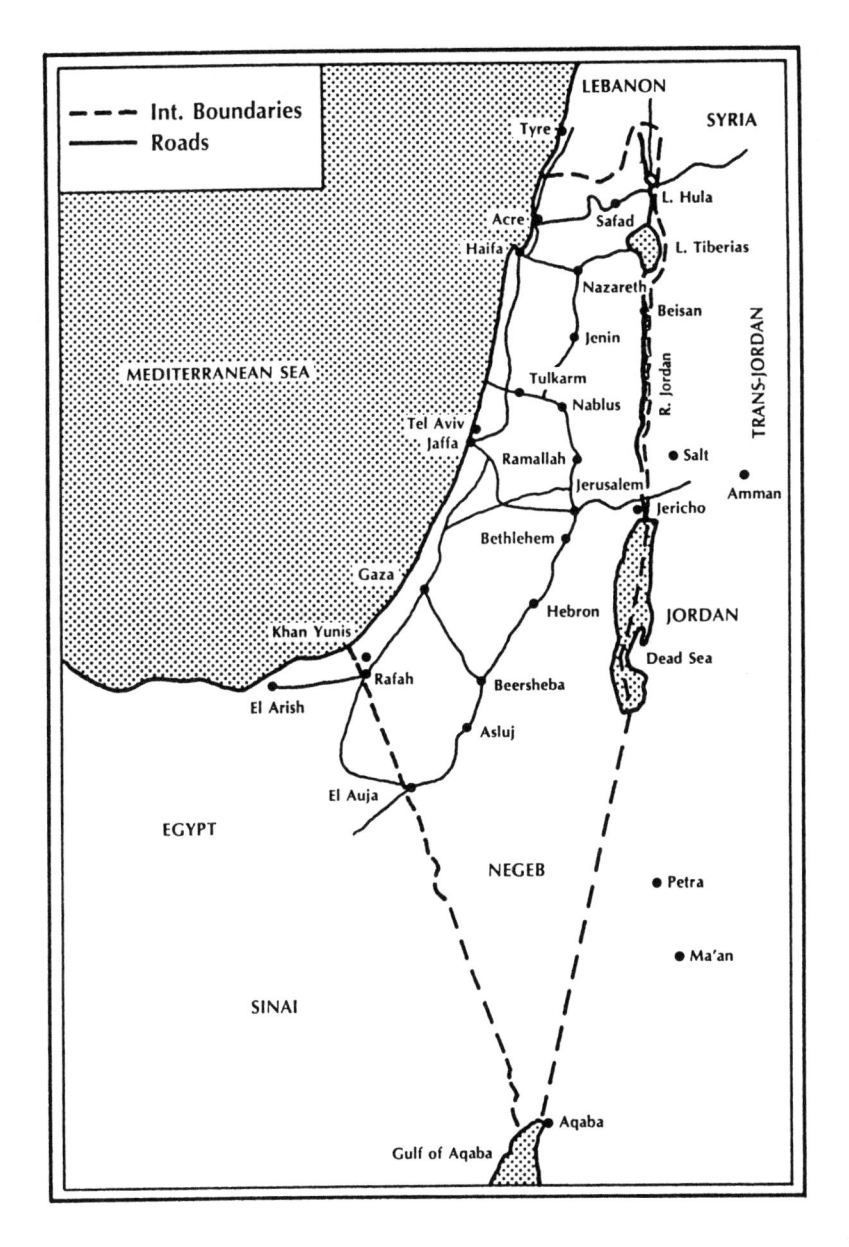

MAP H

Palestine
Classification of Soil

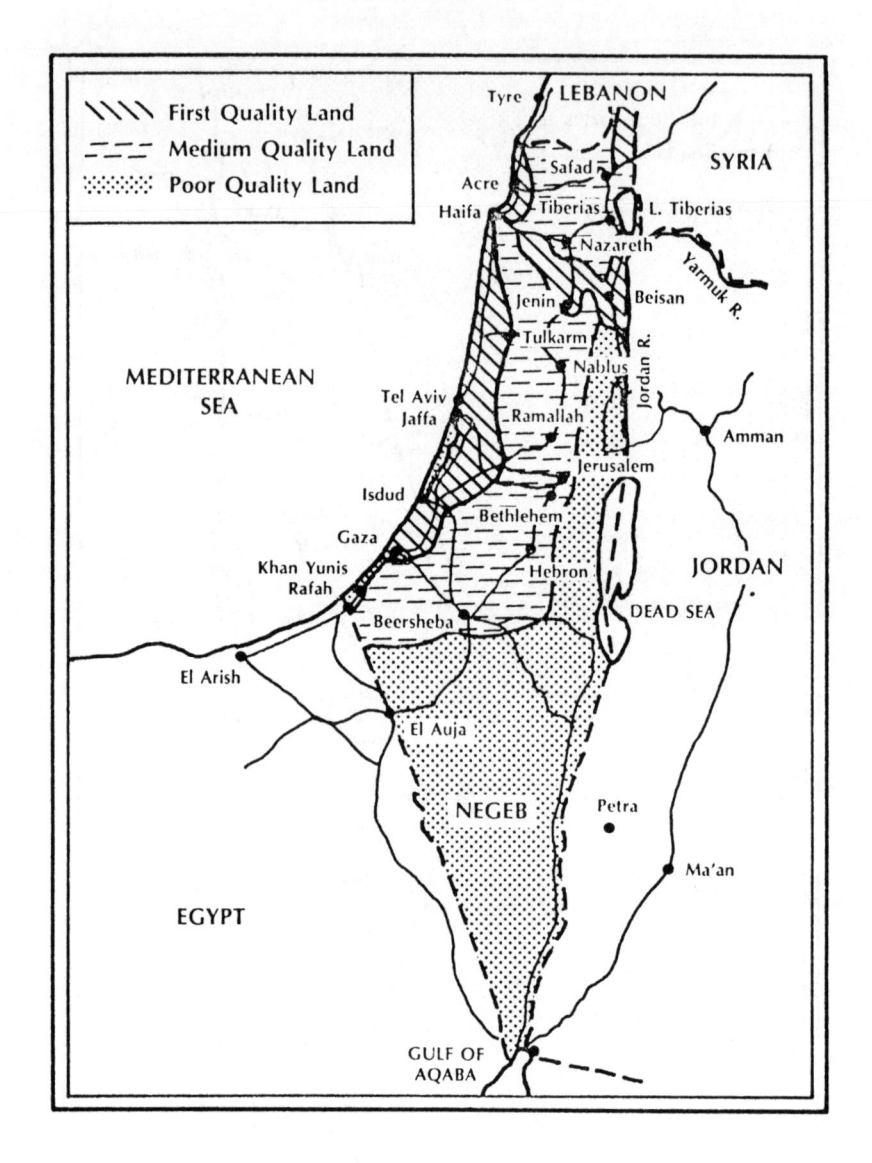

MAP I

Palestine Land Sales Restricted Zones (1940)

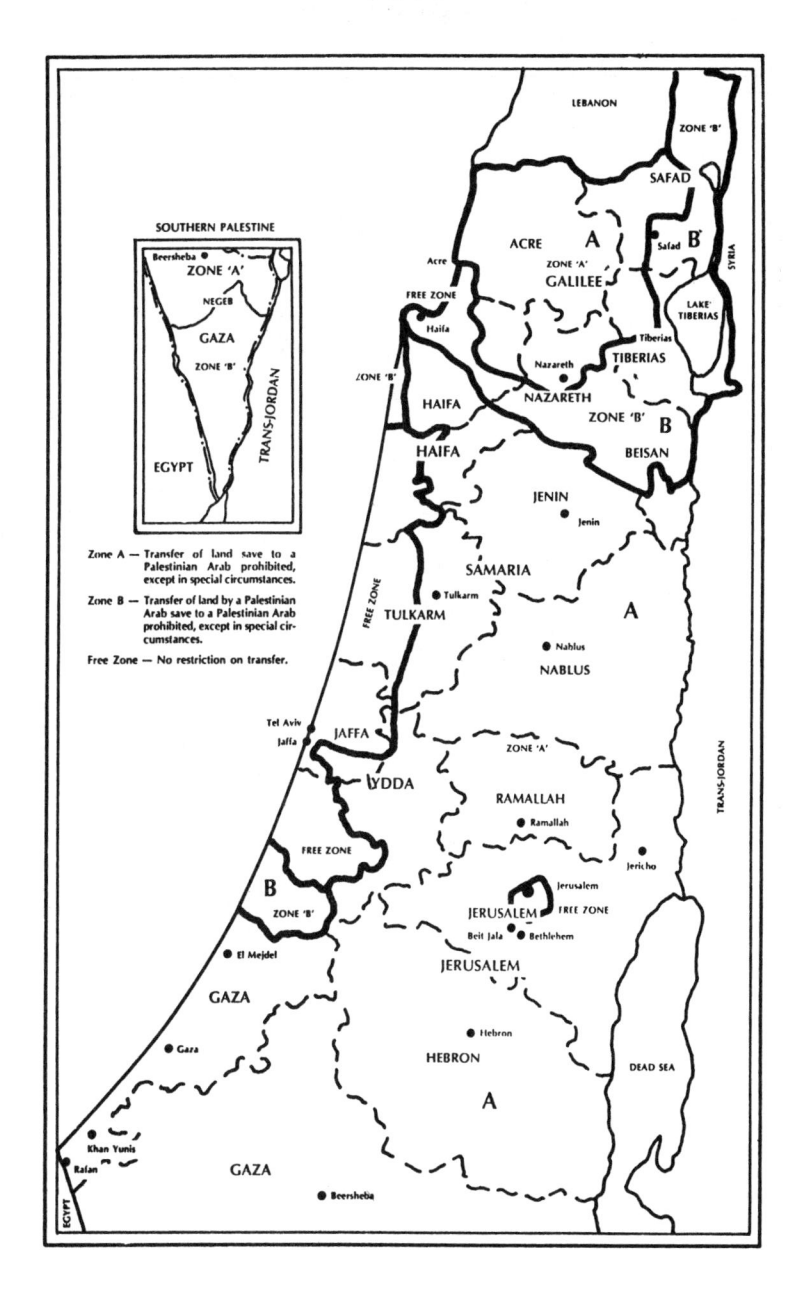

MAP J
Land in Jewish Possession or Occupation (1945)

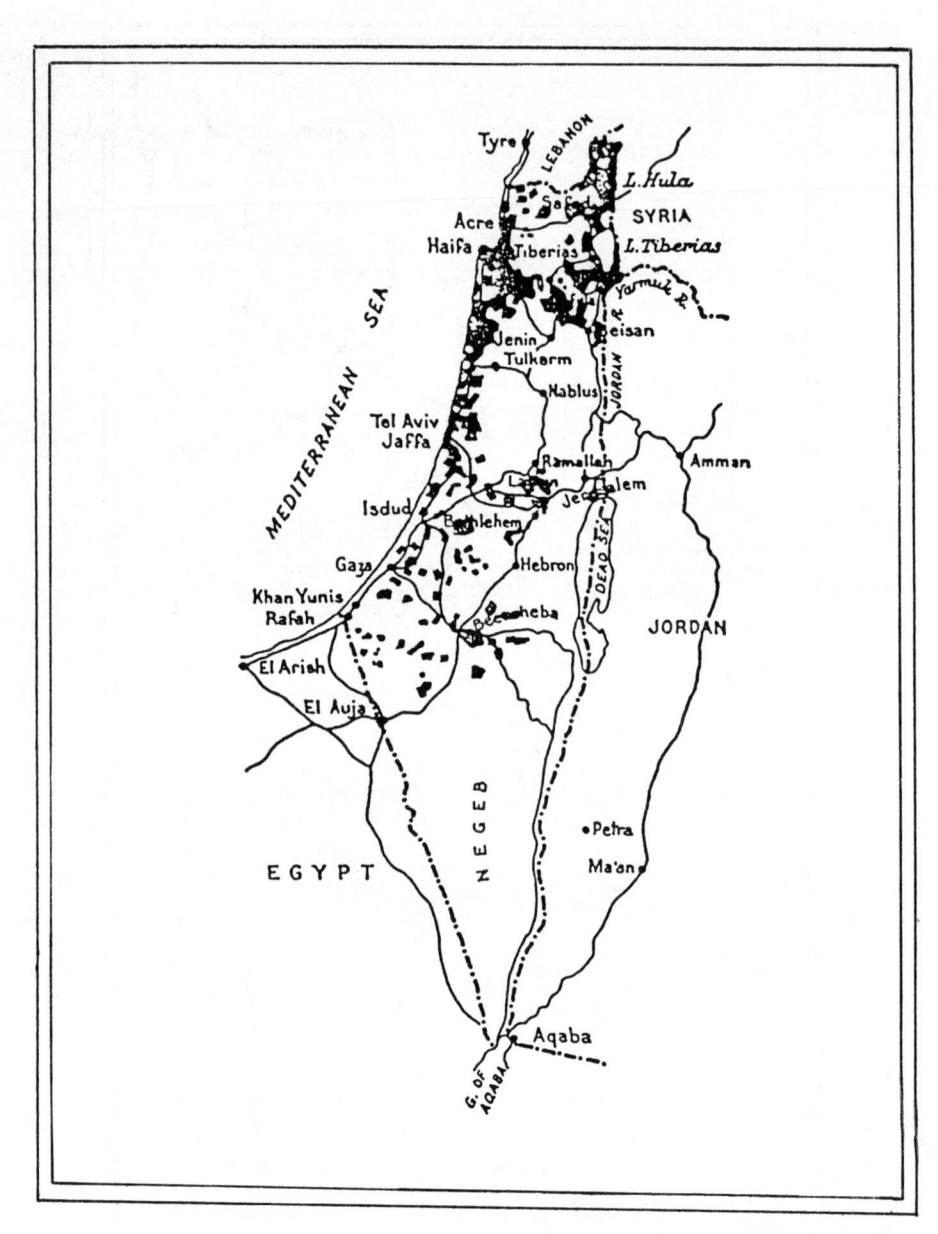

MAP K
Palestine / Map of Partition
UN Resolution 181 (II) of 29 November 1947

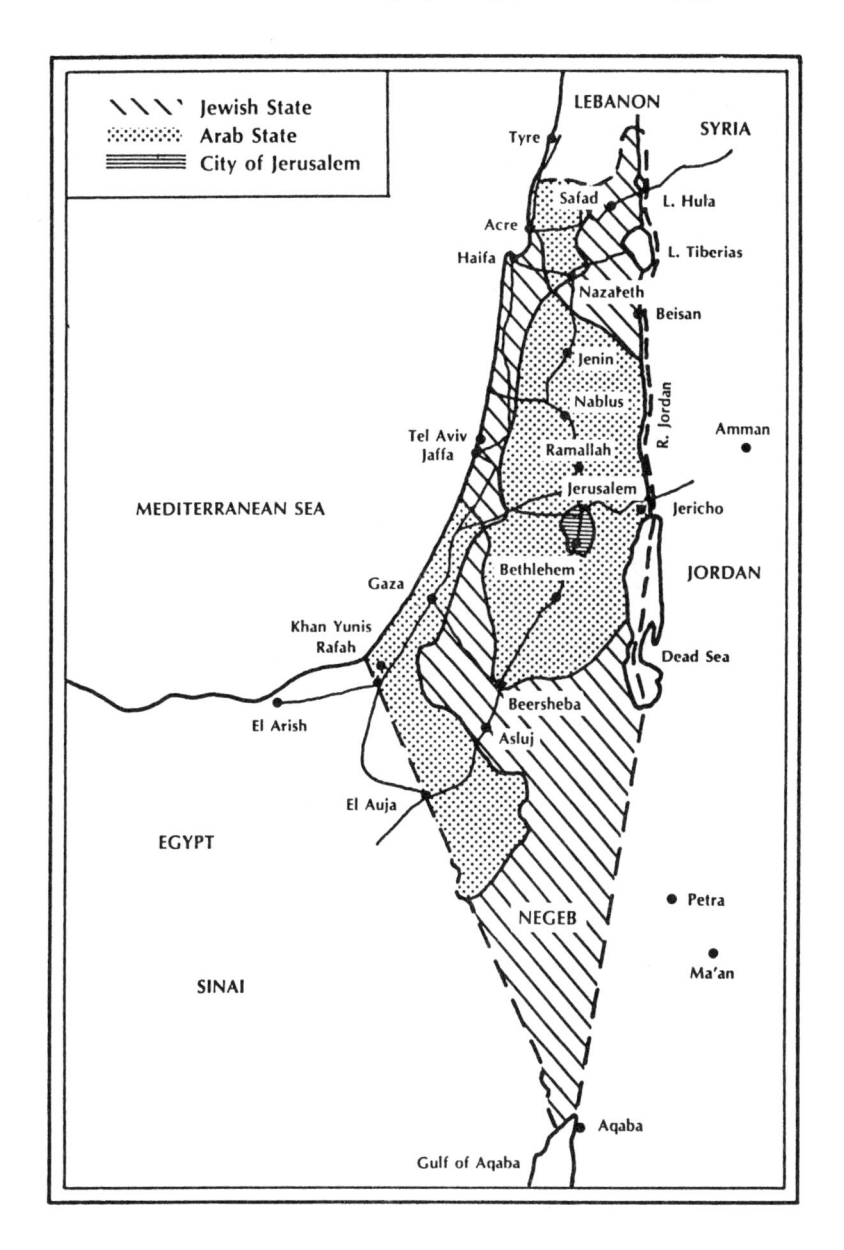

MAP L
Jerusalem International Zone
As Resolved by General Assembly Resolution No. 181 (II) of 29 November 1947

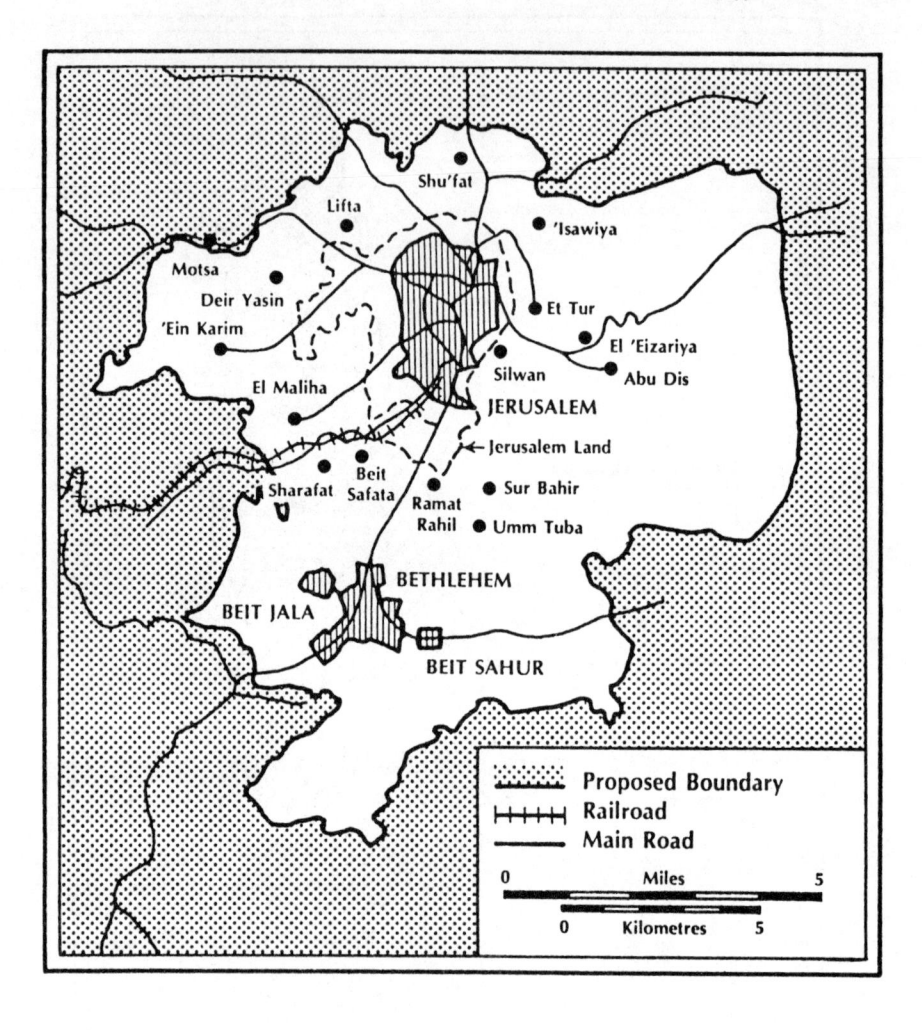

MAP M
Palestine as Result of Armistice Agreements, 1949

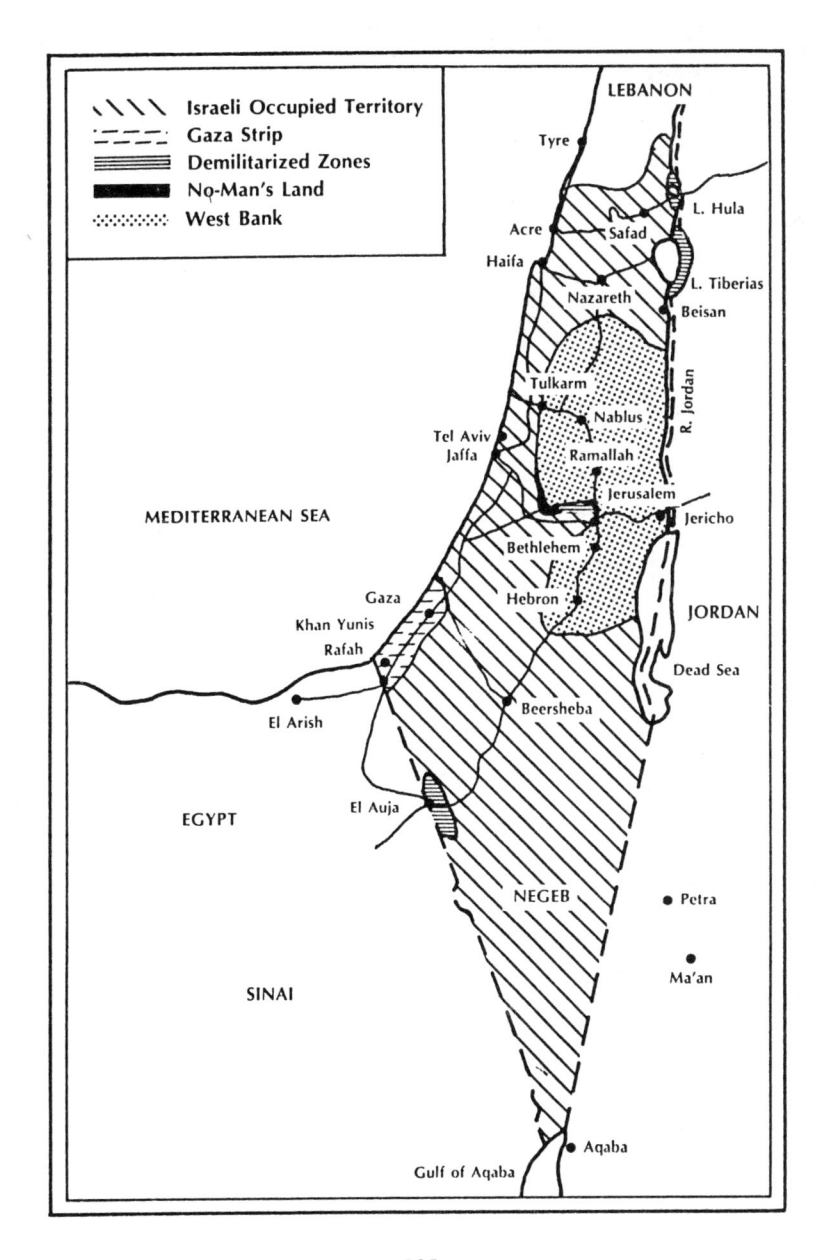

MAP N
Jerusalem According to the General Armistice Agreement, 1949

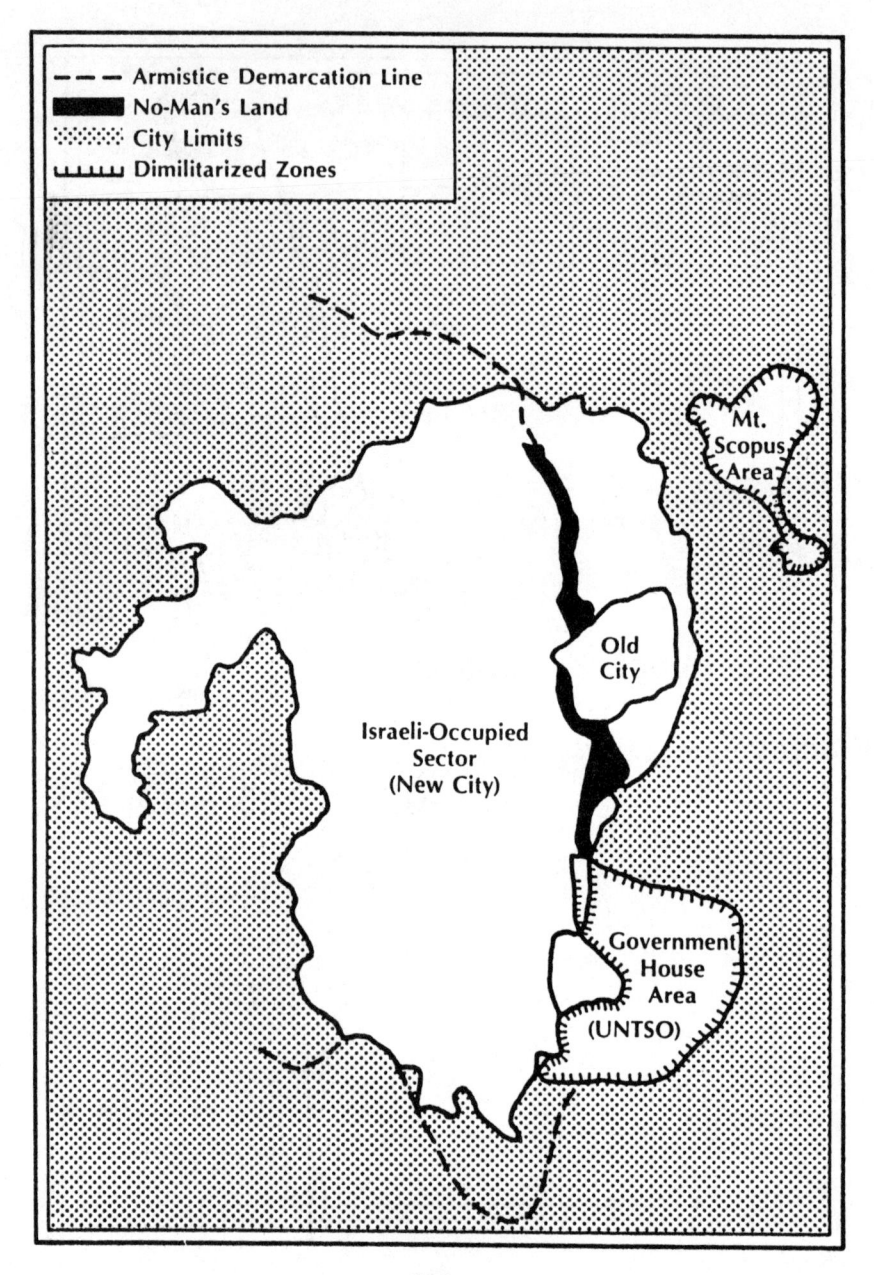

Appendices

Appendix I

**Working Paper
UN Document A/AC. 25W. 81/Rev. 2
(Annexe II)**

Compensation to refugees for loss of or damage to property to be made good under principles of international law or in equity

(Working Paper prepared by the Secretariat in October 1949)

1. Paragraph 11, sub-paragraph 1, of the resolution of the General Assembly of 11 December 1948 provides as follows:

The General Assembly... Resolves that the refugees wishing to return to their homes and live at peace with their neighbours should be permitted to do so at the earliest practicable date, and that compensation should be paid for the property of those choosing not to return and for loss of or damage to the property which, under principles of international law or in equity should be made good by the governments or authorities responsible.

2. It will be noticed that this provision deals with two distinct matters: (1) the right of refugees to return to their homes, and (2) the payment of compensation to them. It will also be seen that the question of payment of compensation presents itself under two different aspects: (a) payment of compensation to refugees not choosing to return to their homes, and (b) payment of compensation to refugees for loss of or damage to property which under principles of international law or in equity should be made good by the governments or authorities responsible.

3. The purpose of the present paper is to throw some light on that part of the provision which provides that compensation shall be paid to refugees for loss of or damage to property which under principles of international law or in equity should be made good by the governments or authorities responsible.

4. For the correct understanding of the question of compensation it is necessary to study the legislative history of paragraph 11, sub-paragraph 1. This Study will make it clear that a distinction must be made between the following

three categories of claims, of which only the first two are dealt with in the resolution of the General Assembly:

A. Compensation claims for property of refugees not choosing to return;
B. Compensation claims for loss of or damage to property, which, under principles of international law or in equity, should be made good;
C. Compensation claims for ordinary war damages.

I

5. A clear distinction between the first two categories of claims was made in the United Nations Mediator's Report. In Part One, Section VIII, it was stated under 4 (i) as a specific conclusion:

> The right of the Arab refugees to return to their homes in Jewish controlled territory at the earliest possible date should be affirmed by the United Nations, and their repatriation, resettlement and economic and social rehabilitation, *and payment of adequate compensation for the property of those choosing not to return,* should be supervised and assisted by the United Nations Conciliation Commission described in paragraph (k) below.*

On the other hand, the following statement was made in Part One, Section V, point 7:

> There have been numerous reports from reliable sources of large-scale looting, pillaging and plundering, and of instances of destruction of villages *without apparent military necessity.* The liability of the Provisional Government of Israel to restore private property to its Arab owners and to indemnify those owners for property wantonly destroyed is *clear, irrespective of any indemnities which the Provisional Government may claim from the Arab States.*

6. In the original draft resolution submitted by the United Kingdom representative to the First Committee of the General Assembly in Paris (A/C. 1/394), the two categories of claims (A. and B.) had been merged into one provision, namely paragraph 11, which reads as follows:

---

* The italics here and following are given for reasons of clarity and are purely editorial.

Appendix I

The General Assembly... Endorses the principle stated in Part One, Section V, paragraph 7, of the Mediator's report and resolves that the Arab refugees should be permitted to return to their homes at the earliest possible date and *that adequate compensation should be paid for the property of those choosing not to return* and *for property which has been lost as a result of pillage, confiscation or of destruction;* and instructs the Conciliation Commission to facilitate the repatriation, resettlement and economic and social rehabilitation of the Arab refugees and the payment of compensation.

7. In the first revision of the United Kingdom draft resolution (A/C. 1/394/Rev. 1), the terms regarding compensation were maintained unaltered. In the second revision (A/C. 1/394/Rev. 2), however, three changes were made. In the first place, the endorsement of the principle in Part One, Section V, paragraph 7, of the Mediator's report was replaced by an endorsement of the conclusions stated in Part One, Section VIII, paragraph 4 (i), of the Mediator's report (see above under paragraph 5). In the second place, the expression 'refugees' had been substituted for 'Arab refugees' which enabled the representative of the United Kingdom to state in the Committee that this part of the resolution now referred to all refugees, irrespective of race or nationality, provided they had been displaced from their homes in Palestine. In the third place, the words 'compensation... for property which has been lost as a *result of pillage, confiscation or of destruction*' were replaced by the expression 'compensation... for loss of or damage to property *which under principles of international law or in equity should be made good by the governments or authorities responsible.*' The relevant paragraph thus came to read as follows:

The General Assembly
Endorses the conclusion stated in Part One, Section VIII, paragraph 4 (i), of the progress report of the United Nations Mediator on Palestine, and *Resolves* that the refugees wishing to return to their homes and live at peace with their neighbours should be permitted to do so at the earliest possible date, *and that compensation should be paid for the property of those choosing not to return* and *for loss of or damage to property which under principles of international law or in equity should be made good by the governments or authorities responsible.*

8. Neither the amendments submitted by the representative of the United States (A/C. 1/351/Rev. 1 and 2) nor those submitted by the representative of Guatemala (A/C. 1/398/Rev. 1. and 2) nor the draft resolution presented by the representative of Colombia (A/C. 1/399) made any reference to the category of

claims mentioned under B. (see above under paragraph 4). All these amendments when dealing with the question of compensation provided only for compensation for property of the refugees not choosing to return. Commenting on paragraph 11 of the original United Kingdom draft resolution (A/C. 1/394), the representative of the United States stated that the paragraph:

> ...endorsed a generally recognized principle and provided a means for implementing that principle. It was not necessary, however, to mention the purely technical question of compensation for losses incurred during the recent fighting. That was a problem which could be dealt with better by the parties concerned, perhaps with the assistance of a claims commission, having regard to the suggestions made in the Mediator's Progress Report (A/675).

In explaining his amendments, the representative of Guatemala stated explicitly:

> ... the omission of any reference to damage and loss had been made intentionally because the question of war damage was separate from the refugee problem. Paragraph 11 of the United Kingdom draft appeared to refer to damage to Jewish and Arab property. The implication seemed to be that the Conciliation Commission would have to assess the whole of the war damage on either side. The Commission should have nothing to do with war damages; that matter ought to be dealt with in the peace treaty... .

9. When the vote in the First Committee took place, the amendment submitted by the representative of Guatemala was rejected by the Committee, which adopted instead paragraph 11 of the second revision of the United Kingdom draft resolution (A/C. 1/394/Rev. 2) with only minor changes made orally by the representative of the United Kingdom. In this way the two categories of claims A. and B. became linked together in paragraph 11 of the draft resolution.

10. In the General Assembly an amendment to paragraph 11 was submitted by seven members (Australia, Brazil, Canada, China, Colombia, France, and New Zealand). This amendment proposed to delete the endorsement at the beginning of the conclusions contained in Part One, Section VIII, paragraph 4 (i), of the Mediator's Report (see above under paragraph 5). This amendment was adopted by 44 votes to none, with 8 abstentions.

Appendix I

II

11. In the following paragraphs some observations shall be made with respect to each of the three categories of compensation claims mentioned under paragraph 4 above.

12. The compensation claims for property of refugees not choosing to return to their homes rest on general legal principles and must be considered in the light of the Assembly's decision that refugees should be given the choice *either* to return to their homes and live at peace with their neighbours *or* to receive compensation for their property if they choose not to return.

13. The compensation claims for loss of or damage to property which, under principles of international law or in equity, should be made good by the governments or authorities responsible, are an intermediate group of claims between the compensation claims under A. and C. The claims in question do arise out of the military events in Palestine but only in an incidental way and they cannot be considered as claims for ordinary war damages. From the legislative history of paragraph 11 of the Resolution of the General Assembly it will appear that the cases which the Assembly particularly had in mind were those of looting, pillaging, and plundering of private property and destruction of property and villages without military necessity. All such acts are violations of the laws and customs of war on land laid down in the Hague Convention of 18 October 1907, the rules of which, as stated in the Nuremberg Judgement in 1939, 'were recognized by all civilized nations and were regarded as being declaratory of the law and customs of war'. Articles 28 and 47 of the Hague regulation, annexed to the Convention, provide *explicitly* that pillage is prohibited. Article 23 (g) prohibits destruction or seizure of the enemy's property unless such destruction or seizure be imperatively demanded by the necessities of war. Article 46 protects private property and Article 56, paragraph 1, provides that the property of municipalities, that of institutions dedicated to religion, charity and education, the arts and sciences, even when State property, shall be treated as private property.

Appendix II

**Working Paper
UN Document A/AC. 25/W. 81/Rev. 2
(Annexe I)**

Historical precedents for restitution of property or payment of compensation to refugees

(Working Paper prepared by the Secretariat, Geneva, March 1950)

1. The underlying principle of paragraph 11, sub-paragraph 1, of the resolution of the General Assembly of 19 December 1948, is that the Palestine refugees shall be permitted *either* to return to their homes and be reinstated in the possession of the property which they previously held *or* that they shall be paid adequate compensation for their property. The purpose of the present paper is to furnish some background for this principle and to recall similar historical situations where claims of restitution of property or payment of compensation were put forward.

2. Such historical background became important during World War II when the question arose whether, according to international law, the Allied nations at the end of the war could protect the property interests of the Axis refugees. At the International Law Conference in London,[1] 1943, a collection of precedents was presented showing that in similar circumstances in the past, states had in fact safeguarded the interests of foreign nationals against their own governments. Of these precedents it would appear that the following three, because of their similarity with the Palestine situation, should be mentioned here: *a)* Article XXI of the Treaty of Nimmeguen of 17 September 1678; *b)* Article XVI of the Treaty of London of 19 April 1839; *c)* Article 144 of the Treaty of Sèvres of 10 August 1920.

3. The Treaty of Nimmeguen, signed by Spain and France on 17 September 1678, provided in Article XXI that:

> All the subjects of the one part as well as the other, both Ecclestiatick and Secular, shall be re-established in the Enjoyment of their Honour, Dignities and Benefices of which they were possessed of before the War as well as in all their Effects, Movables and Immovables and Rents upon Lives seized

Appendix II

and occupied from the said time as well on the occasion of the War as for having followed the contrary Party. Likewise in their Rights, Actions and Successions fallen to them, thought since the War commenced without nevertheless, demanding or pretending anything of the Fruits and Revenues coming from the seizing of the said effects, Immovables, Rents and Benefices till the Publication of this present Treaty.

The Treaty of Nimmeguen followed the war of 1672-1678 between the France of Louis XIV and Holland. The war had spread into the Spanish Netherlands, and though it was the Dutch who fought, it was Spain who lost to the French, giving up Franche Compté and a chain of towns on the north-east frontier of France.

4. The Treaty of London, of 19 April 1839, whereby the independence and neutrality of Belgium was agreed to, provided in Article XVI that:

The Sequestrations which may have been imposed in Belgium during the troubles, for political causes, on any Property or Hereditary Estates whatsoever, shall be taken off without delay, and the enjoyment of the Property and Estates above mentioned shall be immediately restored to the lawful owners thereof.

5. The Peace Treaty with Turkey, signed in Sèvres on 10 August 1920, contained in Article 144 provisions for the compensation of Armenian refugees who had fled from Turkey. Paragraphs 1 and 2 of this Article read:

The Turkish Government recognizes the injustice of the law of 1915 relating to Abandoned Properties (Emval-i-Metroukeh), and of the supplementary provisions thereof, and declares them to be null and void, in the past as in the future.

The Turkish Government solemnly undertakes to facilitate to the greatest possible extent the return to their homes and re-establishment in their businesses of the Turkish subjects of non-Turkish race who have been forcibly driven from their homes by fear of massacre or any other form of pressure since January 1st, 1914. It recognizes that any immovable or movable property of the said Turkish subjects or of the communities to which they belong, which can be recovered, must be restored to them as soon as possible, in whatever hands it may be found. Such property shall be restored free of all charges or servitudes with which it may have been burdened and without compensation of any kind to the present owners or occupiers, subject to any action which they may be able to bring against the persons from whom they derived title.

The Sèvres Treaty, as it will be recalled, was not ratified by Turkey and was finally replaced by the Treaty of Lausanne of 24 July 1923, which did not contain any clause corresponding to Article 144 of the Sèvres Treaty.

6. In the period between World War I and World War II, the question of payment of compensation for immovable property arose in particular in the Hungarian-Romanian land dispute which in 1923 was brought before the Council of the League of Nations by Hungary. This dispute developed out of a Romanian land reform law (Garoflid law) whereby property rights of Hungarian Optants in territory transferred to Romania were confiscated on grounds of absenteeism. For several years this dispute remained unsettled in spite of the conciliatory efforts of the Council. Finally, it was narrowed down to the question of the amount of compensation to be paid to the Optants and was ultimately solved as part of the general financial settlement brought about by the Hague and Paris negotiations in 1930 on reparations in Eastern Europe.

7. During World War II, the Institute of Jewish Affairs of the World Jewish Congress took up the question of indemnities to be paid to Jewish refugees after the war. In a book entitled *Indemnities and Reparations* by Nehemiah Robinson, published in 1944 by the Institute, careful consideration is given to the problem of compensation and all its aspects. The author admits that as a general rule, states are entitled to lodge claims with foreign nations only in respect of their own citizens. He admits further that it normally would be required that the persons for whom they seek indemnification from another state be citizens also at the time the injury occurred. But he points out that if this principle were universally accepted, it would exclude almost all victims of the former Axis countries who are now citizens of other countries, from claims against the Axis for damages inflicted before and during the war. From the viewpoint of international law there seems, in his opinion, to be no reason why diplomatic protection should not be extended to all citizens regardless of the time of injury if the states in question wish to do so. This view has already been expressed by the United States–Peru Mixed Tribunal.

The author calls attention to other precedents of this kind. At the insistence of the French after World War I Germany was compelled to pay indemnities for fines it had imposed during the war on the inhabitants of Alsace-Lorraine[2] although the Alsations became French nationals only as a result of the reannexation of Alsace-Lorraine by France. It was also reported that Estonia, in obedience to German demands, paid indemnification to large landowners whose estates were used for the purposes of agrarian reform; these landowners migrated to Germany and became citizens only after the loss was sustained.

But even if all citizens were granted diplomatic protection, continues the author, there is still the problem of all those emigrants from Europe who have not yet acquired citizenship in their new homelands. Should protection be

Appendix II

denied to them by the states of their refuge, then their claims against the Axis nations and their nationals would in many cases remain without indemnification. To prevent such losses and positively to redress the effects of the Nazi persecution and spoliation, the principle must be accepted by the United Nations (as wartime allied Powers) and those countries where persons of this category reside, that in the question of claims against the Axis the *territorial*, not the *national*, principle be applied.

Finally, there is the case of those who remained in or would be willing to return to their former homeland, and with respect to this category of victims the author makes a strong case that the United Nations must intervene on their behalf. There is, in his opinion, nothing revolutionary in this suggestion, for many cases of such intervention are known. The minorities treaties forced upon a number of states after World War I were just this sort of intervention. To carry out these suggestions, the author argues for the establishment of internationally organized courts or similar bodies, empowered to make decisions and execute them, irrespective of the residence of the respondents and the location of the goods. Only internationally organized jurisdiction and execution would guarantee full impartiality and justice, and would shorten the delays inherent in the usual system of two or three court instances in every case.

8. After World War II, most of the former Axis and Axis-occupied countries passed laws in favour of such persons who had been persecuted or forced to leave the country. In the United States occupied zone of Germany on 10 August 1949, a *General Claims Law* was passed.[3] Article 1 of this law provides:

> Those persons shall be entitled to restitution pursuant to this law who, under the National Socialist dictatorship (30 January 1933 to 8 May 1945), were persecuted because of political convictions or on racial, religious or ideological grounds and have therefore suffered damage to life and limb, health, possessions, property or economic advancement.

Machinery is set up under this law for the filing of individual claims and provisions are made for the payment of compensation.

In the British zone of occupation in Germany, Law No. 59 entitled *Restitution of Identifiable Property to Victims of Nazi Oppression* was passed on 12 May 1949.[4] Article 1 of this law provides:

> The purpose of this law is to effect to the largest extent possible the speedy restitution of identifiable property (tangible and intangible) to persons whether natural or juristic who were unjustly deprived of such property between 30 January 1933 and 8 May 1945 for reasons of race, religion, nationality, political views, or political opposition to National Socialism.

This law also establishes a procedure for the filing of individual claims for restitution with appropriate provisions for compensation.

9. Even before these acts for individual restitution in Germany, the Allied governments in the *Final Act of the Paris Conference on Reparations* of 21 December 1945 and the *Agreement of 14 June 1946* provided for a lump-sum payment into a fund for non-repatriable victims of German action. This allocation for the rehabilitation and resettlement of Nazi victims was to be made up of three items: *a)* all non-monetary gold found by the Allies in Germany; *b)* a sum not exceeding $ 25 million from the proceeds of German Assets in neutral countries; *c)* assets in neutral countries of victims of Nazi action, who had died and left no heirs. This method of collective reparations was not to be prejudicial to the future claims against a future German government.[5]

10. In the Axis and Axis-occupied countries, various laws have been passed for restitution and compensation to the victims of Nazi action. Below is a list of some of these laws and their dates:[6]

a) France — Decree of 14 November 1944, concerning the restitution of property.
b) Romania — Law of 19 December 1944, regarding the restitution of Jewish property rights.
c) Italy — Decree of 5 January 1944, regarding the reinstatement of Jews in property rights.
d) Bulgaria — Decree law of 24 February 1945, concerning the material consequences of the abrogation of anti-Jewish laws.
e) Czechoslovakia — Decree of the President of Czechoslovakia of 19 May 1945, concerning the nullity of certain property transactions made during the period of bondage and the 'national administration' of properties belonging to Germans, Hungarians, traitors, collaborators, and certain organizations and institutions.
f) Holland — Decree of 17 September 1944, concerning the re-establishment of justice.
g) Yugoslavia — Law of 24 May 1945, concerning the procedure with property which the owners were forced to leave at the time of occupation, as well as with property seized by the occupants or their helpers.

11. Finally, reference shall be made to a refugee problem of a comparatively recent date which also presents some similarity with the problem of the Palestine refugees. With the partition of India into the states of India and Pakistan, bloodshed, riots, massacre, and murder caused minority groups on both sides to flee. In spite of official governmental pleas by both India and Pakistan asking the population to remain in their homes, Hindus and Sikhs from

Appendix II

Pakistan fled to India and Muslims in India fled to Pakistan. By the spring of 1948, the total number of transferees exceeded 11 million.[7]

In the early stages of the disorganized two-way flight, when the abandonment of property was considered a temporary phenomenon, the joint Hindu-Muslim Partition Council came to the conclusion (on 6 August 1947) that because:

> no arrangements have so far been made for the management of refugees' property, and because so long as the local population and the majority community in villages and towns maintain a hostile attitude, the refugees will be unable to return and look after their property... the two Governments have decided to appoint managers, at a suitable level, for the administration of refugees' property in the various areas; the expenses of these managers will be paid out of the proceeds of the properties which they were appointed to look after.

It was also decided that, where this had not already been done, provincial governments should be asked to set up machinery for the assessment of damages to both the movable and immovable property of the minority groups involved.[8]

Later on, when the exchange of minorities proved both unprecedented in scope and final in nature, the Pakistan and India governments agreed on the principle that the ownership of refugees' property, movable as well as immovable, should remain vested in the refugees. Custodians were appointed to look after and manage such property on behalf of the owners.[9] Similarly, Registrars of Claims were appointed and instructed to make records of the property left behind by the evacuees.[10] It was agreed that the Custodian's control and management, whether exercised by himself or through a lessee or any other person, would operate only during the absence of the evacuee-owner. It would be open to the owner of such property or his legal heirs to claim its restoration on payment of the excess, if any, of expenditure over receipts during the period the property had been under the Custodian's management.[11]

All these *de jure* guarantees of the inviolability of abandoned property did not seem to reassure the refugees themselves. They repeatedly expressed their anxiety about their property and demanded final settlement of their accounts on the governmental level. It was suggested that in each case 'the Government receiving the refugees should claim compensation on their behalf for the losses they have sustained from the Government from the territory of which the refugees have to come away', and that the same principle should be applied to expenditures incurred during rehabilitation. As an instructive pattern for such procedure, it was recalled that after the disturbances in the province of Bihar, the then government of Bengal claimed that the cost of maintaining and rehabilitating Bihar refugees in Bengal should be borne by the government of Bihar. When this matter was referred to the government of India, which was at the time headed by Pandit Nehru and Liagat Ali Khan, it accepted the validity of the claim and introduced it on an all-India basis. 'Now if that formula had been agreed to, there is no reason why it should not be revived again in the context of Indo-Pakistan population transfer', insisted Bismal Chandra Sinha.[12] In August 1948, the governments of India and Pakistan signed an agreement for the removal and disposal of evacuees' movable property, envisaging the establishment of a joint governmental agency on which the two Dominions would enjoy equal representation. The agency would supervise the execution of agreements and would set up an organization to facilitate the movement of movable property by rail and road.[13]

---

1. The International Law Conference of London, 1943, was held under the auspices of the Institut de Droit International, the International Law Association, the Grotius Society, and the Allied University Professors' Association. Their proceedings have been edited by R. Bissebop.

2. Article 63 of the Versailles Treaty.

3. This law is published in English by the IRO Documentation Branch, IRO/LEG/LS/5, 3 November 1949.

4. This law is published in German and English in *Ruckerstattungs-Gesetz*, by Dr H.G. van Dam, Koblenz, 1949.

5. Reference is made to these agreements in a letter to the FCC of 22 November 1949, from the Chairman of the UN Economic Survey Commission. Also a discussion of these agreements may be found in Nehemiah Robinson, *Indemnification and Reparations*, New York, 1944, Annexe 2, 1946, pp. 157-62.

6. Ibid. No claim is made that this list is complete or up to date.

7. *Joseph B. Schectman*, Population Transfers in Asia, New York, 1949. Chapter on 'Hindu-Moslem Exchange of Population'.

8. *Indian Information*, 1 September 1947.

9. *Ibid.*, 1 January 1948.

10. Ministry of Information and Broadcasting, *Millions on the Move*, Government of India, Delhi, 1948, p. 46.

11. *Indian Information*, 1 December 1947.

12. Bismal Chandra Sinah, 'Economic Relationship between India and Pakistan', *The Modern Review*, February 1948, p. 108.

13. *Indian Information*, 1 January 1948.

Appendix III

Schedule
of vacant sites and total net annual value of buildings owned by Arabs in urban areas[1]

urban area	total area (vacant sites) (dunums)	net annual value (buildings) (£P)	last quinquennial tax year
Acre	636	37,428	1947-1948
Beisan	222	13,588	1944-1945
★ Affula	4		1948-1949
Nazareth	2,387	38,436	1946-1947
Safad	573	13,596	1946-1947
Tiberias	308	17,314	1945-1946
Haifa	4,895	540,527	1947-1948
Shafa 'Amr	1,064	5,091	1944-1945
★ Natanya	47		1946-1947
Jerusalem	4,976	349,393	1944-1945
★ Bat Yam	3		1944-1945
★ Holon	198	14	1944-1945
Jaffa	6,855	401,808	1944-1945
★ Ramat Gan	71		1945-1946
★ Tel Aviv	1,078	4,032	1944-1945
Lydda	2,349	26,302	1944-1945
Majdal	823	20,178	1948-1949
Ramle and Beersheba[2]			

★ Jewish towns and settlements containing Arab-owned lands as shown.

1. As appearing in Appendix A to Report of Land Expert/UN Document A/AC. 25/ W. 84 of 28 April 1964.

2. The Land Expert reported that the statistical information in regard to these two towns was not available to him and could therefore not be included.

Summary schedule showing, by tax Beersheba sub-district) in forms

Sub-District	Area of Sub-District				1,2		3		4	
	Total	RP/1	RP/3	RP/1	RP/3	RP/1	RP/3	RP/1	RP/3
A- Galilee district:									
1 Acre	134,446	99,683	34,763	7,912	263	39	33	6	240
	660,911	408,024	252,887	287	—	—	—	2,940	445
2 Beisan	365,160	146,232	218,928	238	1,377	420	58	311	1,748
	935	935	—	—	—	—	—	37	—
3 Nazareth	409,809	179,444	230,365	49	420	—	—	102	1,899
	81,133	68,901	12,232	—	—	—	—	864	56
4 Safad	461,947	221,815	240,132	246	68	—	—	495	4,062
	234,912	125,895	109,017	—	—	—	—	1,353	530
5 Tiberias	436,218	193,493	242,725	93	1,273	286	1,419	203	3,444
	2,813	946	1,867	—	—	—	2	946	25
B- Haifa district:									
6 Haifa	881,948	352,576	529,372	327	18,335	5	323	549	17,020
	90,364	53,004	37,360	18	—	—	—	1,480	490
C- Samaria district:									
7 Jenin	40,617	35,031	5,586	—	—	—	—	15	—
	216,595	193,376	23,219	4	—	—	—	267	1
8 Nablus	—	—	—	—	—	—	—	—	—
	23,414	23,414	—	—	—	—	—	—	—
9 Tulkaram	425,665	257,790	167,875	15,209	30,701	98	180	97	3,971
	78,011	74,781	3,230	501	—	49	—	862	58
D-Jerusalem district:									
10 Hebron	7,933	7,506	427	—	—	—	—	—	—
	1,154,403	1,137,302	17,101	8	—	—	—	1,032	213
11 Jerusalem	26,262	6,040	20,222	—	—	—	—	—	148
	270,681	215,442	55,239	—	31	—	—	1,512	2,233
12 Ramallah	—	—	—	—	—	—	—	—	—
	6,240	6,240	—	—	—	—	—	—	—
E- Lydda district:									
13 Jaffa	280,665	138,903	141,762	41,994	40,415	268	750	472	9,578
	4,419	1,522	2,897	—	—	—	—	262	2
14 Ramle	597,177	411,620	185,557	37,106	39,883	225	67	665	1,382
	166,304	158,193	8,111	1,874	—	—	—	778	64
F- Gaza district:									
15 Gaza	808,848	670,078	138,770	18,643	4,837	19	16	581	1,087
	6,589	5,905	684	—	—	—	—	1,917	49
Total settled	4,876,695	2,720,211	2,156,484	121,817	137,572	1,360	2,846	3,496	44,579
Total non-settled	2,997,724	2,473,880	523,844	2,692	31	49	2	14,250	4,166
Grand total	7,874,419	5,194,091	2,680,328	124,509	137,603	1,409	2,848	17,746	48,745

1. This schedule appears as Appendix A/1 to UN Document A/AC. 25/W. 84 of 28 April 1964.

2. Two sets of figures are shown for each sub-district: the first represents land the title to which was settled under the Land (Settlement of Title) Ordinance; the second land whose title had not been.

category, settled and non-settled areas (excl. RP/1 and RP/3 (in metric dunums)

Appendix IV

Area classified under tax categories

5-8		9-13		14,15		16A		16B		17	
RP/1	RP/3	RP/1	RP/3	RP/1	RP/3	RP/1	RP/3	RP/1	RP/3	RP/1	RP/3
15,017	1,105	63,451	8,704	4,989	455	8,243	20,671	26	3,292	—	—
71,370	201	154,263	2,565	47,215	3,190	131,898	244,909	51	1,577	—	—
7,973	13,492	126,004	123,003	7,113	5,576	4,161	61,732	12	8,797	—	3,145
33	—	299	—	—	—	556	—	10	—	—	—
14,223	5,282	156,517	123,398	6,520	3,642	2,031	85,061	2	10,663	—	—
6,722	101	33,904	1,449	3,659	—	23,752	10,309	—	317	—	—
61,278	23,049	103,809	56,073	42,374	31,892	13,613	109,982	—	12,845	—	2,161
12,661	236	56,298	1,064	34,651	5,493	20,932	101,029	—	665	—	—
20,829	6,745	153,141	118,528	13,013	24,700	5,925	72,937	3	12,236	—	1,443
—	—	—	55	—	—	—	1,546	—	239	—	—
31,212	32,132	269,160	199,811	37,771	11,668	13,533	220,537	19	27,511	—	2,035
813	73	21,938	7,216	1,999	32	26,754	28,072	2	1,228	—	249
1,952	—	31,836	473	—	—	1,223	4,565	5	548	—	—
6,409	—	123,112	2,564	7,439	25	56,115	20,221	30	408	—	—
—	—	—	—	—	—	—	—	—	—	—	—
5,647	—	540	—	13,729	—	3,498	—	—	—	—	—
15,373	2,007	214,384	99,448	13	—	12,517	18,936	99	12,315	—	317
3,419	—	52,123	1,249	1,841	—	15,986	1,721	—	202	—	—
103	—	5,899	94	—	—	1,503	166	1	167	—	—
10,260	67	242,856	2,620	100,526	1,320	782,620	12,477	—	404	—	—
1,391	1,673	3,048	13,916	143	569	1,458	3,383	—	533	—	—
29,633	1,165	45,711	14,094	22,008	1,447	116,578	34,340	—	1,929	—	—
—	—	1,001	—	196	—	5,043	—	—	—	—	—
13,905	8,860	80,697	58,046	21	394	1,396	10,477	150	13,242	—	—
—	—	—	991	688	—	—	260	2,111	9	96	—	—
54,358	11,121	258,848	64,781	8,046	616	52,194	50,019	178	17,625	—	63
6,305	3	71,690	2,901	8,917	150	68,621	4,181	8	812	—	—
52,782	5,043	575,723	53,263	12,792	676	9,435	57,673	103	16,175	—	—
—	—	3,126	—	—	—	860	116	2	519	—	—
290,396	110,509	2,042,517	919,538	132,795	80,188	127,232	716,139	598	135,949	—	9,164
153,272	1,846	807,852	36,465	242,180	11,657	1,253,473	461,032	112	8,396	—	249
443,668	112,355	2,850,369	956,003	374,975	91,845	1,380,705	1,177,171	710	144,345	—	9,413

3. Form RP/1 denotes land in individual Arab ownership; Form RP/3 denotes land registered or recorded as owned by State, other public authority, Jews, and other non-Arab individuals.

Appendix V

Palestine
Arab Town and Village Lands outside the Territory occupied by Israel under the General Armistice Agreements of 1949

Explanatory Notes

1. Figures appearing in the 'Total' column were extracted from *Village Statistics*, 1945.

2. Figures appearing in the 'Israel' column were taken from the records of the Land Expert of the Palestine Conciliation Commission and are said to be approximate. These lands have been included in Appendix VIII for identification and valuation purposes.

3. Figures under 'West Bank' and 'Gaza Strip' are excluded from the Revised Study.

4. One (*) asterisk indicates that the village built-up area is in the West Bank or the Gaza Strip;
Two (**) asterisks indicate that the village built-up area falls in Israel;
Three (***) indicate that the lands fall in no man's land or in a demilitarized zone and included in Israel.

5. According to the Land Expert of the Palestine Conciliation Commission, 60,000 dunums of the Beersheba sub-district fall in Arab territory. For the purpose of convenience, these have been included in the Gaza Strip.

Appendix V

A - The West Bank of the Jordan Total area: 5,450,297 dunums

sub-district	village	areas (in dunums) in West Bank	in Israel	total
Beisan	a) Whole villages Nil	Nil		
	b) 'Border' villages			
	** El-Fatur	273	456	729
	** El-Hamra	138	11,373	11,511
	Total	411		
Jenin	a) Whole villages			
	37 units	384,539		
	b) 'Border' villages			
	★ 'Anin	11,319	3,730	15,049
	★ 'Arabbuna	5,584	1,188	6,772
	★ Barta'a	11,064	9,435	20,499
	★ Birqin	19,353	94	19,447
	★ Faqqu'a	9,566	20,613	30,179
	★ Jalama	3,089	2,738	5,827
	★ Jalbun	9,951	24,008	33,959
	★★ Mazar	1,190	13,311	14,501
	★ Mughaiyir	12,505	5,544	18,049
	★★ Muqeibila	849	6,279	7,128
	★ Raba	22,184	3,458	25,642
	★ Rummana	9,740	11,936	21,676
	★ Ti'innik	4,957	27,306	32,263
	★★ Umm El-Fahm	1,649	75,593	77,242
	★ Ya'bad	37,555	250	37,805
	★ Yamun	19,074	1,287	20,361
	★ Zibda	11,564	360	11,924
	★ Zububa	2,097	11,746	13,843
	Total:	577,829		
Nablus	a) Whole villages			
	89 units	1,263,806		
	b) 'Border' villages			
	★ Deir Ballut	10,751	4,038	14,789
	★ Tubas	293,747	19,376	313,123
	Total:	1,568,304		

Palestinian Rights and Losses in 1948

sub-district	village	areas (in dunums) in West Bank	in Israel	total
Ramallah	a) Whole Villages			
	59 units	657,917		
	b) 'Border' villages			
	★ Beit Liqya	12,643	1,715	14,358
	★ Beit Sira	1,962	2,725	4,687
	★ Safa	7,802	1,800	9,602
	Total:	680,324		
Jerusalem	a) Whole villages			
	41 units	1,014,443		(includes sites of three Jewish settlements: Atarot (501 dunums) Neve Yaaqov (489 dunums) and Ramat Rahel (145 dunums))
	★ East Jerusalem	2,000		
	b) 'Border' villages			
	★ Arab El-Rashayda	154,445	4,700	159,145
	Sawahira	67,044	124	67,168
	★ Battir	6,636	1,392	8,028
	★ Beit Iksa	4,773	4,500	9,273
	★★★ Beit I'nan	9,780	325	10,105
	★★★ Beit Mahsir	—	16,268	16,268
	★ Beit Safafa	2,676	638	3,314
	★ Beit Surik	2,316	4,633	6,949
	★ Husan	7,184	68	7,252
	★★ Lifta	2,653	6,090	8,743
	★★ Maliha	667	6,161	6,828
	★★ Qabu	1,222	2,584	3,806
	★★ Qaloniya	439	4,405	4,844
	★ Qatanna	3,766	5,698	9,464
	★ Qubeiba	3,139	45	3,184
	★ Sharafat	1,970	4	1,974
	★★★ Silwan	3,598	1,823	5,421
	★ Sur Baher	7,447	2,024	9,471
	★ Wad Fukin	3,411	6,517	9,928
	★★ Walaja	4,091	13,617	17,708
	Total:	1,303,700		

Appendix V

sub-district	village	areas (in dunums) in West Bank	in Israel	total
Hebron	a) Whole villages			
	13 units	381,519		
	b) 'Border' villages			
	★ 'Arab El-Jahalin	74,000	453,000	527,000
	★ Beit 'Aula	22,185	1,860	24,045
	★ Dhahiriya	88,591	32,263	120,854
	★ Dura	136,121	104,583	240,704
	★ Idna	31,274	2,728	34,002
	★ Jab'a	6,138	1,207	7,345
	★★ Khirbet Umm Burj	1,465	11,618	13,085
	★ Nuba	11,617	11,219	22,836
	★ Sammu'	45,672	93,200	138,872
	★ Surif	27,922	10,954	38,876
	★ Yatta	107,172	67,000	174,172
	Total:	933,676		
Ramle	a) Whole villages	Nil	This sub-district has area of about 62,000 dunums in No Man's Land.	
	b) 'Border' villages			
	★ Beit Nuba	2,811	8,590	11,401
	★★ Budros	3,675	5,747	9,422
	★★ Deir Ayyub	1,000	5,028	6,028
	★ 'Imwas	2,501	2,650	5,151
	★ Khirbet Musmar	1,450	1,704	3,154
	★ Latrun	904	7,472	8,376
	★ Lubban	9,842	12	9,854
	★★ Majdal Yaba	5,747	20,885	26,632
	★★ Midya	1,371	5,649	7,020
	★ Ni'lin	13,484	2,391	15,875
	★ Qibya	2,396	14,108	16,504
	★ Rantis	7,735	23,198	30,933
	★★ Shilta	801	4,579	5,380
	★ Shuqba	13,164	1,849	15,013
	★ Yalu	9,437	5,554	14,991
	Total:	76,318		

Palestinian Rights and Losses in 1948

sub-district	village	areas (in dunums) in West Bank	in Israel	total
Tulkaram	a) Whole villages			
	21 units	177,527		
	b) 'Border' villages			
	★ 'Attil	7,229	108	7,337
	★ Baqa El-Sharqiya	3,950	36	3,986
	★ Deir El-Ghusun	14,838	12,932	27,770
	★ Falama	2,373	7	2,380
	★ Fardisiya	205	887	1,092
	★ Far'un	6,422	2,429	8,851
	★ Habla	6,744	4,159	10,903
	★ 'Illar	13,827	154	13,981
	★ Irtah	1,364	1,585	2,949
	★ Jaiyus	12,513	58	12,571
	★★ Kafr Bara	924	3,035	3,959
	★ Kafr Jammal	9,356	5,589	14,945
	★★ Kafr Qasem	760	12,005	12,765
	★ Kafr Sur	8,867	2,059	10,926
	★ Kafr Thulth	24,488	1,450	25,938
	★ Nazlat 'Isa	2,013	17	2,030
	★ Qaffin	10,695	13,060	23,755
	★ Qalqiliya	11,808	16,107	27,915
	★★ Qaqun	589	41,178	41,767
	★ Shweika	5,443	885	6,328
	★★ Taiyiba	4,581	36,044	40,625
	★ Tulkaram (rural)	3,981	28,626	32,607
	★ Zeita	1,643	4,767	6,410
	Total:	332,142		

Summary by Sub-District

Beisan		411
Jenin		577,829
Nablus		1,568,304
Ramallah		657,917
Jerusalem		1,303,700
Hebron		933,676
Ramle		76,318
Tulkaram		332,142
Total West Bank		5,450,297

Appendix V

B — The Gaza Strip

sub-district	village	areas (in dunums) Gaza Strip	in Israel	total
Gaza	a) Whole villages			
	Abu Middein	8,821		
	Deir El Balah	14,735		
	Gaza (urban)	10,072		
	Jabaliya	11,497		
	Khan Yunis — Urban	2,302		
	Rural	53,820		
	Nazla	4,510		
	Nuseirat	10,425		
	Rafah	40,579		
	Summeiri	3,833		
		160,594		
	b) 'Border' villages			
	★ 'Abasan	14,343	1,741	16,084
	★ Bani Suheila	7,503	3,625	11,128
	★ Beit Hanun	12,136	7,899	20,025
	★ Beit Lahiya	12,953	25,423	38,376
	★★ Dimra	1,883	6,609	8,492
	★ Gaza (rural)	72,795	87,949	160,744
	★ Khirbet Ikhza'a	4,409	3,770	8,179
	Total Gaza s/d:	286,626		
	c) Territory from Beersheba s/d:	60,000		
	Total Gaza Strip:	346,616		

Appendix VI

Palestine
Jewish-owned Land in the Territory Occupied by Israel under the Terms of the General Armistice Agreements

Explanatory Notes

1. In 1948, the year the state of Israel came into existence, the Jewish population of Palestine stood at about 700,000 persons, or about one-third of the total population.

2. In 1948, Jewish-owned land was 1,491,690 dunums, or about 6 per cent of the total land area of Palestine (see *Village Statistics*, 1945).

3. The lands of two German colonies, Sarona and Wilhelma, in the Jaffa sub-district, known to have been acquired by the Jews after World War II, have been shown as owned by Jews.

4. The Huleh Concession Area, in the Safad sub-district, has been included in the land area owned by Jews.

5. Land recorded in the *Village Statistics* under the column *public* has been included under Jewish ownership where such land falls in Jewish settlements.

Appendix VI

area in dunums

sub-district settlement, or village	Jewish land	public	total
Acre sub-district			
Acre (urban)	6		6
'Arraba	40		40
Bassa and Ma'sub	4,178		4,178
Birwa	546		546
Buqei'a	189		189
Damun	687		687
Hanita	3,986	5	3,991
Kafr Yasif	8		8
Khirbet Jiddin	3,349		3,349
Khirbet Samah (Eilon)	3,940	48	3,988
Makr	96		96
Manshiya	1,895		1,895
Ein Sara, Shavei Zion, and Ga'ton (Mazra'a)	4,001		4,001
Nahariya	1,986	190	2,176
Tarshiha and Kabri	90		90
Totals	24,997	243	25,240
Beersheba sub-district			
Tel Tsofim and Ruhama	65,231		65,231
Totals	65,231		65,231
Beisan sub-district			
Sede Eliyahu ('Arida)	1,362		1,362
Ashrafiya	1,293		1,293
Avuqa	885	66	951
Bashatiwa	2,252		2,252
Bawati	1,305		1,305
Beisan (urban)	1		1
Sede Nahum & Messilot (Beisan rural)	9,253		9,253
Beit Alfa	6,616	70	6,686
Beit Hash Shitta	6,644	69	6,713
Danna	206		206
Ein Harod	14,066	198	14,264
Gesher	1,365	91	1,456
Geva	3,114	70	3,184
Ma'oz Haiyim & Neve Eitan (Ghazawiya)	7,625		7,625
Hermonim (Hamidiya)	1,386		1,386
Hamra	2,153		2,153
Heftsi Bah	4,012	82	4,094
Beit Yosef (Jabbul)	20		20
Jisr El-Majami'	289	169	458
Kafr Misr	4,462		4,462
Kefar Yeheziqel	5,396	293	5,689
Khuneizir	1,000		1,000
Kefar Ruppin (Misl El-Jizl)	2,222		2,222
Murassas	3,002		3,002
Qumya	81		81

Palestinian Rights and Losses in 1948

sub-district settlement, or village	Jewish land	public	total
Safa	2,523		2,523
Nir David (Sakhina)	4,985		4,985
Sirin	477		477
Benei Berit (Taiyiba)	8,492		8,492
Tel Esh-Shauk	3,116	504	3,620
Tel Yosef	15,312	418	15,730
Irgun Borokhov (Tira)	2,604		2,604
Tirat Tsevi	836	62	898
Umm 'Ajra	1,218		1,218
Yubla	1,758		1,758
Zab'a	3,424	388	3,812
Totals	124,755	2,480	127,235
Gaza sub-district			
Barqa	226		226
Batani Sharqi	70		70
Beer Tuvya	3,562	161	3,723
Nir 'Am (Beit Hanun)	1,917		1,917
Beit Jirja	116		116
Bi'lin & Ard El-Ishra	294		294
Bureir	618		618
Deir Suneid	483		483
Gan Yavne and Kefar Bitsaron	4,476	219	4,695
Gaza (rural)	6,537		6,537
Hamama	1,693		1,693
Hirbiya	1,226		1,226
Dorot (Huj)	4,236		4,236
Gat ('raq El-Manshiya)	3,468		3,468
Isdud	2,487		2,487
Kefar Warburg	1,605	42	1,647
Masmiya El-Kabira	229		229
Najd	495		495
Negba	2,627	146	2,773
Qastina	3,135		3,135
Sawafir Esh-Shamaliya	450		450
Sawafir Esh Sharqiya	103		103
Summeil	2,620		2,620
Sumsum	3,386		3,386
Tell Et-Turmos	68		68
Yasur	2,871		2,871
Totals	48,998	568	49,566
Haifa sub-district			
'Arab El-Fuqara	2,513		2,513
'Arab El-Ghawarina	526		526
'Arab En-Nufei'at	7,466		7,466
'Atlit	5,262		5,262
Balad Esh-Sheikh	285		285
Bat Shelomo	7,501	404	7,905
Beit She'arim	4,045	159	4,204
Binyamina	14,724	677	15,401

Appendix VI

sub-district settlement, or village	Jewish land	public	total
Bureika	9,384		9,384
Buteimat	4,724		4,724
Daliyat El-Karmil	1,736		1,736
Daliyat El-Ruha & Dalia	9,614		9,614
Dumeira	612		612
'Ein Ghazal	424		424
Ein Hash Shofar	4,542	69	4,611
El-Ro-i	569	85	654
Emeq Zevulun & Jidru	32,342		32,342
Fureidis	132		132
Giv'at Ada	7,562	297	7,859
Giv'at Zeid	1,581	8	1,589
Hadera (urban)	2,254	276	2,530
Hadera (rural)	18,000	814	18,814
Haifa (urban) (estimated)	27,623	7,700	35,323
Haz Zorea'	3,215	103	3,318
Heftzi Bah	4,898	939	5,837
'Isfiya	1,476		1,476
Kabbara	3,487		3,487
Kafr Qari'	3,544		3,544
Karkour	13,302	520	13,822
Kefar 'Atta	5,194	934	6,128
Kefar Brandeis	4,906	49	4,955
Kefar Ham Maccabi	1,660	18	1,678
Kefar Hassidim	16,408	592	17,000
Kefar Yehoshua	7,982	525	8,507
Khirbet El-Burj	4,933	343	5,276
Khubbeiza	2,024		2,024
Khureiba	3,911	3,996	7,907
Mazar	856		856
Meir Shefeiya	2,497	57	2,554
Mesheq Yagur	4,084	195	4,279
Mishmar Ha Emeq	4,736	114	4,850
Nesher	2,748	172	2,920
Pardess Hanna	19,856	1,439	21,295
Qannir	50		50
Qiryat Amal	2,832	93	2,925
Qiryat Haroshet	715	190	905
Qisariya (Caesarea)	874		874
Ramat Hash Shofet	5,459	121	5,580
Ramat Yissai	2,792	202	2,994
Ramat Yohanan	3,536	15	3,551
Sabbarin	4,209		4,209
Sede Ya'aqov	8,417	375	8,792
Sha'ar Ha Amaqim	2,676	195	2,871
Shafa 'Amr (rural)	7,621		7,621
Sindiyana	864		864
Tannura	2,051		2,051
Tira	6,553		6,553
Tiv'on	5,771	45	5,816
Umm El-Zinat	51		51
Usha	894	7	901

Palestinian Rights and Losses in 1948

sub-district settlement, or village	Jewish land	public	total
Wadi 'Ara	1,949		1,949
Ya'arot Ha Karmel	6,213		6,213
Yajur	486		486
Yoqne'am	13,265	790	14,055
Zikhron Ya'aqov	11,860	698	12,558
Totals	364,276	23,216	387,492
Hebron sub-district			
Beit Jibrin	1,008		1,008
Jab'a	1,751		1,751
Surif	314		314
Tell El-Safi	1,120		1,120
Zeita	1,273		1,273
Totals	5,466		5,466
Jaffa sub-district			
Abu Kishk	901		901
Bat Yam (urban)	2,107	998	3,105
Beit Dajan	1,975		1,975
Benei Beraq (urban)	1,142	181	1,323
Benei Beraq (rural)	413	15	428
Biyar 'Adas	109		109
Fajja	1,580		1,580
Gat Rimon	706	29	735
Giv'atayim	781	103	884
Giv'at Hen	812	40	852
Hadar	4,135	219	4,354
Haram	4,745		4,745
Herzliya (urban)	1,103	134	1,237
Herzliya (rural)	7,361	659	8,020
Holon (urban)	1,886	122	2,008
Holon (rural)	5,836	1,692	7,528
Jaffa (urban)	1,374		1,374
Jaffa (rural)	1		1
Jalil El-Qibliya	5,980		5,980
Jalil Esh-Shamaliya	521		521
Jammasin El-Gharbi	714		714
Jammasin El-Sharqi	54		54
Jarisha	93		93
Kafr 'Ana	2,334		2,334
Kefar Gannim	2,868	252	3,120
Kefar Malal	2,099	143	2,242
Kefar Sava (urban)	1,239	153	1,392
Kefar Sava (rural)	5,012	198	5,210
Kheiriya	5,842		5,842
Magdiel	3,508	108	3,616
Miqve Israel	1,632	906	2,538
Muweilih	376		376
Nahalat Yits-haq	480	16	496
Petah Tiqva (urban)	4,011	557	4,568

Appendix VI

sub-district settlement, or village	Jewish land	public	total
Petah Tiqva (rural)	18,354	1,724	20,078
Qiryat Shaul	219	19	238
Ra'anana (urban)	2,861	248	3,109
Ra'anana (rural)	2,493	105	2,598
Ramatiyim	2,109	121	2,230
Ramat Hash Sharon	1,737	126	1,863
Ramat Gan (urban)	4,338	693	5,031
Ramat Gan (rural)	228		228
Rantiya	142		142
Rishpon	2,060	173	2,233
Safiriya	1,722		1,722
Salama	885		885
Saqiya	447		447
Sarona (urban)	1,332	235	1,567
Sarona (rural)	2,895	90	2,985
Shefayim	1,899	89	1,988
Sheikh Muwannis	3,545		3,545
Wilhelma	8,989	519	9,508
Tel Aviv (urban) (Includes Mas'udiya)	9,101	1,776	10,877
Tel Litwinsky	1,454	160	1,614
Yahudiya	1,135		1,135
Yarqona	996	49	1,045
Yazur	1,428		1,428
Totals	144,099	12,652	156,751

Jenin sub-district

Ti'innik	2,540		2,540
Zir'in	1,711		1,711
Totals	4,251		4,251

Jerusalem sub-district

'Arab El-Sawahira	54		54
Battir	533		533
Beit Iksa	1,073		1,073
Beit Naqquba	951		951
Beit Safafa	391		391
Beit Surik	63		63
Beit Thul	421		421
Deir Aban	376		376
Deir Yasin	153		153
'Ein Karim	1,362		1,362
Har Tuv	4,547	157	4,704
Jerusalem West (urban) (estimated)	5,047	1,930	6,977
Jerusalem (rural)	405		405
Jura	247		247
Khirbet El-'Umur	436		436
Lifta	756		756
Maliha	922		922
Motza (Qaloniya)	1,084		1,084
Qaryit El-'Inab	818		818

sub-district settlement, or village	Jewish land	public	total
Qastal	7		7
Qiryat Anavim & Ma'ale	3,498	71	3,569
Saris	132		132
Suba	15		15
Sur Bahir	540		540
Walaja	35		35
Totals	23,866	2,158	26,024
Nazareth sub-district			
'Afula (urban)	679	301	980
'Afula (rural)	15,596	1,633	17,229
Balfourya	8,368	431	8,799
Bu'eina	115		115
Dabburiya	571		571
Gevat	5,356	179	5,535
Ginneigar	3,913	141	4,054
Kefar Barukh	10,172	263	10,435
Kefar Gid'on	3,741	54	3,795
Kefar Ha Horesh	8,547	63	8,610
Kefar Tavor	13,866	482	14,348
Kefar Yeladim	784	34	818
Mahne Yisrael	3,497	140	3,637
Ma'lul	2,719		2,719
Merhavya Settlement	13,979	546	14,525
Merhavya Group	3,014	109	3,123
Mizra'	2,267	61	2,328
Mujeidal	485		485
Nahalal and Shimron	8,023	302	8,325
Na'ura	5,299		5,299
Ramat David & Hash Sharon	8,149	232	8,381
Sarid	4,945	120	5,065
Sulam	3		3
Tamra	5,568		5,568
Tel 'Adashim	7,261	383	7,644
Umm Qubei	15		15
Yafa	450		450
Totals	137,382	5,474	142,856
Ramle sub-district			
Abu Shusha	6,337		6,337
'Aqir	3,222		3,222
Beer Ya'aqov	1,813	63	1,876
Beit Hanan and Neta'im	3,666	174	3,840
Beit 'Oved	5,021	144	5,165
Ben Shemen	2,094	82	2,176
Gan Shelomo	380	6	386
Gedera	4,677	341	5,018
Giv'at Brenner	2,678	25	2,703
Haditha	157		157
Hulda	2,534	62	2,596

Appendix VI

sub-district settlement, or village	Jewish land	public	total
Idhnibba	1,082		1,082
'Innaba	21		21
Kefar Aharon	1,727	84	1,811
Kefar Bilu	655	75	730
Kefar Marmorek	777	70	847
Kefar Menahem	1,272		1,272
Kefar Sirkin	548	8	556
Kefar Uriya	4,452		4,452
Latrun	134		134
Majdal Yaba	596		596
Mansura	102		102
Mazkaret Batyah (Eqron)	8,306	299	8,605
Mughar	2,659		2,659
Mukheizin	1,380		1,380
Muzeiri'a	1,450		1,450
Na'ana	5,832		5,832
Nahalat Yehuda	967	68	1,035
Qatra	2,509		2,509
Qubab	861		861
Qubeiba	1,397		1,397
Qula	271		271
Ramle (rural)	185		185
Rantis	487		487
Rehovot (urban)	2,445	362	2,807
Rehovot (rural)	12,837	488	13,325
Rishon le Zion (urban)	1,840	276	2,116
Rishon le Zion (rural)	21,907	8,660	30,567
Sarafand El-'Amar	761		761
Sarafand El-Kharab	1,611		1,611
Seidun	1,221		1,221
Shahma	220		220
Tina	949		949
Tirat Shalom	389	36	425
Umm Kalkha	96		96
Wadi Hunein (Nes Tsiyona)	3,211	192	3,403
Yibna	2,845		2,845
Zarnuqa (Gibbeton)	1,578		1,578
Totals:	122,159	11,515	133,674

Safad sub-district

Abil El-Qamh	1,327		1,327
Aiyelet Hash Shahar and Yarda	6,549	457	7,006
Biriya	5,170	1	5,171
Buweiziya	503		503
Dafna	2,189	222	2,411
Dan	3,054	371	3,425
Dhahiriya El-Fauqa	15,997	307	16,304
'Ein Zeitim	3,707	1,358	5,065
Fir'im	163		163
Ghuraba	478		478
Harrawi	1,471		1,471

Palestinian Rights and Losses in 1948

sub-district settlement, or village	Jewish land	public	total
Hatzor	2,104	113	2,217
Hule Concession Area	41,326		41,326
Hunin	486		486
Jahula	583		583
Ja'una	7		7
Jish	24		24
Kefar Gil'adi	4,184	1,554	5,738
Kefar Szold ('Abisiya)	1,257		1,257
Kefar Nehemya (Dawwara)	2,753		2,753
Khisas	2,738		2,738
Khiyam El-Walid	3,901		3,901
Kirad El-Baqqara	121		121
Kirad El-Ghannama	175		175
Lazzaza and Beit Hillel	942		942
Mahanayim	2,407	13	2,420
Mallaha and 'Arab Zubeid	294		294
Manara	935		935
Mansura	175		175
Mazari' El-Daraja	1,829		1,829
Meirun	5,839		5,839
Metulla	5,002	78	5,080
Mishmar Ha-Yarden	5,208	54	5,262
Muftakhara	3,596		3,596
Mughr El-Kheit	384		384
Na'ima	2,414		2,414
Qadas	3,491		3,491
Qeitiya	183		183
Rosh Pina	6,847	91	6,938
Safad (urban)	153		153
Safad (rural)	103		103
Salihiya	789		789
Sanbariya	198		198
She'ar Yashuv	1,467	100	1,567
Tuba	2,307		2,307
Tuleil and Husseiniya	1,753		1,753
Weiziya and Yarda	3,673	153	3,826
Yesud Ha Ma'ala	10,928	147	11,075
Zuq El-Tahtani	1,630		1,630
Totals:	162,814	5,019	167,833

Tiberias sub-district

Afiqim	640		640
Ashdot Ya'aqov	6,343	807	7,150
Beit Gan	8,221	270	8,491
Beit Zera' (Kefar Gun)	1,398	4	1,402
Beitanya	968	15	983
Dalhamiya	746		746
Deganiya 'A'	1,118	101	1,219
Deganiya 'B'	1,915	76	1,991
'Ein Gev (Nuqeib)	9,851	2,192	12,043
Genossar (Ghweir Abu Shusha)	3,439		3,439

Appendix VI

sub-district settlement, or village	Jewish land	public	total
Hittin	147		147
Kafr Sabt	5,110		5,110
Kefar Hittim	3,929	15	3,944
Kinneret Group	3,288	104	3,392
Kinneret	4,798	329	5,127
Lubiya	1,051		1,051
Ma'dhar	5,287		5,287
Maghar and El-Mansura	1		1
Manara and Nasr-ed-Din	1,410		1,410
Manahayima	8,317	653	8,970
Migdal	5,770	67	5,837
Mitspa	3,621	674	4,295
Nimrin	3,224		3,224
Poriya	2,909	285	3,194
Massada and Sha'ar Hag Golan (in Samakh lands)	8,412		8,412
Samra	1,708		1,708
Sejera (Ilanya)	16,707	418	17,125
Sha'ara and 'Omer	5,985	113	6,098
Shajara	61		61
Sharona	4,814	79	4,893
Shorashim	2,253	115	2,368
Tiberias (urban) (estimated)	1,864	345	2,209
Tiberias (rural) and Haz Zor'im (estimated)	5,947	1,300	7,247
'Ubeidiya	1,139		1,139
'Ulam	7,725		7,725
Yaquq	4,275		4,275
Yavneel and Mishmar Hash Shelosha	23,015	891	23,906
Totals:	167,406	8,853	176,259

Tulkaram sub-district

Avihayel	1,735	127	1,862
Baqa El-Gharbiya	886		886
Beit Yannai	5,160	277	5,437
Beit Yitz-haq	411	36	447
Beit Yehoshua, Kefar Netter, and Tel Yitshaq (In Ghabat Kafr Sur)	10,384	4,776	15,160
Benei Binyamin	741	37	778
Birket Ramadan	231		231
Bitan	859	67	926
'Ein Ha Horesh	985	182	1,167
'Ein Ha Oved	239	15	254
'Ein Vared	1,649	171	1,820
Elyashiv	1,167	177	1,344
Even Yehuda	4,311	237	4,548
Gan Hayim	976	1	977
Ghabet El-'Ababsha	2,223		2,223
Ghabat Jaiyus	1,588		1,588
Ghabat Miska	271		271
Ghabat Taiyiba El-Qibliya	404		404
Ghabat Taiyiba Shamaliya	1,447		1,447
Giv'at Haiyim	951	41	992

Palestinian Rights and Losses in 1948

sub-district settlement, or village	Jewish land	public	total
Giv'at Shapira	2,335	113	2,448
Habla	570		570
Havatselet Hash Sharon	1,572	165	1,737
Herut	753	57	810
Hibbat Zion	1,769	113	1,882
Hogla	1,483	104	1,587
Jaljulia	365		365
Kafr Saba	3,144		3,144
Kafr Thulth	82		82
Kefar Haiyim	1,463	134	1,597
Kefar Ha Roe	1,160	136	1,296
Kefar Hess	1,091	76	1,167
Kefar Vitkin	3,777	339	4,116
Kefar Ya'vetz (Taiyiba)	6,294		6,294
Kefar Yona	2,890	164	3,054
Khirbet Beit Lid	2,220		2,220
Khirbet Manshiya	3,835		3,835
Khirbet El-Zababida	4,884		4,884
Khirbet Zalafa	617		617
Ma'aborot	786	365	1,151
Mishmar Hash Sharon	404	30	434
Miske and Sede Warburg	2,976		2,976
Moshav Gan Haiyim	835	71	906
Natanya (urban)	993	373	1,366
Natanya (rural)	7,719	976	8,695
Nira	150		150
Qadima	4,049	249	4,298
Qalansuwa and Tsur Moshe	7,749		7,749
Qalqilya	787		787
Qaqun	4,642		4,642
Ramat Hak Kovesh	453	15	468
Raml Zeita	1,453		1,453
Tabsar	2,807		2,807
Tel Mond	3,395	245	3,640
Tel Tsur	1,340	87	1,427
Tira	3,720		3,720
Tsofit	1,074	72	1,146
Tulkaram (rural)	3,629		3,629
Umm Khalid	882		882
Wadi Hawarith (North)	2,795		2,795
Wadi Qabbani	9,276		9,276
Yedidya	2,525	176	2,701
Totals:	141,361	5,428	146,789

Summary by Sub-District

Acre	24,997	243	25,240
Beersheba	65,231		65,231
Beisan	124,755	2,480	127,235
Gaza	48,998	568	49,566
Haifa	364,276	23,216	387,492
Hebron	5,466		5,466

Appendix VI

sub-district settlement, or village	Jewish land	public	total
Jaffa	144,099	12,652	156,751
Jenin	4,251		4,251
Jerusalem	23,866	2,158	26,024
Nazareth	137,382	5,474	142,856
Ramle	122,159	11,515	133,674
Safad	162,814	5,019	167,833
Tiberias	167,406	8,853	176,259
Tulkaram	141,361	5,428	146,789
Totals:	1,537,061	77,606	1,614,667

Appendix VII

Palestine
List of Towns and Villages Part of whose Arab Inhabitants Remained in their Homes in Israeli-occupied Territory in 1948

Explanatory Notes

1. *Population*

The 1944 figures were extracted from the Palestine government *Village Statistics,* 1945. The 1948 figures were calculated according to the ratio of increases adopted for previous years (see *A Survey of Palestine* 1946-1947, vol. I, pp. 140-64).

This Appendix estimates the position as it would have existed had normal conditions continued. In addition to the towns and villages listed, some Arabs did remain in their homes in Jaffa, Ramle, and Haifa, in May 1948, but their numbers were insignificant. The estimated number of Arabs who remained in Israeli-occupied territory after hostilities had ceased and the joining of families arranged by the United Nations, was estimated to be 170,000 persons.

2. *Land*

The total figures of land according to ownership were extracted from *Village Statistics,* 1945.

The Land Expert of the Palestine Conciliation Commission made no distinction in his identification of property between 'abandoned' villages and villages part of whose inhabitants remained in their homes. Hence details of the properties of the latter were included in the Revised Study as indicated in Appendix VIII.

Appendix VII

LIST OF TOWNS AND VILLAGES PART OF WHOSE ARAB INHABITANTS REMAINED IN THEIR HOMES IN ISRAELI-OCCUPIED TERRITORY IN 1948

Sub-district, town, or village	population 1944	population 1948	land area (in dunums) Arab	Jewish	public	total
Acre sub-district						
Abu Sinan	820	937	12,871		172	13,043
Acre (urban)	12,310	13,500	1,187	6	345	1,538
Acre (rural)			312		99	411
'Arraba	1,800	2,031	30,852	40	74	30,966
Beit Jann and Ein el-Asad	1,640	1,851	25,594		17,956	43,550
Bi'na	830	937	14,839		57	14,896
Buqei'a	990	1,117	10,276	189	3,731	14,196
Deir el-Asad	1,100	1,241	8,366		7	8,373
Deir Hanna	750	846	15,350		8	15,358
Fassuta	2,300	2,596	26,619		7,392	34,011
Jatt	200	226	5,907		2	5,909
Judeida	280	316	5,215		4	5,219
Julis	820	925	12,835		1,873	14,708
Kafr Sumei'	300	338	7,150		3	7,153
Kafr Yasif	1,400	1,580	6,729	8	26	6,763
Kisra	480	542	10,598		2	10,600
Majd El Kurum	1,400	1,580	17,828		2,214	20,042
Makr	490	553	8,661	96	34	8,791
Mazra'a	430	485	3,116		290	3,406
Mi'ilya	900	1,016	19,136		9,948	29,084
Nahf	1,320	1,490	15,654		91	15,745
Rama	1,690	1,907	23,701		815	24,516
Sajur	350	395	8,172		64	8,236
Sakhnin	2,600	2,934	70,181		11	70,192
Sha'b	1,740	1,964	17,870		121	17,991
Sheikh Dawud and Sheikh Dannun	1,240	1,399	11,771		15	11,786
Tamra	1,830	2,065	30,549		10	30,559
Tarshiha & Kabri	5,360	6,049	37,308	90	10,030	47,428
Yanuh	410	463	12,466		370	12,836
Yirka	1,500	1,693	30,597		1,855	32,452
Totals:	47,270	52,976	501,710	429	57,619	559,758
Haifa sub-district						
'Ar'ara	2,290	2,584	29,537		5,802	35,339
'Arab El-Ghawarna	620	700	2,531	526	371	3,428
Daliyat El-Karmil	2,060	2,324	19,741	1,736	10,253	31,730
Fureidis	780	880	4,220	132	98	4,450
I'billin	1,660	1,874	16,019		2,613	18,632
'Isfiya	1,790	2,020	16,811	1,476	14,260	32,547

Palestinian Rights and Losses in 1948

Sub-district, town, or village	population 1944	population 1948	Arab	Jewish	public	total
Kafr Qari'	1,510	1,704	14,543	3,544	6	18,093
Shafa 'Amr (urban)	6,990	8,020	297		41	338
Shafa 'Amr (rural)			58,428	7,621	31,219	97,268
Wadi 'Ara	230	260	7,846	1,949		9,795
Totals	17,930	20,366	169,973	16,984	64,663	251,620

Jenin sub-district

Barta'a	1,000	1,129	4,320		16,179	20,499
Muqeibila	460	520	2,687		4,441	7,128
Sandala	270	305	3,217		32	3,249
Umm El-Fahm and Mu'awiya Musherifa Musmus	5,490	6,196	68,311		8,931	77,242
Zalafa	340	384	1,285		2,504	3,789
Totals	7,560	8,534	79,820		32,087	111,907

Jerusalem sub-district

Beit Jimal	240	271	4,799		79	4,878
Qaryet El-'Inab (Abu Gosh)	860	971	6,435		337	6,772
Totals	1,100	1,242	11,234		416	11,650

Nazareth sub-district

'Arab Es-Subeih	1,320	1,490	3,740		4,946	8,686
Bu'eina	540	609	6,793	115	2,306	9,214
Dabburiya	1,290	1,456	13,373	571	4,241	18,185
Ed-Dahi	110	124	3,011		5,027	8,038
'Ein Mahil	1,040	1,174	8,268		5,122	13,390
Iksal	1,110	1,252	13,666		2,343	16,009
'Ilut	1,310	1,478	10,891		6,666	17,557
Kafr Kanna	1,930	2,178	18,869		586	19,455
Kafr Manda	1,260	1,422	12,703		2,232	14,935
Kaukab	490	553	2,134		16,540	18,674
Mash-had	660	745	9,852		1,215	11,067
Na'ura	340	384	5,535	5,299	202	11,036
Nazareth (urban)	24,290	27,350	4,398		590	4,988
Nazareth (rural)			8,201		2,025	10,226
Nein	270	305	3,737		950	4,687
Reina	1,290	1,456	15,899		130	16,029
Rummana	590	666	1,485		8	1,493
Sulam	470	530	2,358	3	1,244	3,605
Tamra	160	181	3,604	5,568	264	9,436
Tur'an	1,350	1,523	13,104		16,639	29,743
'Uzeir	150	169	764		2	766
Yafa	1,070	1,208	16,521	450	838	17,809
Totals:	41,040	46,253	178,906	12,006	74,116	265,028

Appendix VII

Sub-district, town, or village	population 1944	population 1948	land area (in dunums) Arab	Jewish	public	total
Safad sub-district						
Akbara	390	440	3,167		57	3,224
Hurfeish	830	937	14,623		2,281	16,904
Jish	1,090	1,210	12,430	24	148	12,602
Tuba ('Arab El-Heib)	590	666	13,684	2,307	1	15,992
Totals:	2,900	3,253	43,904	2,331	2,487	48,722
Tiberias sub-district						
Eilabun	550	621	11,190		3,522	14,712
Mughar and El-Mansura	2,140	2,415	45,590	1	9,992	55,583
Totals:	2,690	3,036	56,780	1	13,514	70,295
Tulkaram sub-district						
Baqa El-Gharbiya	2,240	2,528	21,116	886	22	22,024
Jaljulia	740	835	11,873	365	447	12,685
Jatt	1,120	1,264	9,623		8	9,631
Kafr Bara	150	169	3,956		3	3,959
Kafr Qasim	1,460	1,648	12,718		47	12,765
Qalansuwa	1,540	1,738	17,249		2,498	19,747
Taiyiba	4,290	4,842	32,750		1,581	34,331
Tira	3,180	3,589	26,803	3,720	836	31,359
Totals:	14,720	16,613	136,088	4,971	5,442	146,501

SUMMARY

Sub-district:	population 1944	population 1948	land area (in dunums) Arab	Jewish	public	total
Acre	47,270	52,976	501,710	429	57,619	559,758
Haifa	17,930	20,366	169,973	16,984	64,663	251,620
Jenin	7,560	8,534	79,820	—	32,087	111,907
Jerusalem	1,100	1,242	11,234	—	416	11,650
Nazareth	41,040	46,253	178,906	12,006	74,116	265,028
Safad	2,900	3,253	43,904	2,331	2,487	48,722
Tiberias	2,690	3,036	56,780	1	13,514	70,295
Tulkaram	14,720	16,613	136,088	4,971	5,442	146,501
Totals:	135,210	152,273	1,178,415	36,722	250,344	1,465,481

Note: No information is available for the nomad bedouin tribes of the Beersheba sub-district.

Appendix VIII

Palestine
Revised Schedule of Property Claimed to be Arab-owned in the Territory Occupied by Israel under the Terms of the General Armistice Agreements of 1949

Explanatory Notes

1. This Appendix includes all land claimed to be Arab-owned irrespective of method of registration or recording in the records of the Palestine government.

A indicates land appearing in the column 'Arab' in *Village Statistics*, 1945 of the Palestine government.

P indicates land appearing under the column 'Public' and claimed to be collectively owned by Arabs.

T stands for 'Total'.

2. The term 'Arab' includes non-Jews, such as Armenians, Greeks, Germans, etc.

3. This Appendix *excludes* lands of 'Border' villages whose lands fall outside the territory held by Israel (see Appendix V);

excludes Jewish settlements and Jewish-owned land in Arab villages (see Appendix VI);

includes villages part of whose inhabitants remained in their homes in 1948 (see Appendix VII).

4. Total areas of villages correspond with those appearing in the *Village Statistics*, 1945.

5. One asterisk (*) indicates 'border' village with built-up area in the West Bank or Gaza Strip.

Two asterisks (**) indicate built-up area in Israel.

Three asterisks (***) indicate no-man's land.

6. Population: 1944 figures are extracted from *Village Statistics;* 1948 figures are estimated according to ratio of annual increases used for previous estimates. Figures for villages whose built-up areas fall outside Israeli-held territory are shown in brackets and excluded from the total.

Appendix VIII

7. For a definition of the land tax categories in rural areas, see Chapter 8, p. 48.

8. Population figures appearing in brackets are not included in Grand Totals.

9. Differences between total of village and total of categories represent Jewish-owned land.

10. Division of Appendix VIII: (A) stands for urban areas; (B) stands for rural areas; (C) stands for Arab lands in Jewish settlements.

Appendix VIII (A)
URBAN AREAS

Town	Arab Population 1944	Arab Population 1948	area (in dunums) land	area (in dunums) buildings	area (in dunums) total
1. *Arab Towns*					
Acre	12,310	13,985	1,272	266	1,538
Beersheba	5,570	6,282	3,717	173	3,890
Beisan	5,180	5,684	592	71	663
Haifa	62,800	75,465	52,712	1,593	54,305
Jaffa	66,310	73,425	12,043	1,028	13,071
★ Jerusalem	60,080	68,465	18,304	1,027	19,331
Lydda	16,760	18,954	3,688	167	3,855
Majdal	9,910	11,338	1,064	282	1,346
Nazareth	14,200	16,396	4,678	310	4,988
Ramle	15,160	15,963	1,688	81	1,769
Safad	9,530	10,527	1,238	191	1,429
Shafa 'Amr	3,630	4,050	293	45	338
Tiberias	5,310	5,999	2,966	139	3,105
Sub-totals:	298,557	326,531	104,255	5,373	109,628
2. *Arab Property in Jewish Urban Areas*					
'Affula			12		12
Bat Yam			13		13
Hadera			4		4
Holon			165		165
Natanya			2		2
Ramat Gan			252		252
Tel Aviv	660	745	1,666	179	1,845
Sub-totals:	660	745	2,114	179	2,293
Grand totals:	299,217	327,276	106,369	5,552	111,921

★ City divided by Armistice Demarcation line.

Appendix VIII (B)

SUMMARY — RURAL AREAS

Sub-District	Arab Population 1944	Arab Population 1948	1–3	4	5–8	9–13	14–15	16 A	16 B	Total
Acre	53,070	59,901	8,858	3,424	86,435	216,680	55,696	399,358	2,427	772,878
Beisan	11,390	12,850	722	467	13,385	149,458	9,455	57,828	7,460	238,775
Gaza	58,740	66,343	18,940	2,560	56,078	530,958	85,384	65,040	16,174	775,134
Haifa	50,520	56,122	126	2,400	34,056	311,786	37,392	214,791	10,693	611,244
Hebron	18,530	22,367	8	1,246	10,154	246,803	100,155	802,552	573	1,161,491
Jaffa	41,340	46,647	45,308	756	18,624	85,300	35	9,926	6,956	166,905
Jenin	8,910	10,057	4	282	8,361	156,523	7,464	82,050	992	255,676
Jerusalem	23,810	26,873	31	2,433	32,458	71,520	23,077	150,286	2,073	281,878
Nablus					5,647	540	13,729	3,498		23,414
Nazareth	50,480	56,907	59	1,066	19,639	208,751	6,379	119,653	5,240	360,787
Ramallah						1,001	196	5,043		6,240
Ramle	56,418	64,161	40,543	1,580	67,438	351,665	16,527	164,306	15,046	657,105
Safad	37,380	42,183	228	2,490	78,731	166,495	72,867	198,943	5,920	525,674
Tiberias	22,790	25,720	411	1,382	21,262	158,257	13,690	65,079	4,580	264,661
Tulkaram	26,130	29,489	15,979	999	18,516	270,734	1,855	38,269	5,027	351,379
Totals:	459,508	519,620	131,217	21,085	470,784	2,926,471	443,901	2,376,622	83,161	6,453,241
Beersheba	47,980	55,000								12,452,000
	507,488	574,620								18,905,241

Total Area: 12,577,000
Less Jewish-owned: 65,000
In Gaza Strip: 60,000   125,000

Total:

Appendix VIII (B)
RURAL AREAS

Appendix VIII

Sub-District: Acre

Village	Arab population 1944	Arab population 1948	Village area		1-3	4	5-8	9-13	14-15	16A	16B	Total
'Arab El-'Aramisha	360	406	11,463	A			16	2,637		8,793		11,446
				P							17	17
				T			16	2,637		8,793	17	11,463
'Arab El-Samniya	200	226	1,872	A			58	888	666	227		1,835
				P				13			20	37
				T			58	901	666	227	20	1,872
Abu Sinan	820	936	13,043	A		69	2,171	7,865		2,010	170	12,115
				P				70		688		928
				T		69	2,171	7,935		2,698	170	13,043
Acre (Rural)			411	A			312					312
				P							99	99
				T			312				99	411
'Amqa	1,240	1,399	6,068	A		36	1,812	3,143	83	986	8	5,977
				P								91
				T		36	1,812	3,143	83	986	8	6,068
'Arraba	1,800	2,031	30,966	A		140	3,297	3,834	10,886	12,690		30,847
				P			5		14	48	12	79
				T		140	3,302	3,834	10,900	12,738	12	30,926
Bassa	2,950	3,329	29,535	A	614	132	4,699	14,598	706	4,509		25,258
				P						3	96	99
				T	614	132	4,699	14,598	706	4,512	96	25,357
Beit Jann & 'Ein El-Asad	1,640	1,851	43,550	A		67	2,530	1,686	5,720	15,591		25,594
				P						17,899	57	17,956
				T		67	2,530	1,686	5,720	33,490	57	43,550

Palestinian Rights and Losses in 1948

Village	Arab population 1944	Arab population 1948	Village area		1-3	4	5-8	9-13	14-15	16A	16B	Total
Bi'na	830	937	14,896	A		57	1,771	4,668	734	7,609		14,839
				P							57	57
				T		57	1,771	4,668	734	7,609	57	14,896
Birwa	1,460	1,648	13,542	A		59	1,795	8,221		2,864		12,939
				P							57	57
				T		59	1,795	8,221		2,864	57	12,996
Buqei'a	990	1,117	14,196	A		38	1,565	2,090	1,251	5,403		10,347
				P						3,652	8	3,660
				T		38	1,565	2,090	1,251	9,055	8	14,007
Damun	1,310	1,478	20,357	A		111	1,024	17,068	218	764		19,185
				P						430	55	485
				T		111	1,024	17,068	218	1,194	55	19,670
Deir El-Assad	1,100	1,241	8,373	A		38	1,412	204	1,046	5,666		8,366
				P							7	7
				T		38	1,412	204	1,046	5,666	7	8,373
Deir Hanna	750	846	15,358	A		40	2,799	4,398	844	7,269		15,350
				P							8	8
				T		40	2,799	4,398	844	7,269	8	15,358
Fassuta, Deir El-Qasi, Mansura	2,300	2,596	34,011	A		247	1,630	6,397	124	18,221		26,619
				P						7,350	42	7,392
				T		247	1,630	6,397	124	25,571	42	34,011
Ghabisiya, Sh. Daud, Sheikh Dannun	1,240	1,399	11,786	A		58	1,290	4,562	3,393	2,468		11,771
				P							15	15
				T		58	1,290	4,562	3,393	2,468	15	11,786
Iqrit	490	553	24,722	A		68	458	1,233	655	19,297		21,711
				P						3,008	3	3,011
				T		68	458	1,233	655	22,305	3	24,722
Jatt	200	226	5,909	A		29	553	680	526	4,118		5,906
				P							3	3
				T		29	553	680	526	4,118	3	5,909

Appendix VIII

Judeida	280	316	5,219	A P T	39 39	1,997 1,997	2,060 2,060		1,119 1,119	4 4	5,215 5,219
Julis	820	925	14,708	A P T	63 63	1,721 1,721	5,304 5,304	1,085 1,085	4,857 1,643 6,500	35 35	13,030 1,678 14,708
Kabul	560	632	10,339	A P T	56 56	1,236 1,236	4,906 16 4,922	538 538	3,584 3,584	3 3	10,320 19 10,339
Kafr I'nan	360	406	5,827	A P T	45 45	438 438	4,410 412 4,822	218 218	278 26 304		5,389 438 5,827
Kafr Sumei'	300	338	7,153	A P T	40 40	689 689	842 842	723 723	4,856 4,856	3 3	7,150 3 7,153
Kafr Yasif	1,400	1,580	6,763	A P T	75 75	3,733 3,733	2,803 2,803		118 118	26 26	6,729 26 6,755
Khirbet Jiddin			7,587	A P T			22 22		4,216 4,216		4,238 4,238
Kisra	480	542	10,600	A P T	37 37	285 285	450 450	1,363 1,363	8,463 8,463	2 2	10,598 2 10,600
Kuweikat	1,050	1,185	4,733	A P T	26 26	1,780 1,780	2,784 2,784		80 80	63 63	4,670 63 4,733
Majd El-Kurum	1,400	1,580	20,042	A P T	74 74	2,522 2,522	1,470 1,470	4,292 4,292	9,465 2,041 11,506	178 178	17,823 2,219 20,042
Makr	490	553	8,791	A P T	26 26	831 831	7,144 7,144		564 564	96 34 96 34	8,661 34 8,695

Palestinian Rights and Losses in 1948

Village	Arab population 1944	Arab population 1948	Village area		1-3	4	5-8	9-13	14-15	16A	16B	Total
Manshiya	810	914	14,886	A	260	27	628	11,132	223	353	208	12,623
				P				5		155		368
				T	260	27	628	11,137	223	508	208	12,991
Mazra'a	430	485	7,407	A	610	14	853	1,713		42	174	3,190
				P						42	174	216
				T	610	14	853	1,713		42	174	3,406
Mi'ar	770	869	10,788	A		37	120	1,574	1,323	7,731	3	10,785
				P							3	3
				T		37	120	1,574	1,323	7,731	3	10,788
Mi'ilya	900	1,016	29,084	A		123	1,509	2,676	207	14,621	31	19,136
				P						9,917	31	9,948
				T		123	1,509	2,676	207	24,538	31	29,084
Nahf	1,320	1,490	15,745	A		44	1,160	4,631	500	9,319	91	15,654
				P							91	91
				T		44	1,160	4,631	500	9,319	91	15,745
Nahr	610	688	5,261	A	2,182	28	1,939	1,094			18	5,243
				P							18	18
				T	2,182	28	1,939	1,094			18	5,261
Rama	1,690	1,907	24,516	A		57	8,310	2,850		12,484	128	23,701
				P						687		815
				T		57	8,310	2,850		13,171	128	24,516
Ruweis	330	372	1,163	A		15	254	758	62	70	4	1,159
				P							4	4
				T		15	254	758	62	70	4	1,163
Sajur	350	395	8,236	A	4	7	1,380	1,405	528	4,848	64	8,172
				P							64	64
				T	4	7	1,380	1,405	528	4,848	64	8,236
Sakhnin	2,600	2,934	70,192	A		169	3,622	14,884	14,482	37,024	11	70,181
				P							11	11
				T		169	3,622	14,884	14,482	37,024	11	70,192

Appendix VIII

					A/P/T						
Sha'b	1,740	1,964	17,991		A P T		231 231	3,248 3,248	6,602 6,602		7,789 121 7,789	121 121	17,870 121 17,991
Suhmata	1,130	1,275	17,056		A P T		135 135	1,901 1,901	2,726 2,726	564 564	4,246 7,478 11,724	6 6	9,574 7,484 17,056
Sumeiriya	760	858	8,542		A P T	632 632	28 28	354 354	6,854 16 6,870		67 342 409	249 249	7,935 607 8,542
Tamra	1,830	2,065	30,559		A P T		206 206	1,929 1,929	14,434 14,434		13,980 13,980	10 10	30,549 10 30,559
Tarbikha, Nabi Rubin, Suruh	1,000	1,129	18,563		A P T		112 112	634 634	2,342 2,342	859 859	8,605 6,005 14,610	6 6	12,552 6,011 18,563
Tarshiha, Kabri	5,360	6,049	47,428		A P T	743 743	252 252	5,278 5,278	13,831 13,831	225 225	16,979 10,000 26,979	30 30	37,308 10,030 47,338
Umm El-Faraj	800	903	825		A P T	745 745	15 15	42 42	5 5	13 13	1 1	4 4	821 4 825
Yanuh	410	463	12,836		A P T		40 40	823 823		1,625 1,625	9,978 368 10,346	2 2	12,466 370 12,836
Yirka	1,500	1,693	32,452		A P T		140 140	5,858 5,858	5,809 5,809		18,790 1,839 20,629	16 16	30,597 1,855 32,452
Zeeb and Manawat	1,910	2,156	12,607		A P T	2,972 2,972	74 74	2,164 2,164	4,461 4,461		2,767 2,767	169 169	12,438 169 12,607
Grand Totals:	53,070	59,901	787,957			8,858	3,424	86,435	216,680	55,696	399,358	2,427	772,878

☐ **Sub-District: Beersheba**

tribes and sub-tribes	cultivable land			uncultivable land	total
	Arab	public	total		
Ahyawat	1,936,380	2,279	1,938,659	10,573,110	12,577,000
'Azazima					
Hanajira					
Jubarat					
Sa'idiyin					
Tarabin: Ghawaliya, Jarawin, Najmat					
Tayaha: 'Alamat, Bani 'Uqwa, Budeinat, Qalazin					
Dhullam					
Hukuk					
Nutush					
Rawashida					
'Urur					
Qatatiwa					
Qudeirat					
Ramadin					
Shallaiyin					

Notes:

1. To be excluded from the total figure of 12,577,000 for an area of 65,231 dunums owned by Jews.

2. Also to be excluded an area of 60,000 dunums which remained in Arab territory. See Appendix V under Gaza Strip.

3. Nomad bedouin population was estimated in 1944 to have been 47,980 persons. It is not known how many of these remained in the Beersheba sub-district after 1948.

Appendix VIII

☐ Sub-District: Beisan

Village	Arab population 1944	Arab population 1948	Village area		1-3	4	5-8	9-13	14-15	16A	16B	Total
'Arida	150	169	2,280	A				600		100		700
				P						174	44	218
				T				600		274	44	918
Ashrafiya	230	260	6,711	A	130		4,458	7		104	123	137 5,281
				P	13			583				
				T	143		4,458	590		104	123	5,418
Bashatiwa	1,560	1,761	20,739	A	13		694	11,939	1,378	486	962	14,510
				P				9		3,006		3,977
				T	13		694	11,948	1,378	3,492	962	18,487
Bawati (Hakimiya)	520	587	10,641	A			2,225	3,111	24	52	1,374	5,412
				P				268		2,282		3,924
				T			2,225	3,379	24	2,334	1,374	9,336
Beisan (rural)			28,294	A	340		1,408	12,631		101	970	14,480
				P	6		220	1,341		2,024		4,561
				T	346		1,628	13,972		2,125	970	19,041
Bira	260	293	6,566	A		52	48	4,667		86	96	4,853
				P				14		1,903		2,013
				T		52	48	4,681		1,989	96	6,866
Danna	190	214	6,614	A		15	14	5,097		51	75	5,177
				P				35		1,121		1,231
				T		15	14	5,132		1,172	75	6,408
Farwana	330	372	4,996	A		11	42	3,847		42	80	3,942
				P				396		578		1,054
				T		11	42	4,243		620	80	4,996
** Fatur	110	124	729	A				447		3		450
				P							6	6
				T				447		3	6	456
Ghazawiya	1,020	1,151	18,408	A	13		34	5,185		91	351	5,323
				P				1,561		3,548		5,460
				T	13		34	6,746		3,639	351	10,783

Areas of Arab lands by tax categories (in dunums)

Palestinian Rights and Losses in 1948

Village	Arab population 1944	Arab population 1948	Village area		1-3	4	5-8	9-13	14-15	16A	16B	Total
Hamidiya	220	248	10,902	A		10	8	4,343	52	401		4,814
				P				711	155	3,565	271	4,702
				T		10	8	5,054	207	3,966	271	9,516
**Hamra	730	824	11,511	A	164		32	6,553		12	6	6,767
				P				1,874		356	223	2,453
				T	164		32	8,427		368	229	9,220
Jabbul	250	282	15,127	A		33	5	4,367		1,002		5,407
				P				1,330		8,212	158	9,700
				T		33	5	5,697		9,214	158	15,107
Kafra	430	485	9,172	A		18	36	7,284		71		7,409
				P				1,095		415	253	1,763
				T		18	36	8,379		486	253	9,172
Kafr Misr	330	372	13,230	A		16	3	4,175	150	285		4,629
				P				1,438	1,688	791	222	4,139
				T		16	3	5,613	1,838	1,076	222	8,768
Kaukab El-Hawa	300	338	9,949	A		56	170	3,775	2,064	60		6,125
				P				12		3,649	163	3,824
				T		56	170	3,787	2,064	3,709	163	9,949
Khuncizir	260	293	3,107	A	18		1,658	256		34		1,966
				P						90	51	141
				T	18		1,658	256		124	51	2,107
Misl El-Jizl	100	113	5,873	A				702		22		724
				P			252	447		2,067	161	2,927
				T			252	1,149		2,089	161	3,651
Murassas	460	520	14,477	A		26	16	8,572	1,322	1,112		9,936
				P							427	1,539
				T		26	16	8,572	1,322	1,112	427	11,475
Qumiya	440	496	4,898	A		15	33	4,205		463		4,716
				P						8	93	101
				T		15	33	4,205		471	93	4,817

Areas of Arab lands by tax categories (in dunums)

Appendix VIII

				A P T						
Safa	650	733	12,518	A P T			7,362 922 8,284	87 87	100 1,381 1,481	143 143	7,549 2,446 9,995
Sakhnin	530	598	6,400	A P T	825 3 828		260 47 307		108 108	172 172	1,085 330 1,415
Samiriya	250	282	3,873	A P T	21 21		2,801 824 3,625		18 121 139	77 77	2,851 1,022 3,873
Sirin	810	914	28,445	A P T	113 18 131	413 413	12,426 381 12,807	2,428 107 2,535	1,209 10,486 11,695	387 387	16,589 11,379 27,968
Taiyiba	280	316	15,874	A P T	22 22		7,013 7,013		92 54 146	201 201	7,127 255 7,382
Tal Esh-Shauk	120	135	3,685	A P T	14 14		33 33		18 18		65 65
Tira	150	169	10,207	A P T	29 29	56 56	4,326 298 4,624		52 2,694 2,746	148 148	4,463 3,140 7,603
Umm 'Ajra	260	293	6,443	A P T			2,688 2,334 5,022		20 142 162	41 41	2,708 2,517 5,225
Wad el-Bira	70	79	5,195	A P T	25 25	514 514	2,551 2,551		2,105 2,105		5,195 5,195
Yubla	210	237	5,165	A P T	12 12	37 37	1,971 344 2,315		31 830 861	182 182	2,051 1,356 3,407
Zab'a	170	192	3,968	A P T	156 156						156 156
Grand Totals:	11,390	12,850	306,297		722	467	13,385 149,458	9,455	57,828	7,460	238,775

257

Sub-District: Gaza

Village	Arab population 1944	Arab population 1948	Village area		1–3	4	5–8	9–13	14–15	16A	16B	Total
*'Abasan	(2,230)	(2,516)	16,084	A			4	1,421	237			1,662
				P							79	79
				T			4	1,421	237		79	1,741
'Arab Sukreir	390	440	40,224	A	725		679	12,538	460	1,564		15,966
				P				1,511	452	21,942	353	24,258
				T	725		679	14,049	912	23,506	353	40,224
*Bani Suheila	(3,220)	(3,634)	11,128	A				3,534				3,534
				P							91	91
				T				3,534			91	3,625
Barbara	2,140	2,718	13,978	A	132	70	2,960	9,622		710		13,494
				P						99	385	484
				T	132	70	2,960	9,622		809	385	13,978
Barqa	890	1,004	5,206	A	667	26	47	3,814		99		4,653
				P						188	139	327
				T	667	26	47	3,814		287	139	4,980
Batani Gharbi	980	1,106	4,574	A	170	34	96	4,160		16		4,476
				P							98	98
				T	170	34	96	4,160		16	98	4,574
Batani Sharqi	650	734	5,764	A	319	32	474	4,650		33		5,508
				P						72	114	186
				T	319	32	474	4,650		105	114	5,694
Beit 'Affa	700	790	5,808	A		26	14	5,657		10		5,707
				P							101	101
				T		26	14	5,657		10	101	5,808
Beit Daras	2,750	3,104	16,357	A	832	88	463	14,413		68		15,864
				P						70	423	493
				T	832	88	463	14,413		138	423	16,357

Appendix VIII

*Beit Hanun	(1,680)	(1,896)	20,025	A P T	236 236	 4 4	 90 340 430	4,242 1,264 5,506		662 913 1,575	 148 148	5,230 2,669 7,899
Beit Jirja	940	1,061	8,481	A P T	434 434	25 25	625 625	6,955 6,955		27 27	2 297 299	8,068 297 8,365
*Beit Lahiya	(1,700)	(1,919)	38,376	A P T			8 8	1,360 11,420 12,780		687 11,881 12,568	67 67	2,055 23,368 25,423
Beit Tima	1,060	1,196	11,032	A P T	60 60		197 197	10,412 32 10,444		52 40 92	239 239	10,721 311 11,032
Bi'lin & Art El-Ishra	180	203	8,036	A P T	6 6		143 143	6,972 20 6,992		294 153 447	154 154	7,415 327 7,742
Bureir	2,740	3,092	46,184	A P T	130 130		405 405	38,499 38,499	4,929 4,929	387 504 891	712 712	44,350 1,216 45,566
Deir Suneid	730	824	6,081	A P T	158 158	13 13	502 10 512	4,361 19 4,380		45 220 265	270 270	5,079 519 5,598
**Dimra	520	598	8,492	A P T	17 6 23		359 359	5,552 242 5,794	18 18	226 72 298	117 117	6,172 437 6,609
Faluja	4,670	5,271	38,038	A P T	517 517		87 87	36,590 36,590		65 83 148	696 696	37,259 779 38,038
*Gaza (rural)	(78,460)	(89,240)	160,744	A P T	27 27		6,417 6,417		72,122 72,122	1,458 1,458	1,388 1,388	80,024 1,388 81,412
Hamama	5,010	5,654	41,366	A P T	1,016 1,016	167 167	1,698 1,698	26,048 26,048	4,239 4,239	562 4,856 5,418	5 1,082 1,087	33,735 5,938 39,673

Palestinian Rights and Losses in 1948

Village	Arab population 1944	Arab population 1948	Village area		1-3	4	5-8	9-13	14-15	16A	16B	Total
Hatta	970	1,095	5,305	A		45	4	5,108		36		5,193
				P							112	112
				T		45	4	5,108		36	112	5,305
Hirbiya	2,240	2,258	22,312	A	2,765	42	6,817	7,142		436		17,202
				P				2,037		1,435	412	3,884
				T	2,765	42	6,817	9,179		1,871	412	21,086
Huj	810	914	21,988	A		34	93	16,248		378		16,753
				P						683	316	999
				T		34	93	16,248		1,061	316	17,752
Huleiqat	420	474	7,063	A		18	115	6,648		130		6,911
				P							152	152
				T		18	115	6,648		130	152	7,063
Huraniya (Masmiya Es-Saghira)	530	608	6,478	A	147	18	7	6,111		2		6,285
				P				14		51	128	193
				T	147	18	7	6,125		53	128	6,478
'Ibdis	540	609	4,593	A		18	149	4,307		12		4,486
				P						7	100	107
				T		18	149	4,307		19	100	4,593
'Iraq El-Manshiya	2,010	2,268	17,901	A		168	53	13,440		167		13,828
				P				14		175	416	605
				T		168	53	13,454		342	416	14,433
'Iraq Suweidan	660	745	7,529	A		35	9	7,325		11		7,380
				P							149	149
				T		35	9	7,325		11	149	7,529
Isdud	4,620	5,214	47,871	A	1,921	131	8,171	22,656		509		33,388
				P			5,303	466		5,211	1,016	11,996
				T	1,921	131	13,474	23,122		5,720	1,016	45,384
Jaladiya	360	406	4,329	A		63		4,151		2		4,216
				P				35		13	65	113
				T		63		4,186		15	65	4,329

Appendix VIII

					A						
Jiya	1,230	1,388	8,506	A P	189	45	39	8,004		24	8,301
											205
				T	189	45	39	8,004		24	8,506
Julis	1,030	1,162	13,584	A P	1,360	30	930	10,607 230		82	13,009 575
				T	1,360	30	930	10,837		82	13,584
Jura	2,420	2,731	12,224	A P	481	45	7,180	2,896 100		367 705	10,969 1,255
				T	481	45	7,180	2,996		1,072	12,224
Juseir	1,180	1,332	12,361	A P		54		11,852 11		109 77	12,015 346
				T		54		11,863		186	12,361
Karatiya	1,370	1,546	13,709	A P		48	321	12,928		49 12	13,346 363
				T		48	321	12,928		61	13,709
Kaufakha	500	564	8,569	A P		31	87	5,731	2,037	549	5,849 2,720
				T		31	87	5,731	2,037	549	8,569
Kaukaba	680	767	8,542	A P		40	166	8,184			8,390 152
				T		40	166	8,184		152	8,542
*Khirbet Ikhza'a	(990)	(1,100)	8,179	A P				2,812	890		3,702 68
				T				2,812	890	68	3,770
Khirat Khisas	150	169	6,269	A P	191	10	2,609 6	479		19 2,917	3,308 2,961
				T	191	10	2,615	479		2,936	6,269
Majdal (rural)			42,334	A P	2,354		2,863 22	33,493 1,974		179 313	38,889 3,445
				T	2,354		2,885	35,467		492	42,334
Masmiya El-Kabira	2,520	2,844	20,687	A P	1,005	135	618	17,658 407		28 143	19,444 1,014
				T	1,005	135	618	18,065		171	20,458

Palestinian Rights and Losses in 1948

Village	Arab population 1944	Arab population 1948	Village area		1-3	4	5-8	9-13	14-15	16A	16B	Total
Muharraqa	580	654	4,855	A		29	12	4,622		2		4,665
				P						48	142	190
				T		29	12	4,622		50	142	4,855
Najd	620	700	13,576	A	10	26	511	11,916		274		12,737
				P						80	264	344
				T	10	26	511	11,916		354	264	13,081
Negba			5,376	A			8	2,578				2,586
				P				69			94	163
				T			8	2,647			94	2,749
Ni'ilya	1,310	1,478	5,233	A	1,084	29	1,445	2,225		145		4,928
				P						124	181	305
				T	1,084	29	1,445	2,225		269	181	5,233
Qastina	890	1,004	12,019	A	235	37	770	7,317		79		8,438
				P						129	317	446
				T	235	37	770	7,317		203	317	8,884
Sawafir El-Gharbiya	1,030	1,162	7,523	A		25	585	6,663		34		7,307
				P						4	212	216
				T		25	585	6,663		38	212	7,523
Sawafir Esh-Shamaliya	680	767	5,861	A	481	21	10	4,632		22		5,166
				P						119	125	245
				T	481	21	10	4,633		141	125	5,411
Sawafir Esh-Sharqiya	970	1,095	13,831	A	930	40	387	11,820		23		13,200
				P						214	314	528
				T	930	40	387	11,820		237	314	13,728
Summeil	950	1,072	19,304	A		31	54	16,093		83		16,261
				P				8		103	312	423
				T		31	54	16,101		186	312	16,684
Sumsum	1,290	1,456	16,797	A	240	44	250	12,086		51		12,671
				P				121		315	304	740
				T	240	44	250	12,207		366	304	13,411

Appendix VIII

				A P							
Tal Et-Turmus	760	858	11,508		172	35	686	10,258		55	11,206
				T	172	35	686	10,258		74	234
				A						129	160
Yasur	1,070	1,208	16,390	P	636	35	180	12,173		78	11,440
				T	636	35	180	12,173		95	13,102
										173	322
											13,519
Grand totals:	58,740	66,343	900,483	A P	18,940	2,560	56,078	530,958	85,384	65,040	775,134
										16,174	

☐ Sub-District: Haifa

Abu Shusha	720	813	8,960	A P			1,034	4,855	13 5,902
				T			1,034	4,855	2,844 3,058
									214
									214 8,960
Abu Zureiq	550	621	6,493	A P	1		274 8	4,092	21 4,388
				T	1		282	4,092	1,948 2,105
									149
									1,969 6,493
									149
'Ar'ara	2,290	2,584	35,339	A P		45	2,830 322	21,947 2,485	366 25,188
				T		45	3,152	24,432	6,404 10,151
									940
									6,770 35,339
									940
'Arab El-Fuqara	310	350	2,714	A P					15 15
				T					15 15
'Arab El-Ghawarina	620	700	3,428	A P		69	6	674	1,782 2,531
				T		69	6	674	314 371
									57
									2,096 2,902
									57
'Arab El-Nufe'at	820	925	8,937	A P				87	9 96
				T				87	1,375 1,375
									1,384 1,471

263

Palestinian Rights and Losses in 1948

Village	Arab population 1944	Arab population 1948	Village area		1-3	4	5-8	9-13	14-15	16A	16B	Total
'Atlit	150	170	9,083	A						1		4
				P				3				
				T				3		1		4
Balad Esh-Sheikh	4,120	4,650	9,849	A		221	408	4,410		845		5,884
				P				153		3,222	305	3,680
				T		221	408	4,563		4,067	305	9,564
Beit Lahm	370	417	7,526	A	6	51	278	4,796		2,308		7,439
				P						74	13	87
				T	6	51	278	4,796		2,382	13	7,526
Bureika	290	327	11,434	A		15	78	1,538		233		1,864
				P							186	186
				T		15	78	1,538		233	186	2,050
Buteimat	110	124	8,557	A		10	8	2,374	134	1,307		3,833
				P								
				T		10	8	2,374	134	1,307		3,833
Daliyat El-Carmel	2,060	2,324	31,730	A		60	1,507	18,174		9,186		19,741
				P				177			890	10,253
				T		60	1,507	18,351		9,186	890	29,994
Daliyat El-Ruha	280	316	10,008	A		24	98	56				178
				P								
				T		24	98	56				178
Dumeira	620	700	1,387	A				263		512		775
				P								
				T				263		512		775
'Ein Ghazal	2,170	2,450	18,079	A		145	1,662	10,490	459	4,540		17,296
				P						359		359
				T		145	1,662	10,490	459	4,899		17,655
'Ein Haud	650	734	12,605	A		50	1,461	2,585	1,638	880		6,614
				P					184	5,503	304	5,991
				T		50	1,461	2,585	1,822	6,383	304	12,605

Areas of Arab lands by tax categories (in dunums)

264

Appendix VIII

Fureidis	780	880	4,450	A	33	545	1,577		2,076	87	4,231
				P						87
				T	33	545	1,577		2,076	87	4,318
El-Ghubaiyat	1,130	1,275	12,139	A		209	10,883		515	244	11,851
				P					288		288
				T		209	10,883		803	244	12,139
I'billin	1,660	1,874	18,632	A	95	2,723	10,085	1,604	4,115		18,622
				P						10	10
				T	95	2,723	10,085	1,604	4,115	10	18,632
Ijzim	2,970	3,352	46,905	A	183	1,576	15,337	11,084	1,095	14	29,275
				P					17,616		17,630
				T	183	1,576	15,337	11,084	18,711	14	46,905
'Isfiya	1,790	2,020	32,547	A	74	1,119	15,570		122	956	16,885
				P			311		12,919		14,186
				T	74	1,119	15,881		13,041	956	31,071
Jaba'	1,140	1,286	7,012	A	60	450	3,551	656	42	206	4,759
				P			36	12	1,999		2,253
				T	60	450	3,587	668	2,041	206	7,012
Kabara	120	135	9,831	A		20	1,001		47		1,048
				P	2		3,309		1,445	520	5,296
				T	2	20	4,310		1,492	520	6,344
Kafrin	920	1,038	10,882	A	18	147	9,776		40	207	9,981
				P			135		559		901
				T	18	147	9,911		599	207	10,882
Kafr Lam	340	383	6,838	A	14	131	4,774		182	230	5,101
				P		2	220		1,285		1,737
				T	14	133	4,994		1,467	230	6,838
Kafr Qari'	1,510	1,704	18,093	A	25	1,656	6,046	6,404	418		14,549
				P							—
				T	25	1,656	6,046	6,404	418		14,549
Khirbet Ed Damum	340	384	2,797	A		280	1,619		858	35	1,904
				P	5						893
				T	5	280	1,619		858	35	2,797

265

Palestinian Rights and Losses in 1948

Village	Arab population 1944	Arab population 1948	Village area		1-3	4	5-8	9-13	14-15	16A	16B	Total
Khirbet Lid	640	722	13,572	A P T		52 52	103 103	13,063 12 13,075		 44 44	 298 298	13,218 354 13,572
Khubbeiza	290	327	4,854	A P T		11 11	94 94	1,215 1,215	1,257 1,257	251 251	 2 2	2,828 2 2,830
Mansi ('Arab Baniha)	1,200	1,354	12,272	A P T		17 17	1,391 1,391	5,984 655 6,639		309 3,669 3,978	 247 247	7,701 4,571 12,272
Mazar	210	237	7,976	A P T	5 5	39 39	473 473	3,633 3,633	117 117	165 2,510 2,675	 178 178	4,432 2,688 7,120
Qannir	750	846	11,331	A P T		22 22	946 946	2,834 2,834	6,655 6,655	369 450 819	 5 5	10,826 455 11,281
Qasariya	960	1,083	31,786	A P T	18 18	28 28	108 108	625 386 1,011	395 395	19,785 9,465 29,250	 102 102	20,959 9,953 30,912
Rihaniya	240	271	1,930	A P T		46 46	73 73	1,761 1,761		5 5	 45 45	1,885 45 1,930
Sabbarin	1,700	1,919	25,307	A P T		179 179	352 352	15,707 15,707		4,860 4,860		21,098 21,098
Sarafand	290	327	5,409	A P T		6 6	22 22	3,238 3,238		214 1,738 1,952	 191 191	3,480 1,929 5,409
Shafa 'Amr (rural)	3,560	4,018	97,268	A P T	63 63		5,032 83 5,115	44,093 2,668 46,761		9,157 26,184 35,341	 2,367 2,367	58,345 31,302 89,647

Appendix VIII

Sindiyana	1,250	1,411	15,172	A P		90	525		1,844 4,596		9,712 4,596
				T		90	525	7,253	6,440		14,308
Tantura	1,490	1,681	14,520	A P	26	119	287 287	6,594 184	4,733 82	444	11,759 710
				T	26	119	287	6,778	4,815	444	12,469
Tira	5,270	5,948	45,262	A P		368	3,543	16,219 85	3,954 13,658	882	24,084 14,625
				T		368	3,543	16,304	17,612	882	38,709
Umm Esh-Shauf	480	542	7,426	A P		31	283	702	6 865	229	6,332 1,094
				T		31	283	702	871	229	7,426
Umm El-Zinat	1,470	1,659	22,156	A P		80	1,682	10,049	6,994 1,817		20,288 1,817
				T		80	1,682	10,049	8,811		22,105
Wadi 'Ara	230	260	9,795	A P				6,400	1,446		7,846
				T				6,400	1,446		7,846
Waldheim (Umm El-'Amad)	260	293	9,225	A P		102 102	170 170	4,776 4,776	4,146 4,146	31 31	9,194 31 9,225
Yajur	610	688	2,720	A P		18	57	261	8 1,785	105	344 1,890
				T		18	57	261	1,793	105	2,234
Grand Totals:	50,520	56,122	694,236		126	2,400	34,056	311,786	214,791	10,693	611,244
								37,392			

☐ Sub-District: Hebron

Village	Arab population 1944	Arab population 1948	Village area		1-3	4	5-8	9-13	14-15	16A	16B	Total
*'Arab El-Jahhalin	(1,000)	(2,257)	517,000	A P						453,000		453,000
				T						453,000		453,000
'Ajjur	3,730	4,210	58,074	A P		171	2,428	24,885	342	16,945 13,280	23	44,771 13,303
				T		171	2,428	24,885	342	30,225	23	58,074
Barqusiyia	330	372	3,216	A P		31	28	2,460		695	2	3,214 2
				T		31	28	2,460		695	2	3,216
*Beit 'Aula	(1,310)	(1,478)	24,045	A P				441	17	1,402		1,860
				T				441	17	1,402		1,860
Beit Jibrin	2,430	2,742	56,185	A P		287	2,477	20,083 82	10,530 106	21,585 6	21	54,962 215
				T		287	2,477	20,165	10,636	21,591	21	55,177
Beit Nattif	2,150	2,427	44,587	A P		162	688	17,961	2,188	11,763 11,816	9	32,762 11,825
				T		162	688	17,961	2,188	23,579	9	44,587
Dawayima	3,710	4,187	60,585	A P		179	1,199 7	27,709	1,482	29,984	25	60,553 32
				T		179	1,206	27,709	1,482	29,984	25	60,585
Deir Ed-Dubban	730	824	7,784	A P		58		5,102	256	2,361	7	7,777 7
				T		58		5,102	256	2,361	7	7,784
Deir Nakhkhas	600	677	14,476	A P		22	362	3,472	1,415	3,652 5,548	5	8,923 5,553
				T		22	362	3,472	1,415	9,200	5	14,476

Appendix VIII

★ Dhahiriya	(3,760)	(4,243)	120,854	A P T		2 2	6,938 6,938	258 258	32,003 260 32,263
★ Dura	(9,700)	(10,948)	240,704	A P T	70 70	55,456 55,456	49,057 49,057		104,583 104,583
★ Idna	(2,190)	(2,471)	34,002	A P T		574 574	1,714 1,714	440 440	2,728 2,728
★ Jab'a	(210)	(237)	7,345	A P T		548 548	567 567	92 92	1,207 1,207
★★ Khirbet Umm El-Burj	140	158	13,083	A P T	15 15	2,378 2,378	8,485 5 8,490	707 707	11,609 9 11,618
Kidna	450	508	15,774	A P T	15 15	6,505 6,505	4,262 4,133 8,395		11,607 4,137 15,774
Mughallis	540	609	11,459	A P T	23 23	7,277 7,277	3,898 3,898	173· 173	11,286 173 11,459
★ Nuba	(760)	(858)	22,836	A P T	28 28	3,869 3,869	7,312 10,000 17,312		11,209 10,000 21,209
Qubeiba	1,060	1,196	11,912	A P T	35 35	8,109 8,109	3,657 103 3,760	8 8	11,801 111 11,912
Ra'na	190	214	6,925	A P T	14 14	5,882 5,882	915 915	2 2	6,923 2 6,925
★ Sammu'	(2,520)	(2,844)	138,872	A P T		2,913 2,913	66,745 66,745	23,542 23,542	93,200 93,200

Village	Arab population 1944	Arab population 1948	Village area		1–3	4	5–8	9–13	14–15	16A	16B	Total
*Surif	(2,190)	(2,472)	38,876	A			34	315	4,370	5,535		10,254
				P					600	100		700
				T			34	315	4,970	5,635		10,954
Tel Es-Safi	1,290	1,456	28,925	A	8	68	742	19,603		7,267		27,688
				P				1,214		12	11	1,237
				T	8	68	742	20,817		7,279	11	28,925
*Yatta	(5,260)	(5,936)	174,172	A					27,318	39,682		67,000
				P								
				T					27,318	39,682		67,000
Zakariya	1,180	1,331	15,320	A		70	998	6,487		7,743		15,298
				P			8			5	9	22
				T		70	1,006	6,487		7,748	9	15,320
Zeita	330	373	10,490	A		32		7,214	1,685	293		9,224
				P			36	1,214		13	3	1,266
				T		32	36	8,428	1,685	306	3	10,490
Zikrin	960	1,083	17,195	A		64		15,048		2,066		17,178
				P						8	9	17
				T	—	64		15,048		2,074	9	17,195
Grand Totals:	18,530	22,367	1,694,666		8	1,246	10,154	246,803	100,155	802,552	573	1,161,491

Appendix VIII

☐ **Sub-District: Jaffa**

				A/P/T					
Abu Kishk	1,900	2,144	18,470	A	2,487		226	14,018	390		17,121
				P					50	398	448
				T	2,487		226	14,018	440	398	17,569
Beit Dajan	3,840	4,333	17,327	A	7,990	60	3,195	676	340		12,261
				P					2,537	554	3,091
				T	7,990	60	3,195	676	2,877	554	15,352
Biyar 'Adas	300	338	5,492	A	1,604	14	181	3,413	20		5,232
				P				3	42	106	151
				T	1,604	14	181	3,416	62	106	5,383
Fajja	1,200	1,354	4,919	A	602	7	53	2,457	96		3,215
				P						124	124
				T	602	7	53	2,457	96	124	3,339
Haram	520	586	8,065	A	136	18	256	2,096	175		2,681
				P				234	53	352	639
				T	136	18	256	2,330	228	352	3,320
Jaffa (rural)			4,439	A				1,095	1,338		2,433
				P					1,996	10	2,006
				T				1,095	3,334	10	4,439
Jalil El-Qibliya	470	530	15,207	A	1,029	7	4,929	6,390	581		12,936
				P				43	36	456	535
				T	1,029	7	4,929	6,433	617	456	13,471
Jalil Esh-Shamaliya	190	214	2,450	A	183	7	22	1,605	83		1,900
				P						29	29
				T	183	7	22	1,605	83	29	1,929
Jammasin El-Gharbi	1,080	1,219	1,365	A	202		169	155	3		529
				P					31	91	122
				T	202		169	155	34	91	651
Jammasin Esh-Sharqi	730	824	358	A	46		160	80			286
				P						18	18
				T	46		160	80		18	304

271

Palestinian Rights and Losses in 1948

Village	Arab population 1944	Arab population 1948	Village area		1-3	4	5-8	9-13	14-15	16A	16B	Total
Jarisha	190	214	555	A	302	3	89			3		397
				P						21	44	65
				T	302	3	89			24	44	462
Kafr 'Ana	2,800	3,160	17,353	A	2,214	90	597	11,022		435		14,358
				P						52	609	661
				T	2,214	90	597	11,022		487	609	15,019
Kheiriya	1,420	1,602	13,672	A	3,359	26	1,275	2,355		167		7,182
				P				40		15	593	648
				T	3,359	26	1,275	2,395		182	593	7,830
Mirr (Mahmudiya)	170	192	51	A	2	2				6		41
				P							10	10
				T	2	2		31		6	10	51
Muweilih	360	406	3,342	A	949		27	1,796		23		2,795
				P							171	171
				T	949		27	1,796		23	171	2,966
Rantiya	590	666	4,389	A	505	13	173	3,444		20		4,155
				P							92	92
				T	505	13	173	3,444		20	92	4,247
Safiriya	3,070	3,464	12,842	A	3,539	95	3,766	2,974		171		10,545
				P							575	575
				T	3,539	95	3,766	2,974		171	575	11,120
Salama	6,730	7,595	6,782	A	2,853	114	370	2,266		30		5,633
				P							264	264
				T	2,853	114	370	2,266		30	264	5,897
Saqiya	1,100	1,241	5,850	A	2,422	30	145	2,534		20		5,151
				P						42	210	252
				T	2,422	30	145	2,534		62	210	5,403
Sawalima	800	902	5,942	A	923		191	4,537		193		5,844
				P						9	89	98
				T	923		191	4,537		202	89	5,942

Areas of Arab lands by tax categories (in dunums)

Appendix VIII

Sheikh Muwannis	1,930	2,178	15,972	A P	3,810	41	86	7,052	35	432	935	11,456
				T	3,810	41	86	7,072	35	448	935	12,427
Yahudiya ('Abbasiya)	5,650	6,376	20,540	A P	3,879	142	993	12,333		152	611	17,499
				T	3,879	142	993	13,535		245	611	19,405
Yazur	4,030	4,548	11,807	A P	6,272	87	1,721	1,429		255	615	9,764
				T	6,272	87	1,721	1,429		255	615	10,379
Nomads	2,270	2,561		A P T								
Grand Totals:	41,340	46,647	195,189		45,308	756	18,624	85,300	35	9,926	6,956	166,905

☐ Sub-District: Jenin

★ Anin	(390)		15,049	A P		92	1,131	2,507	1,223
				T		92	1,131	2,507	2,507
★ 'Arabbuna	(210)	(237)	6,772	A P			312	876	3,730
				T			312	876	1,188
★ Barta'a, Khirbet Tura Gharbiya	(1,000)	(1,129)	20,499	A P		1,291	3,448 65	4,433	5 193	4,744 4,691
				T		1,291	3,513	4,438	193	9,435

273

Palestinian Rights and Losses in 1948

Village	Arab population 1944	Arab population 1948	Village area		1-3	4	5-8	9-13	14-15	16A	16B	Total
*Birqin	(1,540)	(1,738)	19,477	A				94				94
				P								
				T				94				94
'Ein El-Mansi	90	102	1,297	A		2	496	626		109		1,233
				P						10	54	64
				T		2	496	626		119	54	1,297
*Faqqu'a	(880)	(993)	30,179	A			400	6,548		13,614		20,562
				P						51		51
				T			400	6,548		13,665		20,613
*Jalama	(460)	(520)	5,827	A			9	2,506		108		2,515
				P				25			90	223
				T			9	2,531		108	90	2,738
*Jalbun & Mujadda'a	(610)	(688)	33,959	A			287	7,616	5,433	10,664		24,000
				P						8		8
				T			287	7,616	5,433	10,672		24,008
**Mazar	270	305	14,501	A		9	229	5,087		7,957		5,325
				P							29	7,986
				T		9	229	5,087		7,957	29	13,311
*Mughaiyir	(220)	(248)	18,049	A				865	2,000	2,579		5,450
				P						94		94
				T				865	2,000	2,673		5,544
**Muqeibila	460	520	7,128	A		12	194	5,345		44		5,595
				P				408		124	152	684
				T		12	194	5,753		168	152	6,279
Nuris	570	643	6,256	A	4	36	243	2,935		3,029		6,247
				P							9	9
				T	4	36	243	2,935		3,029	9	6,256
*Raba and Umm Sirhan	(870)	(982)	25,642	A			10	100		3,298		3,408
				P						50		50
				T			10	100		3,348		3,458

Appendix VIII

Village										
*Rummana and Khirbet Salim	(880)	(993)	21,676	A P T		590 8,769 8,769		96 2,405 2,501	25 25	9,455 2,481 11,936
Sandala	270	305	3,249	A P T	7 7	2 3,109 3,109		99 99		3,217 32 3,249
*Ti'innik	(100)	(113)	32,263	A P T	82 82	24,582 2,540 27,122		10 10	32 32	24,664 2,642 27,306
**Umm El-Fahm etc.	5,490	6,196	77,242	A P T	127 127	4,371 43,810 43,810		24,827 2,365 27,192	93 93	73,135 2,458 75,593
*Ya'bad	(3,480)	(4,000)	37,805	A P T				250 250		250 250
*Yamun	(2,520)	(2,844)	20,361	A P T		1,277 1,277		10 10		1,287 1,287
Zalafa	340	384	3,789	A P T	8 8	2,677 2,677		1,017 1,017	22 22	3,767 22 3,789
*Zibda	(190)	(214)	11,924	A P T				360 360		360 360
Zir'in	1,420	1,602	23,920	A P T	81 81	20,964 20,964		989 989	175 175	22,034 175 22,209
*Zububa	(560)	(632)	13,843	A P T		11,684 11,684		62 62		11,746 11,746
Grand Totals:	8,910	10,057	450,707		4 282 8,361	156,523	7,464	82,050	992	255,676

275

☐ Sub-District: Jerusalem

Village	Arab population 1944	Arab population 1948	Village area		1-3	4	5-8	9-13	14-15	16A	16B	Total
*'Arab Er-Rashayida			159,145	A P T						4,700 4,700		4,700 — 4,700
*'Arab Es-Sawahira			67,168	A P T				124 124				124 — 124
'Allar	440	497	12,356	A P T		12 12	353 353	1,529 1,529	705 705	7,326 2,428 9,754	3 3	9,925 2,431 12,356
'Aqqur	40	45	5,522	A P T		5 5	174 174	278 278	375 375	4,612 4,612	78 78	5,444 78 5,522
'Artuf	350	395	403	A P T		18 18	61 61	279 279		43 43	2 2	401 2 403
*Battir	(1,050)	(1,155)	8,028	A P T			536 13 549	400 400		295 74 369	74 74	1,231 161 1,392
*Beit Iksa	(1,410)	(1,591)	9,273	A P T			600 20 620	300 300	600 600	2,500 475 2,975	5 5	4,000 500 4,500
Beit 'Itab	540	609	8,757	A P T		14 14	665 665	1,342 1,342	58 58	3,368 3,306 6,674	4 4	5,447 3,310 8,757
***Beit I'nan	(820)	(970)	10,105	A P T						325 325		325 — 325

Appendix VIII

Beit Jimal	240	273	4,878	A				1,185		4,799
				P		715			79	79
				T		715	2,899	1,185	79	4,878
Beit Mahsir	2,400	2,709	16,268	A	77		2,899			15,428
				P	77	1,348	4,195	7,778	40	840
				T		1,348	4,195	800	40	16,268
Beit Naqquba	240	271	2,979	A	9	389		8,578		1,972
				P	9	389	38	1,101		
				T			38	1,101		1,972
*Beit Safafa (divided)	(1,410)	(1,591)	3,314	A	5	81	320			636
				P	5	81		170	2	2
				T			320	170	2	638
*Beit Surik	(480)	(542)	6,949	A				4,198		4,533
				P			38	60		100
				T			38	4,258	2	4,633
Beit Thul	260	293	4,629	A	13	75	786			4,205
				P	13	75		3,297	3	3
				T			786	3,297	3	4,208
Beit Umm El-Meis	70	79	1,013	A	2	71	273			1,013
				P	2	71		667		
				T			273	667		1,013
Bureij	720	813	19,080	A	14	77	9,426			18,856
				P	14	31		9,308	114	224
				T		31	9,426	110	114	19,080
						77		9,418		
Deiraban	2,100	2,370	22,734	A	54	1,580	9,455	5,019		21,578
				P	54	1,580		537	243	780
				T			9,455	5,556	243	22,358
Deir 'Amr	10	11	3,072	A		18	650			3,072
				P		18		2,404		
				T			650	2,404		3,072
Deir El-Hawa	60	68	5,907	A	4	58	294	3,033		4,660
				P	4	58		1,188	59	1,247
				T			294	4,221	59	5,907

Village	Arab population 1944	Arab population 1948	Village area		1-3	4	5-8	9-13	14-15	16A	16B	Total
Deir Rafat	430	485	13,242	A P		10	216	10,563		2,177 213	63	12,966 276
				T		10	216	10,563		2,390	63	13,242
Deir Esh-Sheikh	220	248	6,781	A P		8	291	486	539	42 5,274	141	1,366 5,415
				T		8	291	486	539	5,316	141	6,781
Deir Yasin	610	688	2,857	A P		12		601	155	1,933	3	2,701 3
				T		12		601	155	1,933	3	2,704
'Ein Karem	3,180	3,589	15,029	A P		1,007 17	7,953	1,175		3,314 18	183	13,449 218
				T		1,024	7,953	1,175		3,332	183	13,667
* Husan	(770)	(869)	7,252	A P				38		30		68
				T				38		30		68
Ishwa'	620	700	5,522	A P		18	473	1,070	841	3,054	66	5,456 66
				T		18	473	1,070	841	3,054	66	5,522
'Islin	260	293	2,159	A P		420	122	549	296	770	2	2,157 2
				T		420	122	549	296	770	2	2,159
Jarash	190	214	3,518	A P		5	5	917	418	2,172	1	3,517 1
				T		5	5	917	418	2,172	1	3,518
Jerusalem (rural)			1,459	A P			196	739		62 17	40	997 57
				T			196	739		79	40	1,054
Jura	420	474	4,158	A P		27	1,167	177	648	1,890	2	3,909 2
				T		27	1,167	177	648	1,890	2	3,911

Appendix VIII

Kasla	280	316	8,004	A P T	10 10	440 440	418 418	1,847 1,847	5,286 5,286	3 3	8,001 3 8,004
Khirbet Ismallah	20	23	568	A P T		3 3	485 485		80 80		568 — 568
Khirbet El-Lauz	450	508	4,502	A P T	13 13	728 728	242 242	451 451	3,061 3,061	7 7	4,495 7 4,502
Khirbet El-'Umur	270	305	4,163	A P T	10 10	497 497	1,324 1,324	20 20	1,874 1,874	2 2	3,725 2 3,727
** Lifta	2,550	2,878	8,743	A P T	313 313		2,325 2,325		2,626 2,626	132 132	5,264 132 5,396
** Maliha	1,940	2,190	6,828	A P T	86 86	2,613 2,613	711 711	302 302	2,087 2,087	107 107	5,799 107 5,906
Nataf	40	45	1,401	A P T		176 176	41 41	117 117	1,067 1,067		1,401 1,401
** Qabu	260	293	3,806	A P T	12 12	349 349	595 595		1,614 1,623	9 5	2,570 14 2,584
** Qalonia	910	1,027	4,844	A P T	74 74	717 717	414 414	306 306	1,748 1,748	5	3,259 3,259
Qaryet El-'Inab (Abu Gosh)	860	971	7,590	A P T	21 21	1,402 1,402	2,349 2,366	713 713	1,950 1,987	283 37 283	6,435 337 6,772
Qastal	90	102	1,446	A P T	5 5	247 247		45 45	1,125 1,125	17 17	1,422 17 1,439

279

Palestinian Rights and Losses in 1948

Village	Arab population 1944	Arab population 1948	Village area		1-3	4	5-8	9-13	14-15	16A	16B	Total
***Qatanna	(1,150)	(1,298)	9,464	A			1,442	1,044	229	2,983		5,698
				P								
				T			1,442	1,044	229	2,983		5,698
***Qubeiba	(420)	(474)	3,184	A					45			45
				P								
				T					45			45
Ras Abu 'Ammar	620	700	8,342	A		40	924	1,532	1,362	4,430		8,288
				P						25	29	54
				T		40	924	1,532	1,362	4,455	29	8,342
Sar'a	340	384	4,967	A		16	194	2,979		1,775		4,964
				P							3	3
				T		16	194	2,979		1,775	3	4,967
Saris	560	632	10,699	A		10	399	1,261	2,416	6,374		10,460
				P			27	30		10	100	167
				T		10	426	1,291	2,416	6,384	100	10,627
Sataf	540	609	3,775	A		22	928		465	2,354		3,769
				P							6	6
				T		22	928		465	2,354	6	3,775
*Sharafat	(210)	(238)	1,974	A			4					4
				P								
				T			4					4
***Silwan	(3,820)	(4,500)	5,421	A				976	200	647		1,823
				P								
				T				976	200	647		1,823
Suba	620	700	4,102	A		16	1,438	604	108	1,919		4,085
				P							5	5
				T		16	1,438	604	108	1,919	5	4,090
Sufla	60	68	2,061	A		3		400		311		714
				P						1,347		1,347
				T		3		400		1,658		2,061

Areas of Arab lands by tax categories (in dunums)

Appendix VIII

	1944	1948			5-8	9-13	14-15	16A	Total
* Sur Bahir	(2,450)	(2,765)	9,471	A P		485	878	110	551	2,024
				T		485	878	110	551	2,024
* Wad Fukin	(280)	(316)	9,928	A P			775		5,742	6,517
				T			775		5,742	6,517
** Walaja	(1,650)	(1,862)	17,708	A P	2,188	3,179	71	7,981	13,450
					31				165	165
				T	2,188	3,179	71	7,981	13,615
Grand Totals:	23,810	26,873	576,548		32,458	71,520	23,077	150,286	2,073	281,878
					31					
					2,433					

☐ **Sub-District: Nablus, Ramallah**

Sub-district and village	Arab Population 1944	1948	Total Village Area	Areas in Israel by tax categories (in dunums) 5-8	9-13	14-15	16A	Total
Nablus sub-district								
* Deir Ballut	(720)	(824)	14,789		540		3,498	4,038
* Tubas	(5,530)	(5,980)	313,123	5,647		13,729		19,376
Totals:			327,912	5,647	540	13,729	3,498	23,414
Ramallah sub-district								
* Beit Liqya	(1,040)	(1,300)	14,358		280		1,435	1,715
* Beit Sira	(540)	(670)	4,687		721	196	1,808	2,725
* Safa	(790)	(830)	9,602				1,800	1,800
Totals:			28,647		1,001	196	5,043	6,240

☐ Sub-District: Nazareth

Village	Arab population 1944	Arab population 1948	Village area		1-3	4	5-8	9-13	14-15	16A	16B	Total
Reina	1,290	1,456	16,029	A	10	139	915	10,451		4,384	130	16,029
				P								
				T	10	139	915	10,451		4,384	130	16,029
Rummana	590	666	1,493	A		14	22	1,322		99	36	1,493
				P								
				T		14	22	1,322		99	36	1,493
Saffuriya	4,330	4,887	55,378	A		102	5,298	20,723	1,118	14,495	25	41,736
				P			12			13,605		13,642
				T		102	5,310	20,723	1,118	28,100	25	55,378
Sulam	470	530	3,605	A	4	17	276	2,041		8	76	2,346
				P			15			1,168		1,259
				T	4	17	291	2,041		1,176	76	3,605
Tamra	160	181	9,436	A		46	27	1,601		183	130	1,674
				P				7,449				7,762
				T		46	27	9,050		183	130	9,436
Tur'an	1,350	1,523	29,743	A		34	1,136	11,892		9	620	13,071
				P			16	15		16,021		16,672
				T		34	1,152	11,907		16,030	620	29,743
Umm Qubei			4,651	A	21		329	3,513		518	168	4,381
				P						87		255
				T	21		329	3,513		605	168	4,636
'Uzeir	150	169	766	A		7		737		20	2	766
				P								
				T		7		737		20	2	766
Yafa	1,070	1,208	17,809	A		149	713	12,258		3,401	117	16,521
				P						721		838
				T		149	713	12,258		4,122	117	17,359
Grand Totals:	50,480	56,907	364,456		59	1,066	19,639	208,751	6,379	119,653	5,240	360,787

Areas of Arab lands by tax categories (in dunums)

Appendix VIII

☐ Sub-District: Ramle

Abu El-Fadl (Sautariya)	510	576	2,870	A P	843	42	1,135		697		2,717 153
				T	843	42	1,135		697	153	2,870
Abu Shusha	870	982	9,425	A P		24	203		2,399	270	2,896 192
				T		24	203		2,399	270 192	3,088
'Aqir	2,480	2,799	15,825	A P	1,161	46	1,112		8,909 771	94 13	11,322 1,281
				T	1,161	46	1,112		9,680	107 497	12,603
Barfiliya	730	824	7,134	A P		17	241	740	1,999	4,137	7,134
				T		17	241	740	1,999	4,137	7,134
Barriya	510	576	2,831	A P		55	51		2,627	25	2,758 73
				T		55	51		2,627	25 73	2,831
Bash-shit	1,620	1,828	18,553	A P	66	58	651		17,558	205	18,538 15
				T	66	58	651		17,558	205 15	18,553
Beit Jiz	550	621	8,357	A P		29	175 9		6,405 4	1,594 11	8,203 154
				T		29	184		6,409	1,605 130	8,357
Beit Nabala	2,330	2,629	15,051	A P	226	124	1,733	1,969	8,230	2,148 153	14,430 621
				T	226	124	1,733	1,969	8,230	2,301 468	15,051
* Beit Nuba	(1,240)	(1,400)	11,401	A P			314	3,281	1,927	2,874	8,396 194
				T			314	3,281	1,927	2,874 194	8,590
Beit Shanna	210	237	3,617	A P		44		589	276	2,708	3,617
				T		44		589	276	2,708	3,617

283

Palestinian Rights and Losses in 1948

Village	Arab population 1944	Arab population 1948	Village area		1-3	4	5-8	9-13	14-15	16A	16B	Total
Beit Susin	210	237	6,491	A P		8	114	5,442 1		324 487	109	5,888 603
				T		8	114	5,443	6	811	109	6,491
Bi'lin	210	237	3,992	A P		6	1,450	800		1,735		3,991 1
				T		6	1,450	800		1,735	1	3,992
Bir Ma'in	510	576	9,319	A P		9	176	2,184	696	6,252	2	9,317 2
				T		9	176	2,184	696	6,252	2	9,319
Bir Salim	410	463	3,401	A P	742		510	1,468		568	113	3,288 113
				T	742		510	1,468		568	113	3,401
** Budros	510	576	7,935	A P			355	840	550	3,690	312	5,435 312
				T			355	840	550	3,690	312	5,747
Burj	480	542	4,708	A P		12	6	1,142	1,486	2,008 51	3	4,654 54
				T		12	6	1,142	1,486	2,059	3	4,708
Danyal	410	463	2,808	A P		15	37	2,453 145		83	75	2,588 220
				T		15	37	2,598		83	75	2,808
Deir Abu Salama	60	68	1,195	A P			41	695		459		1,195
				T			41	695		459		1,195
** Deir Ayub	320	361	6,028	A P		26	120	1,929	319	2,557	77	4,951 77
				T		26	120	1,929	319	2,557	77	5,028
Deir Muheisin	460	519	10,008	A P		72	78	7,852 29		1,702 21	254	9,704 304
				T		72	78	7,881		1,723	254	10,008

Appendix VIII

					A/P/T					
Deir Qaddis	440	496	8,224		A		8	1,815	1,069	5,330	2	8,222
					T		8	1,815	1,069	5,330	2	8,224
Deir Tarif	1,750	1,975	8,756		A P	1,241	51	487	5,717	442	466	352	8,404
					T	1,241	51	487	5,717	442	466	352	8,756
Haditha	760	858	7,110		A P	10	16	246	3,801	618	1,853	206	6,544
									2		201		409
					T	10	16	246	3,803	618	2,054	206	6,953
Idhnibba	490	553	8,103		A P		25	85	5,277		1,440	149	6,827
											45		194
					T		25	85	5,277		1,485	149	7,021
*'Imwas	(1,450)	(1,636)	5,151		A P				2,639		11		2,650
					T				2,639		11		2,650
'Innaba	1,420	1,602	12,857		A P	111	54	512	10,652		1,174	354	12,503
													354
					T	111	54	512	10,652		1,174	354	12,857
Jilya	330	373	10,347		A P	8	7		6,631	1,078	2,621	2	10,345
													2
					T	8	7		6,631	1,078	2,621	2	10,347
Jimzu	1,510	1,704	9,681		A P	77	50	1,605	5,176	418	2,145	210	9,471
													210
					T	77	50	1,605	5,176	418	2,145	210	9,681
Jindas			4,448		A P	290		540	3,457		38	123	4,325
													123
					T	290		540	3,457		38	123	4,448
Khalayil			12,127		A P			23	8,408		3,515	170	11,946
											11		181
					T			23	8,408		3,526	170	12,127
Kharbata	650	733	7,120		A P	9	2,788	591		3,730	2	7,118
													2
					T	9	2,788	591		3,730	2	7,120

285

Palestinian Rights and Losses in 1948

Village	Arab population 1944	Arab population 1948	Village area		1-3	4	5-8	9-13	14-15	16A	16B	Total
Kharruba	170	192	3,374	A P		3	25	1,050	570	1,725	—	3,373 1
				T		3	25	1,050	570	1,725	—	3,374
Kheima	190	214	5,150	A P		9	4	5,007		20	110	5,040 110
				T		9	4	5,007		20	110	5,150
Khirbet Beit Far	300	338	5,604	A P			19	5,337		101 68	79	5,457 147
				T			19	5,337		169	79	5,604
Khirbet Buweira	190	214	1,150	A P			59	533		521	37	1,113 37
				T			59	533		521	37	1,150
Khirbet Dhudeiriya	100	113	1,341	A P			66	1,224		51		1,341
				T			66	1,224		51		1,341
*Khirbet Musmar			3,154	A P				26		1,678		1,704
				T				26		1,678		1,704
Khirbet Qubeiba			1,082	A P				717		365		1,082
				T				717		365		1,082
Khirbet Zakaria			4,538	A P				2,070	91	2,377		4,538
				T				2,070	91	2,377		4,538
Khulda	280	316	9,461	A P		8	9	8,994		338	112	9,349 112
				T		8	9	8,994		338	112	9,461
Kuneiyisa	40	45	3,872	A P		20	64	2,432		1,288	68	3,804 68
				T		20	64	2,432		1,288	68	3,872

Appendix VIII

** Latrun	190	214	8,376	A P	7	2	346	5,824	277	768	248	7,224 248
				T	7	2	346	5,824	277	768	248	7,472
* Lubban	(340)	(384)	9,854	A P						12		12
				T						12		12
Lydda (rural)			19,868	A P	3,220		7,956	7,282 429		71 247	663	18,529 1,339
				T	3,220		7,956	7,711		318	663	19,868
** Majdal Yaba	1,520	1,715	26,632	A P	2,197 250	59	103	11,912 421		5,018 329	596	19,289 1,596
				T	2,447	59	103	12,333		5,347	596	20,885
Mansura	90	102	2,328	A P		3		2,113 64		7	39	2,123 103
				T		3		2,177		7	39	2,226
** Midya	320	361	7,020	A P			688	379	1,316	3,054 212		5,437 212
				T			688	379	1,316	3,266		5,649
Mughar	1,740	1,964	15,390	A P	1,707 65	31	86	9,070 186		293 906	387	11,187 1,544
				T	1,772	31	86	9,256		1,199	387	12,731
Mukheisin	200	226	12,548	A P				10,969		6 42	151	10,975 193
				T				10,969		48	151	11,168
Muzeiri'a	1,160	1,309	10,822	A P	953	25	35	5,895		2,134	330	9,042 330
				T	953	25	35	5,895		2,134	330	9,372
Na'ana	1,470	1,660	16,129	A P		51	335	9,277		105	529	9,768 529
				T		51	335	9,277		105	529	10,297
Nabi Rubin	1,420	1,603	31,002	A P	1,808		3,315	4,477	256	20,081	734	29,937 734
				T	1,808		3,315	4,477	256	20,081	734	30,671

287

Areas of Arab lands by tax categories (in dunums)

Village	Arab population 1944	1948	Village area		1-3	4	5-8	9-13	14-15	16A	16B	Total
*Ni'lin	(1,420)	(1,603)	15,875	A			2,011	380				2,391
				P								
				T			2,011	380				2,391
Qatra	1,210	1,365	7,853	A	405	26	329	4,320		50		5,130
				P							214	214
				T	405	26	329	4,320		50	214	5,344
Qazaza	940	1,060	18,829	A		38	142	15,192		2,161	527	17,533
				P			5	478		286		1,296
				T		38	147	15,670		2,447	527	18,829
*Qibya	(1,250)	(1,411)	16,504	A				4,486		9,622		14,108
				P								
				T				4,486		9,622		14,108
Qubab	1,980	2,235	13,918	A		54	238	12,385		54		12,731
				P							326	326
				T		54	238	12,385		54	326	13,057
Qubeiba	1,720	1,941	10,737	A	4,771	43	933	3,499		92		9,338
				P							2	2
				T	4,771	43	933	3,499		92	2	9,340
Qula	1,010	1,140	4,347	A		26	105	2,819		939		3,889
				P							187	187
				T		26	105	2,819		939	187	4,076
Ramle (rural)			38,983	A	3,645		16,925	16,094		132		36,796
				P	18		75	784			1,125	2,002
				T	3,663		17,000	16,878		132	1,125	38,798
*Rantis	(1,280)	(1,445)	30,933	A			1,294	5,379		16,355	80	23,028
				P				50		40		170
				T			1,294	5,429		16,395	80	23,198
Sajad	370	418	2,795	A		19	40	1,600		885	89	2,544
				P				47		115		251
				T		19	40	1,647		1,000	89	2,795

Appendix VIII

** Salbit	510	575	6,111	A P T		31 31	16 16	4,066 4,066	1,992 1,992	6 6	6,105 6 6,111
Sarafand El-'Amar	1,950	2,201	13,267	A P T	3,433 3,433	36 36	1,343 338 1,681	3,712 3,080 6,792		564 564	8,524 3,982 12,506
Sarafand El-Kharab	1,040	1,174	5,503	A P T	3,148 3,140	33 33	79 79	245 245	82 20 102	285 285	3,587 305 3,892
Seidun	210	237	7,487	A P T		15 15	86 86	5,207 5,207	791 791	167 167	6,099 167 6,266
Shabtin	150	169	4,423	A P T		7 7	27 27	1,158 1,158	3,229 3,229	2 2	4,421 2 4,423
Shahma	280	316	6,875	A P T	152 152	11 11	33 33	4,921 1,289 6,210	69 69	180 180	5,186 1,469 6,655
** Shilta	100	113	5,380	A P T		6 6	27 27	1,859 1,859	2,687 2,687		4,579 4,579
* Shuqba	(840)	(948)	15,013	A P T			452 452	890 890	507 507		1,849 1,849
Tina	750	847	7,001	A P T	141 141	24 24	17 17	5,511 1,101 6,612	83 83	124 124	5,776 1,225 7,001
Tira	1,290	1,455	6,956	A P T		45 45	78 78	4,271 4,271	1,033 1,033	1,281 1,281 248 248	6,708 248 6,956
Umm Kalkha	60	68	1,405	A P T	21 21		94 94	1,023 108 1,131	32 32	31 31	1,170 139 1,309

Palestinian Rights and Losses in 1948

Village	Arab population 1944	Arab population 1948	Village area		1-3	4	5-8	9-13	14-15	16A	16B	Total
Wadi Hunein	1,620	1,828	5,401	A	1,827		20	150		19		2,016
				P							174	174
				T	1,827		20	150		19	174	2,190
*Yalu	(1,220)	(1,377)	14,992	A			475	1,314	544	3,221		5,554
				P								
				T			475	1,314	544	3,221		5,554
Yibna	5,380	6,072	59,554	A	6,468	127	7,729	15,124		5,109		34,557
				P			3,362	605		16,119	2,066	22,152
				T	6,468	127	11,091	15,729		21,228	2,066	56,709
Zarnuqa	2,380	2,687	7,545	A	1,532	65	1,399	2,628		16		5,640
				P							327	327
				T	1,532	65	1,399	2,628		16	327	5,967
Nomads	3,780	4,266		A								
				P								
				T								
Grand Totals:	56,418	64,161	771,255		40,543	1,580	67,438	351,665	16,527	164,306	15,046	657,105

Areas of Arab lands by tax categories (in dunums)

Appendix VIII

☐ Sub-District: Safad

Abil El-Qamh	330	372	4,615	A P T		13 13	298 1 299	2,535 2 2,537		269 67 336	103 103	3,115 173 3,288
'Abisiya, 'Aziziyat, Ein Fit, Kh. Summan	1,220	1,377	15,429	A P T	33 33	39 39	6,181 6,181	2,988 2,988		4,430 65 4,495	436 436	13,671 501 14,172
Yarda (part of Ayelit Hash Shahar)	20	23	1,367	A P T				464 464	895 895	8 8		1,367 1,367
'Akbara	390	440	3,224	A P T		6 6	464 464	2,188 2,188	321 321	243 243	2 2	3,222 2 3,224
'Alma	950	1,072	19,498	A P T		147 147	983 983	5,311 5,311	2,164 2,164	8,635 2,252 10,887	6 6	17,240 2,258 19,498
'Ammuqa	140	158	2,574	A P T		30 30	195 195	622 622	542 542	1,182 1,182	3 3	2,571 3 2,574
'Arab Shamalina, Khirbet Abu Zeina, Buteiha	650	733	16,690	A P T			238 238	3,842 3,842		12,610 12,610		16,690 16,690
Beisamun	20	23	2,102	A P T			107 107	1,950 1,950			45 45	2,057 45 2,102
Biriya	240	271	5,579	A P T		25 25	53 53	325 325	4 4	2 2		409 409
Buwieziya & Meis	510	575	14,620	A P T		17 17	67 67	6,098 6,098	6,485 6,485	559 761 1,320	130 130	13,226 891 14,117

291

Palestinian Rights and Losses in 1948

Village	Arab population 1944	Arab population 1948	Village area		1-3	4	5-8	9-13	14-15	16A	16B	Total
Dallata	360	406	9,074	A		37	302	1,265	2,386	5,082		9,072
				P							2	2
				T		37	302	1,265	2,386	5,082	2	9,074
Khan El-Duweir (part of Dan)			2,163	A			2,067	96				2,163
				P								
				T			2,067	96				2,163
Darbashiya	310	350	2,883	A			2,763			4		2,767
				P						101	15	116
				T			2,763			105	15	2,883
Dawwara, 'Amir	700	790	5,470	A	68	52	2,114	272		11		2,547
				P						38	132	170
				T	68	52	2,144	272		49	132	2,717
Deishum	590	666	23,044	A			611	1,153	3,548	17,081		22,393
				P				69	571	8	3	651
				T			611	1,222	4,119	17,089	3	23,044
Dhahiriya Tahta	350	395	6,773	A		28	780	3,579	986	1,398		6,771
				P							2	2
				T		28	780	3,579	986	1,398	2	6,773
'Ein El-Zeitun	820	925	1,100	A		35	592	252	69	106		1,054
				P							46	46
				T		35	592	252	69	106	46	1,100
Fara	320	361	7,229	A		38	173	3,340	398	3,276		7,225
				P							4	4
				T		38	173	3,340	398	3,276	4	7,229
Farradiya	670	756	19,747	A		25	1,604	3,184	5,619	9,222		19,654
				P							93	93
				T		25	1,604	3,184	5,619	9,222	93	19,747
Fir'im	740	835	2,191	A		17	1,222	599		185		2,023
				P							5	5
				T		17	1,222	599		185	5	2,028

Areas of Arab lands by tax categories (in dunums)

Appendix VIII

Ghabbatiya	60	68	2,933	A P T		15 15		178 178	234 234	1,954 552 2,506	2,381 552 2,933
Ghuraba	220	248	3,453	A P T	2,928 2,928				7 23 30	17 17	2,935 40 2,975
Harrawi			3,726	A P T		551 551			1,704 1,704		2,255 2,255
Hula Concession (Arab area)			15,608	A P T	13,443 13,443	2,165 2,165					15,608 15,608
Hunin, Hula & 'Udeisa	1,620	1,820	14,224	A P T	81 81	867 867	5,429 5,429	722 722	6,629 6,629	10 10	13,728 10 13,738
Hurfeich	830	937	16,904	A P T	91 91	1,039 1,039	2,199 2,199	11,294 2,278 13,572	3 3		14,623 2,281 16,904
Jahula	420	474	3,869	A P T	64 64	1,626 1,626		301 1,157 1,458	138 138		1,991 1,295 3,286
Ja'una	1,150	1,298	839	A P T	43 43	190 190	230 230	361 361	8 8		824 8 832
Jish	1,090	1,230	12,602	A P T	71 71	1,502 11 1,513	4,124 82 4,206	2,512 2,512	4,248 20 4,268	8 8	12,457 121 12,578
Jubb Yusuf	170	192	11,325	A P T			4,291 4,291		6,939 6,939	95 95	11,230 95 11,325
Kafr Bir'im	710	801	12,250	A P T	96 96	1,101 1,101	1,622 1,622	2,096 2,096	7,329 7,329	6 6	12,244 6 12,250

293

Palestinian Rights and Losses in 1948

Village	Arab population 1944	Arab population 1948	Village area		1-3	4	5-8	9-13	14-15	16A	16B	Total
Khalisa	1,840	2,077	11,280	A P		20	5,586	3,775		1,392	507	10,773 507
				T		20	5,586	3,775		1,392	507	11,280
Khirbet El-Hiqab			3,280	A P			30	1,800	479	930	41	3,239 41
				T			30	1,800	479	930	41	3,280
Khisas	470	530	4,795	A P		34	1,458			15	550	1,507 550
				T		34	1,458			15	550	2,057
Khiyam El-Walid	280	316	4,215	A P			153			8 119	34	161 153
				T			153			127	34	314
Kirad El-Baqqara	360	406	2,262	A P	10		15	2,087		29		2,141
				T	10		15	2,087		29		2,141
Kirad El-Ghannama	350	395	3,975	A P	94	64	131	3,535		151		3,975
				T	94	64	131	3,535		151		3,975
Lazzaza	230	260	1,586	A P		27	235	95		20	267	377 267
				T		27	235	95		20	267	644
Mallaha & 'Arab Zubaid	890	1,004	2,168	A P		30	639	1,122		47	36	1,838 36
				T		30	639	1,122		47	36	1,874
Malakiya, 'Eitarun	360	406	7,328	A P		55		1,284	2,941	3,046	2	7,326 2
				T		55		1,284	2,941	3,046	2	7,328
Manara			2,550	A P				235	556	824		1,615
				T				235	556	824		1,615

Appendix VIII

Mansura	360	406	1,544	A	5					1,261
				P					108	108
				T	5	1,256			108	1,369
Mansurat El-Kheit	200	226	6,735	A	17		5,360		5	5,382
				P					1,353	1,353
				T	17	1,256	5,360		1,358	6,735
Marus	80	90	3,183	A	8	108	670	233	2,162	3,181
				P						2
				T	8	108	670	233	2,162	3,183
Mazari' Ed-Daraja, Dardara, Dureijat, Ein Tina, Jalabina, Weiziya ('Almin)	100	113	6,361	A		1,322	2,281	552	328	4,483
				P					49	49
				T		1,322	2,281	552	328	4,532
Meirun	290	327	14,114	A	35		883	5,845	2	6,765
				P				2	1,153	1,510
				T	35		883	5,847	1,155	8,275
Deir Mamas, Hura, Kafr Kila (in Metulla)			2,010	A		22	1,300		688	2,010
				P						
				T		22	1,300		688	2,010
Muftakhira, & Barjiyat	350	395	9,215	A		392	4,425		802	5,619
				P						
				T		392	4,425		802	5,619
Mughr El-Kheit	490	553	6,627	A	31	758	3,191	740	1,421	6,141
				P						102
				T	31	758	3,191	740	1,421	6,243
Nabi Yusha'	70	79	3,617	A	16		64	576	2,960	3,616
				P						1
				T	16		64	576	2,960	3,617
Na'ima	1,030	1,162	7,155	A	112	4,122	156		60	4,450
				P					15	291
				T	112	4,122	156		75	4,741

295

Palestinian Rights and Losses in 1948

Village	Arab population 1944	Arab population 1948	Village area		1-3	4	5-8	9-13	14-15	16A	16B	Total
Qabba'a, Jazayir Hindaj, Mughr Ed-Duruz	460	519	13,817	A		66	379	5,421	2,545	5,332		13,743
				P						32	42	74
				T		66	379	5,421	2,545	5,364	42	13,817
Qadas & Buleida	390	440	14,139	A	4	21	193	4,967	742	4,717		10,644
				P							4	4
				T	4	21	193	4,967	742	4,717	4	10,648
Qaddita	240	271	2,441	A		31	150	1,376	76	807		2,440
				P							1	1
				T		31	150	1,376	76	807	1	2,441
Qeitiya	940	1,061	5,390	A	19	93	4,465	44		61		4,682
				P						39	486	525
				T	19	93	4,465	44		100	486	5,207
Qudeiriya	390	440	12,487	A			79	2,953	3,789	5,547		12,368
				P							119	119
				T			79	2,953	3,789	5,547	119	12,487
Ras El-Ahmar	620	700	7,934	A		61	1,008	2,485	2,243	2,134		7,931
				P							3	3
				T		61	1,008	2,485	2,243	2,134	3	7,934
Rihaniya	290	327	6,137	A		89	271	4,725		1,049		6,134
				P							3	3
				T		89	271	4,725		1,049	3	6,137
Sabalan	70	79	1,798	A		14	144		421	1,218		1,797
				P							1	1
				T		14	144		421	1,218	1	1,798
Safad (rural)			3,002	A			1,037	304	1,240	190		2,771
				P							128	128
				T			1,037	304	1,240	190	128	2,899
Safsaf	910	1,027	7,391	A		62	761	1,465	1,121	1,927		5,336
				P						2,049	6	2,055
				T		62	761	1,465	1,121	3,976	6	7,391

Areas of Arab lands by tax categories (in dunums)

Appendix VIII

					A P T					
Saliha, Marun Er-Ras, Yarun	1,070	1,208	11,735	A P T	58 58	422 422	4,687 4,687	2,714 2,714	3,849 3,849	5 5	11,730 5 11,735
Salihiya	1,520	1,715	5,607	A P T	94 94	23 23	4,249 4,249		181 181	271 271	4,547 271 4,818
Sammu'i	310	350	15,135	A P T	27 27	1,136 1,136	4,358 4,358	3,293 3,293	576 5,336 5,912	409 409	9,390 5,745 15,135
Sanbariya	130	140	2,532	A P T		539 539	1,739 1,739		6 6	50 50	2,284 50 2,334
Sa'sa'	1,130	1,276	14,796	A P T	48 48	1,382 22 1,404	4,496 18 4,514		8,816 7 8,823	7 7	14,742 54 14,796
Shauqa Et-Tahta and Mughr El-Shab'an	200	226	2,132	A P T	17 17	1,476 369 1,845	140 140		7 7	123 123	1,640 492 2,132
Shuna	170	192	3,660	A P T			619 619	2,823 2,823	218 218		3,442 218 3,660
Teitaba	530	598	8,453	A P T	61 61	585 585	1,342 1,342	3,836 3,836	2,623 2,623	6 6	8,447 6 8,453
Tuba ('Arab El-Heib)	590	666	15,992	A P T	48 48	15 15	2,413 2,413	4,119 4,119	7,089 7,089	1 1	13,684 1 13,685
Tulcil and Husseiniya	340	384	5,324	A P T	48 48	57 57	3,388 3,388		63 63	15 15	3,556 15 3,571
'Ulmaniya	260	293	1,169	A P T	9 9		1,146 1,146		14 14		1,169 1,169

Village	Arab population 1944	Arab population 1948	Village area		1-3	4	5-8	9-13	14-15	16A	16B	Total
Zanghariya	840	948	27,918	A				14,671		13,179		27,850
				P							68	68
				T				14,671		13,179	68	27,918
Zawiya	760	858	3,958	A		195		3,593		9		3,797
				P						32	129	161
				T		195		3,593		41	129	3,958
Zuq El-Fauqani			1,832	A			503	1,286				1,789
				P							43	43
				T			503	1,286			43	1,832
Zuq Et-Tahtani	1,050	1,185	11,634	A		39	5,547	2,145		1,637		9,368
				P						278	358	636
				T		39	5,547	2,145		1,915	358	10,004
Nomads	820	925										
Grand Totals:	37,380	42,183	573,518		228	2,490	78,731	166,495	72,867	198,943	5,920	525,674

☐ Sub-District: Tiberias

Village	Arab population 1944	Arab population 1948	Village area		1-3	4	5-8	9-13	14-15	16A	16B	Total
Dalhamiya	410	463	2,852	A			29	1,709		18		1,756
				P						263	87	350
				T			29	1,709		281	87	2,106
'Eilabun	550	621	14,712	A		26	2,079	6,502	471	2,112		11,190
				P						3,518	4	3,522
				T		26	2,079	6,502	471	5,630	4	14,712

Appendix VIII

Nuqeib (part of Ein Gev)	320	361	2,720	A P T	26 26	30 30	141 141	2,514 2,514		9 9		2,720 2,720
Ghuweir Abu Shusha	1,240	1,399	12,098	A P T	99 99	100 100	1,088 1,088	961 961	1,877 1,877	4,484 4,484	50 50	8,609 50 8,659
Hadatha	520	587	10,310	A P T		38 38	199 199	8,379 8,379		6 1,440 1,446	248 248	8,622 1,688 10,310
Hamma	290	327	1,692	A P T			1,097 8 1,105			205 205	382 382	1,097 595 1,692
Hittin	1,190	1,343	22,764	A P T		70 70	1,979 1,979	9,643 9,643	4,545 4,545	5,849 523 6,372	8 8	22,086 531 22,617
Kafr Kama	660	745	8,819	A P T		108 108		8,278 15 8,293		9 50 59	359 359	8,395 424 8,819
Kafr Sabt	480	542	9,850	A P T		30 30	7 7	4,108 4,108	150 150	275 275	170 170	4,295 445 4,740
Khirbet El-Wa'ara Es-Sauda (Mawasi & Wuheib)	1,870	2,110	7,036	A P T		10 10	34 34	4,090 4,090		2,902 2,902		7,036 7,036
Lubiya	2,350	2,652	39,629	A P T		208 2 210	1,645 1,645	31,080 233 31,313		6 4,241 4,247	1,163 1,163	32,939 5,639 38,578
Ma'dhar	480	542	11,666	A P T		63 63	498 498	3,393 3,393	2,086 2,086	5 153 158	181 181	6,045 334 6,379
Mughar & Mansura	2,140	2,415	55,583	A P T	20 20	143 143	7,918 7,918	24,750 24,750		12,759 9,980 22,739	12 12	45,590 9,992 55,582

299

Palestinian Rights and Losses in 1948

Village	Arab population 1944	Arab population 1948	Village area		1-3	4	5-8	9-13	14-15	16A	16B	Total
Majdal	360	406	103	A	28	6	17	41				92
				P							11	11
				T	28	6	17	41			11	103
Manara & Nasr-ed-Din	580	655	6,797	A		13		4,172		946	108	4,185
				P				148			108	1,202
				T		13		4,320		946	108	5,387
Nimrin	320	361	12,019	A		64	335	7,905		2	301	8,306
				P						188	301	489
				T		64	335	7,905		190	301	8,795
Samakh	5,460	6,162	18,611	A	176	239		8,523		327	624	9,265
				P		22		55		233		934
				T	176	261		8,578		560	624	10,199
Samakiya	380	429	10,526	A			66	9,873		535	52	10,474
				P								52
				T			66	9,873		535	52	10,526
Samra & Kafr Harib	290	327	12,563	A	30	23	21	6,828		10	121	6,912
				P						3,822		3,943
				T	30	23	21	6,828		3,832	121	10,855
Shajara	770	869	3,754	A		100	550	2,104		11	164	2,765
				P				4		760		928
				T		100	550	2,108		771	164	3,693
Tabigha	330	372	5,389	A	7		287	2,728		2,265	102	5,287
				P							102	102
				T	7		287	2,728		2,265	102	5,389
Tiberias (rural)			12,624	A	22		15	1,054	2,399	589	422	4,079
				P				671		1,505		2,598
				T	22		15	1,725	2,399	2,094	422	6,677
'Ubeidiya	870	982	5,173	A	3	24	2,261	919		824	3	4,031
				P							3	3
				T	3	24	2,261	919		824	3	4,034

Appendix VIII

'Ulam	720	813	18,546	A P T		50 50	971 971	4,836 4,836	2,162 2,162	2,797 2,797	5	10,816 10,821
Yaquq	210	237	8,507	A P T		13 13	17 17	2,741 2,741		1,458 1,458	3	4,229 4,232
Grand Totals:	22,790	25,720	314,643	411	1,382	21,262	158,257	13,690	65,079	4,580	264,661

☐ Sub-District: Tulkaram

★ 'Attil	(2,650)	(2,991)	7,337	A P T							108 108
Baqa El-Gharbiya	2,240	2,528	22,024	A P T	70 70	75 75	806 806	18,550 275 18,825		693 9 702	19 19	20,194 303 20,497
★ Baqa El-Sharqiya	(480)	(542)		A P T				36 36				36 36
Birket Ramadan			5,554	A P T				196 12 208		4,819 286 5,105	10 10	5,015 308 5,323
★ Deir El-Ghusun, etc.	(2,860)	(3,228)	27,770	A P T	183 183	20 20	2,705 2,705	9,016 74 9,090		648 16 664	270 270	12,572 360 12,932
★ Falama	(120)	(135)	2,380	A P T					4 4	3 3		7 7

301

Village	Arab population 1944	Arab population 1948	Village area		1-3	4	5-8	9-13	14-15	16A	16B	Total
** Fardisiya	20	23	1,092	A P		14	237	284		352		887
				T		14	237	284		352		887
* Far'un	(710)	(801)	8,851	A P			73	2,242 13		9 9	92	2,324 105
				T			73	2,255		9	92	2,429
Ghabat El-'Ababisha			4,834	A P	50			2,368 55		2 14	122	2,420 191
				T	50			2,423		16	122	2,611
Ghabat Jaiyus			2,442	A P				804		3		807 47
				T				804		3	47	854
Ghabat Kafr Sur		740	835	19,666	A P	1,432		46	2,700 158		431 4,257	258	4,609 4,673
				T	1,432		46	2,858		4,688	258	9,282
Ghabat Miska			5,882	A P				5,572		1	38	5,573 38
				T				5,572		1	38	5,611
Ghabat El-Taiyiba El-Qibliya			1,528	A P	144		51 28	776 106			19	971 153
				T	144		79	882			19	1,124
Ghabat Et-Tayiba El-Shamaliya			2,062	A P	276			331		3 3	5	610 5
				T	276			331		3	5	615
* Habla	(580)	(655)	10,903	A P	126		35	3,251 119		171 411	46	3,583 576
				T	126		35	3,370		582	46	4,159
* Illar	(1,450)	(1,636)	13,981	A P				154				154
				T				154				154

Appendix VIII

* Irtah	1,060	1,196	2,949	A P T		1 1	1,366 63 1,429		5 66 71	84 84	1,372 213 1,585
* Jaiyus	(830)	(937)	12,571	A P T				58 58			58 58
Jaljuliya	740	835	12,685	A P T	2,638 2,638	15 15	8,999 7 9,006		46 87 133	353 353	11,873 447 12,320
Jatt	1,120	1,264	9,631	A P T		31 31	1,241 1,241		133 133	8 8	9,623 8 9,631
** Kafr Bara	150	169	3,959	A P T	10 10	14 14	1,482 1,482	204 204	1,310 1,310	3 3	3,032 3 3,035
* Kafr Jammal	(690)	(779)	14,945	A P T		10 10	2,361 2,361		2,368 850 3,218		4,739 850 5,589
** Kafr Qasem	1,460	1,648	12,765	A P T	239 239	58 58	8,531 8,531		2,640 9 2,649	47 47	11,949 56 12,005
Kafr Saba	1,270	1,433	9,688	A P T	1,026 1,026	26 26	4,600 4,600		12 53 65	451 451	6,040 504 6,544
* Kafr Sur	(460)	(519)	10,926	A P T		56 56	673 673		1,121 200 1,321	9 9	1,850 209 2,059
* Kafr Thulth	(1,290)	(1,456)	24,938	A P T			338 63 401	50 50	980 19 999		1,368 82 1,450
Khirbet Beit Lid	460	519	5,336	A P T		22 22	2,878 2,878		6 6	146 146	2,970 146 3,116

Palestinian Rights and Losses in 1948

Village	Arab population 1944	Arab population 1948	Village area		1-3	4	5-8	9-13	14-15	16A	16B	Total
Khirbet Khureish	260	293	3,655	A P T	283 283	20 20	70 70	1,726 1,726	524 524	1,032 1,032		3,655 3,655
Khirbet Manshiya	260	293	16,770	A P T	1 1		12 12	12,594 12,594		5 323 323	323 323	12,612 323 12,935
Khirbet Zababida			10,879	A P T	344 344		215 215	3,776 46 3,822		278 1,205 1,483	131 131	4,613 1,382 5,995
Khirbet Zalafa & Kh. Birket Ghaziya	210	237	7,713	A P T	38 38	3 3	6 6	6,798 6,798		20 24 44	207 207	6,865 231 7,096
Miska	880	993	8,076	A P T	1,115 1,115	88 88	304 304	3,247 3,247		8 163 171	175 175	4,762 338 5,100
* Qaffin, Kh. 'Aqqaba, & Sh. Meisar	(1,570)	(1,772)	23,755	A P T		12 12	395 395	5,954 5,954	1,001 1,001	5,692 6 5,698		13,054 6 13,060
Qalansiwa	1,540	1,738	27,496	A P T	473 473	47 47	821 821	15,885 1,103 16,988		23 916 939	479 479	17,249 2,498 19,747
* Qalqiliya	(5,850)	(6,602)	27,915	A P T	3,196 3,196		3,043 3,043	9,201 9,201		629 629	38 38	16,069 38 16,107
** Qaqun	1,970	2,223	41,767	A P T	821 821	137 137	277 277	33,637 33,637		76 76	10 10	34,948 10 34,958
Raml Zeita (Kh. Qazaza)	140	158	14,837	A P T	126 126		27 4 31	12,543 111 12,654		20 253 273	300 300	12,716 668 13,384

304

Appendix VIII

* Shweika	(2,370)	(2,675)	6,328	A		308	569	8	885
				P					
				T		308	569	8	885
Tabsar (Kh. 'Azzun)			5,328	A	722	29	1,578		2,353
				P				168	168
				T	722	29	1,578	168	2,521
** Taiyiba, Kh. 'Amarin, Nuseirat Kh. Takla	4,290	4,842	40,625	A	559	257	3,082	14	3,434	29,091
				P						1
				T	559	257	3,082	14	3,434	29,092
Tira	3,180	3,589	31,359	A	513	96	3,038		420	26,849
				P						790
				T	513	96	3,038		420	27,639
* Tulkaram (rural)			32,610	A	1,547	12	155			23,667
				P						98
				T	1,547	12	155			23,667
Umm Khalid	970	1,095	2,894	A	47	23	1,830		23	1,923
				P						89
				T	47	23	1,830		23	2,012
Wadi Hawarith (North)	1,330	1,501	7,106	A			960		1,555	2,515
				P			1,538		67	1,796
				T			2,498		1,622	4,311
Wadi Qabbani	320	361	9,812	A					19	427
				P			408			
				T			408		19	427
* Zeita	1,780	2,009	6,410	A		338	4,069		360	4,767
				P						
				T		338	4,069		360	4,767
Grand Totals:	26,130	29,489	582,034		15,979	999	18,516	270,734	1,855	38,269	5,027	351,379

Appendix VIII (C)
ARAB RURAL LANDS IN JEWISH SETTLEMENTS

Sub-District and Settlement	1-3	4	5-8	9-13	14-15	16A	Total
Acre sub-district							
Nahariya		13					13
Beisan sub-district							
Beit Hash Shitta						4	4
Gaza sub-district							
Gan Yavne Bitsaron	150			515			665
Kefar Warburg	117			130			247
Negba			8	2,585		10	2,603
Haifa sub-district							
Beit Shelomo				114		2	116
Emek Zevulun		3	97	138	458	97	793
Hadera (rural)				117			117
Heftsi Bah						2	2
Karkur						10	10
Kefar 'Atta						3	3
Kefar Hassidim						2	2
Khirbet El-Burj						15	15
Mesheq Yagur				32			32
Pardess Hanna	233		55	709		116	1,113
Qiryat Haroshet		4					4
Tiv'on						7	7
Ya'arot Hak Karmel				64			64
Yaqna'am				7			7
Zikhron Ya'acov						13	13
Jaffa sub-district							
Givatayim	124			331			455
Holon (rural)		8	100	38	65		211
Magdiel	39		2	3			44
Petah Tiqva (rural)	147		6	1			154
Ramat Gan (rural)	294		71	204			569
Rishpon				33			33
Shafayim				104			104
Jerusalem sub-district							
Har Tuv				45			45
Ramat Rahel				36			36
Nazareth sub-district							
'Affula (rural)				4			4
Mahne Yisrael				379		11	390
Ramle sub-district							
Beit 'Oved	22					8	30
Gedera	30		13	146		7	196
Kefar Aharon	38						38
Kefar Bilu	45		15	201			261
Rehovot (rural)	18						18
Rishon le Zion (rural)				3		200	203
Tirat Shalom	269						269

Appendix VIII

Sub-District and Settlement	1-3	4	5-8	9-13	14-15	16A	Total
Safad sub-district							
Dafna			252				252
'Ein Zeitim						4	4
Hatzor						2	2
Kefar Gil'adi				116		144	260
Mahamayin				41	11		52
Rosh Pinna			153	259	111	278	801
Sha'ar Yashuv						3	3
Yasod Ham Ma'ala						150	150
Tiberias sub-district							
Ashdot Ya'acov					60		60
Beit Gan				84			84
Kefar Hittim				96			96
Migdal			6	19			25
Mitspa				399		151	550
Sejera				94			94
Shorashim				1,297			1,297
Tulkaram sub-district							
Elyashiv						9	9
Even Yahuda				102			102
Herut				21			21
Kefar Yona				49			49
Mosha Gan Haiyim				255			255
Natanya (rural)	90	47	40	2,371		7	2,555
Qadima				40			40
Ramat Hash Kovesh	16		70	30		4	120
Totals:	1,632	75	888	11,212	640	1,324	15,771

Appendix IX

Restitution in Germany

*(Exact Copy of Document No. 1/May 1985
supplied to the author by the German Information
Center, 410 Park Avenue, New York, NY10022,USA)*

The German word for restitution, *Wiedergutmachung*, means literally 'to make something good again'. For more than thirty years, the Government of the Federal Republic of Germany and the individual German states have been striving to 'make good again' the history of injustice inherited from the National Socialist regime. Three decades of effort have been directed at making amends to those who suffered, within and outside of Germany, either because they were considered politically opposed to the Nazis, or simply because they were Jews.

The Beginnings
After the war, the occupation powers enacted laws in their individual zones which restored property confiscated by the Nazis to the original owners. These laws were restricted to property. They did not encompass personal damage to the victims of Nazi persecution – physical and psychological suffering, or unjust deprivation of freedom, or injury to a person's professional or economic potential. Nor did these laws provide for assistance to the widows and orphans of those who had died as a result of Hitler's policies. The occupation forces placed the responsibility for the reparation of such damages on the newly constituted German states (the Federal Republic did not come into existence until 1949).

The Moral Obligation
Both Houses of Parliament in the Federal Republic of Germany, as well as the Federal Government, have often restated the policy that restitution for the crimes of the National Socialists is one of the most important and urgent obligations of the German people.

In the fall of 1949, the late Dr Kurt Schumacher, then chairman of the Social Democratic Party of Germany, called for appropriate legislation. Dr Schumacher had himself spent several years in Nazi concentration camps. Similarly, another internee during the Hitler regime, Dr Konrad Adenauer, the first Chancellor of the Federal Republic of Germany, made the following historic statement before the Bundestag (Parliament) on September 27, 1951:

> The Federal Government and the great majority of the German people are deeply aware of the immeasurable suffering endured by the Jews of Germany and by the Jews of the occupied territories during the period of National Socialism. The great majority of the German people did not participate in the crimes committed against the Jews, and wish constantly to express their abhorrence of these crimes. While the Nazis were in power, there were many among the German people who attempted to aid their Jewish fellow-citizens in spite of the personal danger involved. They were motivated by religious conviction, the urgings of conscience and shame at the base acts perpetrated in the name of the whole German people. In our name, unspeakable crimes have been committed and they demand restitution, both moral and material, for the persons and properties of the Jews who have been so seriously harmed.

Transitional Stage: The Luxembourg Agreement and the Israeli-German Treaty

One of the first acts of the Federal Republic of Germany was an official expression of intent to make restitution. A major provision of the treaty with the three Western occupying powers of May 26, 1952, which was to effect the transition of the Federal Republic of Germany from occupied territory to sovereign state, obligated the new state to make restitution. The Luxembourg Agreement between the Government of the Federal Republic of Germany and the State of Israel and various Jewish organizations defined further the eventual shape of the legislation which was to regulate this restitution.

The Jewish organizations were represented by the Conference on Jewish Material Claims against Germany, or simply, the Claims Conference. Negotiations took place in Luxembourg and at the Hague and the agreement was signed in Luxembourg on September 10, 1952. Among its provisions: the requirement that the Government of the Federal Republic of Germany pay DM 3 billion ($714,300,000)* to the State of Israel and DM 450 million to various Jewish organizations. Payments to Israel, particularly in the form of goods,

---

* The amounts agreed upon were almost exclusively expressed in German marks. The dollar figures are in accordance with the rate of exchange accepted at the respective dates. The totals given in dollars express an average of the different rates in effect over the last thirty years.

recognized the fact that the young nation had assumed a tremendous financial burden in accepting so many victims of Nazi persecution in Europe. Monetary payments to the Claims Conference were designed to aid Jewish organizations throughout the world in resettling Jews who lived outside Israel.

Legislation

Legislation was enacted subsequently to guarantee the compensation promised in the Transitional Treaty and in the Luxembourg Agreement.

The 'Supplementary Federal Law for the Compensation of the Victims of National Socialist Persecution' of October 1, 1953, was followed on June 29, 1956, by the 'Federal Law for the Compensation of the Victims of National Socialist Persecution' (Bundesentschädigungsgesetz, or BEG), which substantially expanded the effectiveness of the 1953 law in favor of those receiving compensation. A 'Final Federal Compensation Law' was enacted on September 14, 1965, to increase the number of persons eligible for compensation and to improve the assistance offered.

Indemnification for Persecution of Persons

The BEG laws compensate those persecuted for political, racial, religious, or ideological reasons – people who suffered physical injury or loss of freedom, property, income, professional and financial advancement as a result of that persecution. In addition to racial and political victims of the Third Reich, the law includes compensation for artists and scholars whose works disagreed with Nazi tenets. It also provides compensation for people who were persecuted merely because they were related to or friendly with victims of the Nazis. Finally, it guarantees assistance to the survivors of the deceased victims.

The BEG legislation extends far beyond the responsibilities assumed by the Government of the Federal Republic of Germany in the Transitional Treaty and in the Luxembourg Agreement. Of 4,393,365 claims submitted under this legislation, between October 1, 1953 and December 31, 1983, 4,390,049 or 99.9 per cent had been settled by January 1, 1984. Up to this date, payments equaling DM 56.2 billion had been made. Approximately 40 per cent of those receiving compensation live in Israel, 20 per cent reside in the Federal Republic of Germany and 40 per cent live in other countries.

An additional DM 400 million in compensation was appropriated by the Bundestag (Parliament) in December 1970. This appropriation is earmarked for Jews whose health was damaged by the Nazi regime but who, because they were unable to comply with the deadline for filing or to qualify because of the residency requirements in the legislation, had not been able to obtain restitution previously.

Appendix IX

In 1981, the Bundestag decided to grant a further amount up to DM 100 million for payments to non-Jewish victims of the Nazi regime in cases similar to the ones mentioned above.

Restitution for Lost Property

Claims for property lost as a result of National Socialist persecution are handled according to the provisions of the Federal Restitution Law (Bundesrückerstattungsgesetz, or BRüG) of July 19, 1957.

As mentioned before, the original restitution statutes were issued by the occupation forces of the three Western zones and Berlin to expedite the return of still-existing property and to settle related legal questions. Difficulties in handling claims for objects that had ceased to exist arose under these statutes; their extent was limited and enforced variously in the different zones. The BRüG recognized the obligation of the Federal Republic of Germany to pay compensation for all objects confiscated by the Third Reich which were no longer existent and which, therefore, could not be returned in their natural state.

This legislation was further developed in four supplementary laws, the last of which was approved on September 3, 1969. Compensation for lost property is made according to the estimated replacement value as of April 1, 1956.

The BRüG legislation is also applicable to property confiscated outside the territory of the Federal Republic of Germany, provided that, at the time of confiscation, it was brought into or kept in territory covered by BRüG legislation.

As of January 1, 1984, 734,952 claims had been made on the basis of the BRüG, 734,786 of which were settled. In addition, claimants who missed the 1959 deadline were able to make hardship applications for lost household goods, precious metals and jewelry in areas outside the Federal Republic of Germany up to 1966. The responsible government office in West Berlin reports that approximately 300,000 claims have been processed on the basis of this provision.

Initially, international agreements had limited the Federal Republic's financial obligations under the BRüG to DM 1.5 billion. The amount actually paid exceeds DM 3.9 billion. It is estimated that when all claims for losses of property will have been settled, the Federal Republic of Germany will have paid DM 4.25 billion as restitution in this category alone.

In addition to this basic legal complex, several other compensatory laws have been enacted to aid those who suffered as a result of the discrimination practiced by the Nazi regime.

On August 22, 1949, a law was passed restoring the rights and privileges of those who had been discriminated against in Nazi social legislation. This law has been steadily improved. On the same day, another law was approved extending the benefits of assistance to war victims ruled ineligible by Nazi law. This law was also considerably improved by new legislation on June 25, 1958. A further law of May 11, 1951, provided for restitution to members of the civil service who had suffered injustice at the hands of the Nazis. Their condition had also been steadily improved by new legislation.

Mention must be made of the lump sum payments made to former concentration camp internees who were the objects of 'medical experimentation' by the Nazis. Lump sum payments were also made to Palestinian prisoners of war who, due to their Jewish background, did not receive the humane treatment guaranteed to all prisoners of war by the provisions of international law. While the BEG legislation attempts to aid persecuted Jews, a special fund was set up to assist those persecuted by the Nazis for having Jewish ancestry although they themselves were not Jews.

Global Agreements

Between 1959 and 1964, the Federal Republic of Germany worked out 'global agreements' with the eleven European nations listed below. As a result of these agreements, the Federal Republic of Germany assumed an obligation of almost DM 900 million to these countries, thus enabling them to compensate citizens not eligible under the BEG for damages incurred as victims of Nazi policies. Their survivors also became eligible for compensation.

Table 1: Payments Made by the Federal Republic of Germany as a Result of Global Agreements with Eleven European Nations

Country	Date of Agreement	million DM
Luxembourg	July 11, 1959	18
Norway	August 7, 1959	60
Denmark	August 24, 1959	16
Greece	March 18, 1960	115
Holland	April 8, 1960	125
France	July 15, 1960	400
Belgium	September 28, 1960	80
Italy	June 2, 1961	40
Switzerland	June 29, 1961	10
United Kingdom	June 9, 1964	11
Sweden	August 3, 1964	1
	Total:	876

Appendix IX

Austria

At the time when the discriminatory policies of the National Socialists took effect, Austria was an integral part of the German Reich and thus, according to international law, was itself responsible for injustices committed within its territory. The Federal Republic of Germany, nevertheless, made available to the Austrian government DM 102 million for compensatory payments. Of this amount, DM 96 million were used for the establishment of two funds: to compensate for loss of income to the victims of political persecution in Austria, and to aid such victims in other countries. The remaining DM 6 million were set aside to pay claims for lost property.

Summary

By December 31, 1983, the Federal Republic of Germany and the individual German states had paid more than DM 70 billion in restitution to victims of the National Socialist regime. Table 2 itemizes the individual amounts.

It is estimated that another DM 15.7 billion will be spent for the same purpose, bringing the total to DM 85.84 billion.

Table 2: Public Expenditures in Restitution for Nazi Damages (as of January 1, 1984)

		In billion DM
I.	Expenditure thus far:	
	Compensation of Victims (BEG)	56.200
	Restitution for Lost Property (BRÜG)	3.912
	Israel Agreement	3.450
	Global agreements with 12 nations incl. Austria	1.000
	Other (Civil Service etc.)	5.200
	Final Restitution in Special Cases	0.356
		70.118
		In billion DM
II.	Anticipated future expenditures:	
	Compensation of Victims (BEG)	13.800
	Restitution for Lost Property (BRÜG)	0.338
	Other (Civil Service etc.)	1.400
	Final Restitution in Special Cases	0.184
		15.722

III. Total (in round figures):

Compensation of Victims (Beg)	70.000
Restitution for Lost Property (Brüg)	4.250
Israeli Agreement	3.450
Global agreements with 12 nations incl. Austria	1.000
Other (Civil Service etc.)	6.600
Final Restitution in Special Cases	0.540
	85.840

No matter how large the sum, no amount of money will ever suffice to compensate for National Socialist persecution. On this, the Federal Republic of Germany, its Western allies and responsible independent organizations have always concurred.

But in dealing with the legacy of the Hitler regime, the Federal Republic of Germany has established a precedent; namely that of making restitution for injustice.

Appendix X

VALUATION OF PALESTINIAN RURAL LAND LOSSES USING VILLAGE SPECIFIC DATA OF 1946 (WEIGHTED AVERAGES)

($£$P million)

Sub-district	Valuation 1	Valuation 2
Acre	46.042	43.177
Beersheba	25.000	25.000
Beisan	7.979	8.391
Gaza	31.176	31.176
Haifa	19.642	22.459
Hebron	36.034	36.034
Jaffa	53.085	55.452
Jenin	9.249	9.249
Jerusalem	10.941	10.745
Nablus	-.836	-.836
Nazareth	12.390	12.390
Ramallah	-.193	-.193
Ramle	29.556	28.063
Safad	24.073	24.073
Tiberias	8.165	8.233
Tulkaram	14.130	13.967
Totals:	328.491	329.438

Note: This Appendix is too extensive to be included in full in this volume. If required by any writer, researcher, or library, it can be obtained from the Publishers at a certain fee.

Appendix XI

PROPERTY HOLDINGS IN URBAN AREAS (1945)

(in dunums)

urban area	Arabs	Jews	public	others	roads & railways	total
Acre	1,137	6	293	50	52	1,538
Beersheba	1,526	80	1,815	5	464	3,890
Beisan	561	1	26		75	663
Haifa	6,269	27,623	7,881	6,642	5,890	54,305
Jaffa	9,012	1,374	418	307	1,960	13,071
Jerusalem	7,738	5,047	556	2,685	3,305	19,331
Lydda	3,090		74	46	645	3,855
Majdal	1,141		2	3	200	1,346
Nazareth	3,176		187	1,222	403	4,988
Ramle	1,455		77	37	200	1,769
Safad	991	153	64	7	214	1,429
Shafa 'Amr	297		7		34	338
Tiberias	478	1,864	257	74	432	3,105
Tel Aviv	1,192	9,101	744	653	1,032	12,722
Totals:	38,063	45,249	12,401	11,731	14,906	122,350

Source: Government of Palestine, *Village Statistics*, 1945.

Appendix XI

VALUATION OF PALESTINIAN URBAN PROPERTY LOSSES (1947)

(in dunums)

urban area	total area	area of vacant land*	area of buildings	area of land and buildings
Acre	1,538	1,479	266	1,745
Beersheba	3,890	3,256	169	3,425
Beisan	663	590	72	662
Haifa	54,305	15,421	1,490	16,911
Jaffa	13,071	9,683	1,035	10,718
Jerusalem	19,331	10,798	1,043	11,841
Lydda	3,855	3,210	167	3,377
Majdal	1,346	1,146	282	1,428
Nazareth	4,988	4,585	310	4,895
Ramle	1,769	1,569	81	1,650
Safad	1,429	1,053	191	1,244
Shafa 'Amr	338	304	45	349
Tiberias	3,105	611	127	738
Tel Aviv	12,722**	1,970	190	2,160
Totals:	122,350	55,675	5,468	61,143

* Includes only Arab, others, and the share of this group in public lands. The latter share is calculated on the basis of their share in the total area.

** If only Arab holdings and those classified under 'Others' are added up, the total land in Tel Aviv would be 1,845 dunums (see Appendix VIII-A). To be consistent with the rest of the figures in this column, the total for Tel Aviv includes Jewish holdings, public land, and roads and railway tracks.

Note: This Appendix is too extensive to be included in full in this volume. If required by any writer, researcher, or library, it can be obtained from the Publishers at a certain fee.

Notes

CHAPTER 1

1. Albert Hourani, *Ottoman Reform and the Politics of Notables* (quoted in: A.W. Kayyali, *Palestine. A Modern History*, Billing & Sons, Ltd, London, p. 12).

2. Dispatch from Viscount Palmerston to Viscount Ponsonby, 11 August 1840 (FO. 78/390, No. 134) (quoted in Kayyali, p. 13).

3. Halil Cin, *The Legal Status of Jordan and Palestine During the Ottoman Period*, pp. 2-3 (quoted in: Kamal Oke, *Abdul Hamid II, the Zionists, and the Palestinians During the Ottoman Period*, pp. 12-13).

4. Cin, p. 53; also Oke, pp. 141-2.

5. Cin, p. 76ff.

6. *Ibid.*, p. 85ff.

7. *Ibid.*, pp. 76-7; also Oke, p. 97.

8. See Kayyali, pp. 11-42.

9. *Ibid.*, pp. 29-30 (quoted from: *Falastin*, 5 June 1913).

10. *Ha'olam* newspaper, vol. 5 (1911), quoted by Moshe Pearlman, 'Chapters of Arab-Jewish Diplomacy', *Jewish Social Studies*, 1944 (quoted in: Kayyali, p. 27).

CHAPTER 2

1. Cmd. 5957, *The Hussein-McMahon Correspondence* (letter dated 14 July 1915), London.

2. *Ibid.* (letters dated 24 October and 14 December 1915).

3. Liddell Hart, *Colonel Lawrence: The Man Behind the Legend*, Dodd, Mead & Co., New York, 1934, pp. 162-3.

4. Joseph M.N. Jeffries, *Palestine: The Reality*, Longmans, Green & Co., New York, 1939, pp. 234-5.

5. E.L. Woodward and R. Butler, *Documents on British Foreign Policy 1919-1939*, 1st ser., vol. 4, pp. 241-51.

6. George Antonius, *The Arab Awakening,* Hamish Hamilton, London, 1938, p. 248.

7. Harry Luke and Edward Keith-Roach, *The Handbook of Palestine,* Macmillan & Co., London, 1934, p. 28.

8. Cmd. 5974, *The Maugham Commission Report,* London, 16 March 1939, App. II.

9. Jeffries, pp. 216-17.

10. Antonius, pp. 433-4.

11. Jeffries, pp. 237-8.

12. Cmd. 5974.

13. Cmd. 5957.

14. *Ibid.,* Annexe C., pp. 30-8.

CHAPTER 3

1. Theodor Herzl, *The Jewish State,* H. Pordes, London, 1967.

2. Authorities on the Old and New Testaments dispute the claim that only the Jews are entitled to the benefits of the 'Divine Promise', and they argue that the Arabs are equally entitled to claim descent from Abraham through his son Ishmael. They point out that when the Promise was made, Ishmael had been born and circumcised; Isaac had not even been conceived. (See Sami Hadawi, *Bitter Harvest,* Caravan Books, New York, 1979, pp. 19-28.)

3. There is ample evidence to repudiate the claim that all Jews of today are the descendants of the ancient Hebrews.

Firstly, Professor Juan Comas of the National University of Mexico argues, among other things, that 'The anthropological fact is that Jews are racially heterogeneous and there is no foundation for the claim that there is a Jewish race.' (See article in *Issues* (magazine of the American Council for Judaism), 1965-6, pp. 21-3, quoted in Hadawi, pp. 24-6.)

Secondly, Arthur Koestler traces the origin of the Ashkenazi Jews to the Khazars, a pagan tribe in Russia which embraced Judaism in the mid-eighth century. He admits that the right of the state of Israel to exist is not based on the hypothetical origins of the Jewish people, nor on the mythological covenant of Abraham with God; it is based, he states, on international law, i.e. on the United Nations decision in 1947 to partition Palestine *(The Thirteenth Tribe,* Pan Books, London, 1976, p. 198).

4. Leonard Stein, *The Balfour Declaration,* Simon & Schuster, New York, 1916, p. 529.

5. Memorandum by Arthur Balfour dated 11 August 1919 in Woodward and Butler, 1st series, vol. 4.

6. William Ziff, *The Rape of Palestine,* Longmans & Green, New York, 1938, p. 171.

7. Cmd. 1700, *The Churchill Memorandum,* 3 June 1922.

8. David Hunter Miller, *My Diary at the Conference in Paris,* New York, 1924, vol. 5, pp. 15-29.

Notes

9. From a report submitted by General Patrick J. Hurley, Personal Representative of President Roosevelt in the Middle East, dated 3 May 1943 — *Foreign Relations of the United States*, vol. 4, pp. 776-7.

CHAPTER 4

1. League of Nations: Responsibilities of the League Arising Out of Article 22 – Mandates, No. 20/48/161, Annexe I, p. 5.

2. Joseph M.N. Jeffries, *Palestine: The Reality*, Longmans, Green, & Co., New York, 1939, pp. 284-5.

3. Herbert Hoover, *Ordeal of Woodrow Wilson*, McGraw-Hill Book Co., New York, 1958, pp. 20-5.

4. *The American Journal of International Law*, vol. 17, 1923, p. 51.

5. *Report of King-Crane Commission dated 28 August 1919* (Foreign Relations of the US Paris Peace Conference 1919), Washington, DC, 1944, vol. 12, pp. 787-99.

CHAPTER 5

1. Kenneth W. Stein, *The Land Question in Palestine 1917-1939*, The University Press, North Carolina, 1984, pp. 214-15.

2. Document FO.371/5121, *The Palin Commission Report*, London, 1 July 1920.

3. Cmd. 1785, *A Survey of Palestine 1945-1946*, Jerusalem, vol. I, chapter I, p. 5.

4. Sami Hadawi, *Bitter Harvest*, Caravan Books, New York, 1979, p. 44.

5. Harry Luke and Edward Keith-Roach, *The Handbook of Palestine*, Macmillan & Co., London, 1934, pp. 57-8.

6. David Millard, *Journal of Travels: Egypt, Arabia, Petrae, and the Holy Land 1841-2*, Erastus Shepard, Rochester, 1843, pp. 847-8.

7. Cmd. 1785, vol. I, p. 144.

8. See Statement by the British Foreign Secretary in the House of Commons – Supplementary Memorandum submitted by the Palestine Government to the United Nations Special Committee on Palestine (UNSCOP), p. 27.

CHAPTER 6

1. Areas calculated by the writer on the basis of the divisions made by the Palestine Department of Surveys as shown on Map H.

CHAPTER 7

1. See Cmd. 1785, *A Survey of Palestine 1945-1946*, Jerusalem, vol. 1, chapter 8, pp. 225-33.
2. *Ibid.*, p. 244.

CHAPTER 8

1. *Laws of Palestine*, 1944, vol. I, p. 32; and Ordinance No. 8 of 1945, Supplement No. 1, p. 47.
2. Cmd. 1785, *A Survey of Palestine 1945-1946*, Jerusalem, vol. I, pp. 251-2.
3. Cmd. 5479, *The Royal (Peel) Commission Report*, London, chapter 9, para. 48, p. 236.
4. A. Granovsky, *The Land Issue in Palestine*, 1936, pp. 61-2.
5. *Ibid.*, p. 64.
6. Cmd. 3686, *Report by Sir John Hope Simpson on Immigration, Land Settlement, and Development*, London, 1930, p. 20.

CHAPTER 9

1. Cmd. 3686, *The Hope Simpson Report*, London, 1930, pp. 34-5.
2. *Ibid.*, p. 35.
3. *Ibid.* This requirement was restored in 1931 mainly by reason of the recrudescence at that time of large-scale land sales by Arabs to Jews and the emergence of the problem of the landless Arab.
4. *Ibid.*, pp. 35-6. In 1933, a committee of inquiry found that some 644 Arab families who had been displaced by land sales had been unable to obtain other holdings on which to establish themselves, or to find other equally satisfactory occupation.
5. *Laws of Palestine*, 1939, vol. 2, p. 459.
6. Cmd. 1785, *A Survey of Palestine 1945-1946*, Jerusalem, vol. 1, p. 293.
7. Kenneth W. Stein, *The Land Question in Palestine 1917-1939*, The University Press, North Carolina, 1984, p. 215.

CHAPTER 10

1. See American Jewish Alternative to Zionism, Inc., *Report No. 47*, November 1984, p. 6.
2. American Jewish Alternative to Zionism, Inc., *Report No. 48*, p. 18.
3. *Ibid.*, p. 3.
4. See Sami Hadawi, *Revised Edition of Village Statistics 1945*, Palestine Research Centre, Beirut, 1970, p. 59.

Notes

5. Cmd. 1785, *A Survey of Palestine 1945-1946*, Jerusalem, vol. I, p. 243.

6. A. Granott, *The Land System in Palestine*, Eyre & Spotiswoode, London, 1952, p. 278.

7. Cmd. 1785, vol. I, p. 244. See Map J.

8. Granott, pp. 275-7.

9. For a detailed list of Palestinian Arabs, their personal positions, and location of land sold to Jews between 1918 and 1945, see Stein, *The Land Question in Palestine 1917-1939*, The University Press, North Carolina, 1984, Appendix 3, pp. 228-38.

10. Granott, Table 32, p. 277.

11. This sale displaced 1,746 Arab farmer families comprising 8,730 persons (see Cmd. 3530, *The Shaw Commission Report*, p. 118).

12. See Hadawi, pp. 27 and 28.

CHAPTER 11

1. Cmd. 1785, *A Survey of Palestine 1945-1946*, Jerusalem, vol. I, p. 17.

2. In the United States a year later, Chaim Weizmann, President of the World Zionist Organization, disclosed: 'I was mainly responsible for the appointment of Sir Herbert Samuel to Palestine. Sir Herbert Samuel is our friend. At our request he accepted that difficult position. We put him in that position. He is our Samuel' (J. Jeffries, *Palestine: The Reality*, Longmans, Green, & Co., New York, 1939, p. 37).

3. Matiel E.T. Moghannam, *The Arab Woman*, Herbert Joseph Ltd, London, 1937, pp. 140-1.

4. Hans Kohn, 'Zion and the Jewish National Idea', *Menorah Journal*, Autumn-Winter 1958, vol. XLVI, Nos. 1 and 2, p. 36.

5. Cmd. 1540, *British Parliamentary Papers*, London.

6. Report of Great Britain to the League of Nations on the Administration of Palestine for 1929, p. 4.

7. Cmd. 3530, *The Shaw Commission Report*, London, 1930.

8. Cmd. 3686, *The Hope Simpson Report*, London, 20 October 1930.

9. Cmd. 3692, The Statement of Policy known as the *Passfield White Paper*, London, October 1930.

10. Letter from British Prime Minister Ramsay MacDonald to Chaim Weizmann dated 13 February 1931, *The Times* (London), 14 February 1931.

11. Kenneth W. Stein, *The Land Question in Palestine 1917-1939*, The University Press, North Carolina, 1984, p. 128.

12. R.I.I.A., *Great Britain and Palestine, 1915-1939*, p. 74.

13. A.W. Kayyali, *Palestine. A Modern History*, Billing & Sons, Ltd, London, p. 158.

14. Cmd. 5479, *The Royal (Peel) Commission Report*, London, 22 June 1937.

15. Cmd. 5513, *Statement of Policy*, London, 7 July 1937.

16. Cmd. 6019, British *Statement of Policy* known as the *MacDonald White Paper,* London, 17 May 1939.

CHAPTER 12

1. Walter Millis, *The Forrestal Dairies,* The Viking Press, New York, 1951, pp. 359-65.
2. UN Resolution 181 (II).
3. Official Records of the 128th Meeting of the General Assembly, vol. 2, p. 1426.
4. For functions and responsibilities of the UN Commission, see UN Resolution No. 181(II) of 29 November 1947, Part I, Section B, paragraphs 1-15.
5. Menachem Begin, *The Revolt,* W.H. Allen, London, 1951, pp. 161, 348.
6. William Zukerman, *The Jewish Newsletter,* 3 October 1960. See also Sami Hadawi, *Bitter Harvest,* Caravan Books, New York, 1979, p. 80.
7. James Macdonald, *My Mission to Israel,* Simon & Schuster, New York, 1951, p. 176.
8. UN Library Document UNX/956,9 – A/658.
9. UN Documents S/1264/Rev. 1; S/1296/Rev. 1; S/1302/Rev. 1; and S/1353/Rev. 1.
10. Similar resolutions were adopted by other organs of the United Nations, such as the Economic and Social Council, the Commission on Human Rights, the International Conference on Human Rights, the Commission on the Status of Women, the Trusteeship Council, UNESCO, and the World Health Organization.

CHAPTER 13

1. Arnold Toynbee, 'The Arab Conflict', *Arizona Republic,* 15 June 1967.
2. Don Peretz, *Israel and the Palestine Arabs,* Middle East Institute, Washington DC, 1958, pp. 250-1.
3. *Ibid.,* p. 180.
4. UN Resolution 181(II) of 29 November 1947, Part I, Chapter 2, Article 8, Section C and Chapter 4(I).
5. Henry Cattan, *Palestine, the Arabs and Israel,* Longman Group Ltd, London, 1969, pp. 78-80.
6. UN Document A/648, pp. 14, 47.
7. UN Document A/689, p. 1.
8. W. de St. Aubin, 'Peace and Refugees in the Middle East', *Middle East Journal,* 1949, p. 252.
9. *Middle East Journal,* 1949, p. 14.
10. George Kirk, *The Middle East,* 1945-1950, Oxford University Press, London, 1954, p. 263.

Notes

11. S.G. Thicknesse, *Arab Refugees*, Institute of International Affairs, London, 1949, pp. 27-8.

12. From the Report of the Israeli Custodian to the Knesset Finance Committee, 18 April 1949, quoted in Peretz, p. 148.

13. Cattan, p. 80.

CHAPTER 14

1. UN Resolution No. 189(S-2).
2. UN Document A/648, 16 September 1948, pp. 14, 18.
3. UN Resolution No. 194 (III).
4. UN Document A/AC. 25/W. 81/Rev. 2, Annexe II.
5. *Ibid.*, Annexe I.
6. According to a statement (No. 1/May 1985) supplied by the West German Consulate-General in New York, the Federal Republic of Germany and the individual government states had processed 4,393,365 claims submitted under the 'BEG' legislation of which 4,390,049 or 99.9 % had been settled by 1 January 1984. Up to this date, payments equalling DM 56,200 million had been made. Approximately 40 % of those receiving compensation live in Israel, 20 % reside in the Federal Republic of Germany, and 40 % live in other countries. The final total compensation figure is stated to be DM 85,840 million. For full details, see Appendix IX.
7. According to the *New York Times* of 14 August 1959, 'The Supreme International Restitution Court in Berlin has recognized the claims of four Jewish families for the return of valuable estates and houses sold to foreign diplomatic agencies during the Nazi era.'

The Tribunal, the highest restitution court in West Berlin, 'ruled that the property was to be returned to the former owners because they had been forced to sell for fear of racial persecution under the Hitler regime'.

8. UN Resolution No. 394(V).
9. The writer can state from personal experience and knowledge gained on the spot that the number of persons who were able to remove their belongings was negligible because the exodus was sudden, members of families in their haste to escape lost sight of each other, transport was extremely rare because of chaos and lack of facilities, and those who had the opportunity to move their belongings were turned back by Arab vigilante groups.
10. For full report of land Specialist, see UN Document A/AC.25/W.31/Rev.2, Annexe V, dated 2 October 1961.
11. UN Document A/AC.25/W.84 of 28 April 1964.
12. The Land Expert reported in Appendix A to his Report that statistical information in regard to Ramle and Beersheba was not available to him and was therefore not included in the figures. According to the *Village Statistics*, 1945, information relating to these two towns appears as follows:

	area	urban tax
Ramle	1,769 dunums	£P 3,746 or an approximate net annual value of £P 37,460
Beersheba	3,890	£P 1,566 or an approximate net value of £P 15,660

13. In 1947 UNSCOP estimated Arab-owned land to be 85 % of the lands of Palestine, or 22,374,567 dunums out of a total land area of 26,323,000 dunums (see UN Document A/364); and in 1961, the Land Specialist of the Palestine Conciliation Commission estimated Arab-owned land to be 16,324,000 dunums (UN Document A/AC.25/W.81/Rev.2, Annexe 5, of 2 October 1961).

14. The procedure laid down when land settlement operations were first introduced in 1928 provided for the inclusion of land not in individual ownership in the name of 'the Mukhtar (headman) for the time being in trust for the village'. Among the first lands in which land settlement operations had been completed were those of Bnei Braq, a Jewish settlement near Tel Aviv. The road passing through the settlement was registered in the name of the Mukhtar who decided to enforce his so-called right of ownership by closing the road on Saturdays and on other days by charging a fee on any Arab who used the road on his way to his village. This created a problem, and the Commissioner of Lands, the Director of Land Registration, the Director of Surveys, and the Attorney General, with the writer acting as secretary, met to consider the situation. It was decided that, in order to meet such contingencies in future, all lands of a non-individual character should be registered in the name of 'The High Commission for the time being in trust for the Government of Palestine'.

15. As general inspector of urban assessments, the writer became aware of many cases where the net annual value of properties occupied by their owners was assessed well below similar rented properties. A case worth mentioning is one where the property was assessed in 1936 at a net annual value of £P 65. This assessment was maintained during the years of World War II when restrictions were placed on new constructions followed by rent control. If the formula of $16\frac{2}{3}\%$ were applied to the net annual value of £P 65, it would produce a capital value of £P 1,083. The writer was aware at the time that the owner had been offered in 1942 a sum of £P 8,000, but refused to sell.

16. For full details, see Progress Reports of the Palestine Conciliation Commission with particular reference to the Twenty-third Report for period 1 May 1964 to 22 December 1965 (UN Document A/6225).

CHAPTER 15

1. The assessment of the estimated capital value of immovable property left behind by the Palestinians, and the revenues and incomes expected from them since 1948, will be dealt with separately in Part Five.

2. Cmd. 3686, *The Hope Simpson Report,* London, 20 October 1930, p. 59. Article 6

Notes

of the Mandate provides: '...that the rights and position of other [than Jewish] sections of the population are not prejudiced'.

3. Cmd. 1785, *A Survey of Palestine* 1945-1946, Jerusalem, vol. 1, pp. 255-6.

4. *Ibid.*, This figure coincides with the figures in category 16 (1,544,575 dunums) which appear as 'public' lands and 'Roads, etc.' in the summary statement of *Village Statistics*, 1945 (p. 3) for the whole country except the Beersheba sub-district, p. 267.

5. *Ibid.*, p. 256.

CHAPTER 16

1. Federal Republic of Germany, *Focus on Restitution in Germany*, German Information Centre, New York, No. 1, May 1985, p. 1. See Appendix IX for details.

2. Readers unfamiliar with economics may wish to skip this technical sub-section.

3. See J.R. Hicks, *A Revision of Demand Theory*, Oxford University Press, Oxford, 1951; and D.M. Winch, *Analytical Welfare Economics*, Penguin, Baltimore, 1971.

4. Nechemiah Robinson, *Indemnification and Reparations: Jewish Aspects*, International Press, New York, 1944, pp. 84-5.

5. The US dollar equivalent of this value is approximately $480 million at the then rate of $4.03 to the Palestine pound (UN Document A/AC.25/W.81/Rev. 2, Annexe V dated 2 October 1961).

6. While the Land Expert who followed the Land Specialist in 1956 was appointed to carry out the work of identification and valuation of Arab losses in immovable property, he did not report the aggregate estimates in his Report of 1964 (UN Document A/AC. 25/W. 84, Appendix A).

7. The value of land, for instance, was derived as the capitalization of taxes. This has led to substantial underestimation inasmuch as these taxes were very low and were out of line with the market value of the assets. These points will be studied in detail as we present our alternative valuations.

8. The detailed assumptions made by the AHC in assessing losses will be dealt with in detail in the next section.

9. Unfortunately, we do not have the full details of the procedures used by this Expert Group.

CHAPTER 17

1. The accuracy of the procedure of valuation followed by the PCC Land Expert has been questioned by the officer who served as Inspector of Assessments and Official Valuer in the Palestine administration (see Chapter 14).

2. These estimates are based on the study *Arab Property and Blocked Accounts in Occupied Palestine*, League of Arab States, Cairo, 1956, p. 20.

3. 20 shillings to the pound sterling.

4. Cmd. 1785, *A Survey of Palestine*, 1945-1946, Jerusalem, p. 555.

5. *Arab Property and Blocked Accounts in Occupied Palestine*, pp. 29-31.

6. Ibid., p. 31.

7. Yusif A. Sayigh, *The Israeli Economy*, PLO Research Centre, Beirut, 1966, pp. 92-133.

8. Professor Sayigh uses Palestinian pounds, but since the value of a Palestinian pound was equivalent to one pound sterling we continue to use the sterling symbol (£).

9. Cmd. 1785, p. 568.

CHAPTER 18

1. The information used here is based on Federal Republic of Germany, *Focus on Restitution in Germany*, No. 1, May 1985, and on the BEG documents: *Sweites Gesetz Zur Änderung des Bundesentschädigungsgesetzes* (BEG – Schlubgesetz), 14 September 1965. See Appendix IX.

2. See Chapter 14, note 7.

3. Nehemiah Robinson, *Indemnities and Reparations*, New York, 1944, pp. 93-4.

4. Data on price changes in the FRG were obtained from the IMF, *International Financial Statistics*, December 1983.

CHAPTER 19

1. R. Loftus, *National Income of Palestine*, Government Printer, Jerusalem, 1944.

2. The year 1936 is the only inter-war year for which direct estimates of Palestine's product by 'ethnic' origin are available. According to the input-output tables of A.L. Gaathon (*National Income and Policy in Palestine*, 1936, 2nd edn, Jerusalem, Bank of Israel, 1978, pp. 19-35), Robert Szereszewski (*Essays on the Sturcture of the Jewish Economy in Palestine and Israel*, Jerusalem, Falk Institute, 1968, pp. 27-69), the 1936 Jewish net domestic product was about 55 % of the entire economy. For the rest of the inter-war period, the annual figures for Jewish net domestic product are those estimated by Szereszewski for the years 1922 to 1947. On the basis of these estimates, the Jewish share in 1945 is put at 52.5 %. The estimates of Loftus put the Arab share at 51.2 % in 1944. These two independent estimates appear to be marginally different. We opted, therefore, to use Loftus's estimate throughout this Study, although we still felt that it underestimated the Palestinians' share, as we shall show later.

3. This is based on the identification of 302,000 workers and an average wage of about 500 fils per day. See Cmd. 1785, *A Survey of Palestine* 1945-1946, Jerusalem, p. 731.

4. Statistically, the man-farmer is the head of the family, but in point of fact, in the Arab world, the whole farming family, big and small, male and female, are engaged in the cultivation and harvesting of the produce.

5. See *ibid.*, pp. 563-9.

Notes

6. *ibid.*, p. 563.

7. This is made up of a 4 % real rate of growth and 6 % inflation.

8. *Ibid.*, p. 569.

9. These figures were based on an estimated 5 persons per household.

10. Loftus, pp. 1-15.

11. A rate of increase of 10 % was used again – 4 % for real increases and 6 % for inflation.

12. Yusif A. Sayigh, *The Israeli Economy*, PLO Research Centre, Beirut, 1967, p. 108.

13. Said Himadeh, *The Economic Organization of Palestine*, American University of Beirut, Beirut, 1938, pp. 464-84.

14. Cmd. 1785, p. 554.

15. *Ibid.*, p. 556.

16. The annual rate of growth of deposits between 1943 and 1945 was 42.6 %. Half of it is 21 %, which is the assumed rate of growth.

17. The assets of the Arab Bank and the Arab National Bank are not included and left to cover for any margin of error the estimates above might include.

18. See Chapter 16 for some examples of these practices.

19. Cmd. 1785, pp. 565-6.

20. *Ibid.*

21. *United Nations Conciliation Commission for Palestine*, A/AC. 25/W. 81, Rev. 2, p. 46.

22. Constantino Lluch, Allan Powell, and Ross Williamson, *Patterns in Household Demand and Saving*, Oxford University Press, Oxford, 1977, pp. 40-1.

CHAPTER 20

1. International Association of Assessing Officers, *Assessing and the Appraisal Process*, Chicago, 1974.

2. International Association of Assessing Officers, *Application of Multiple Regression Analysis in Assessment Administration*, Chicago, 1974.

3. R. Carbone and R. Longini, 'A Feedback Model For Automated Real Estate Assessment', *Management Science*, vol. 24, n° 3, November 1977, pp. 241-8.

4. R.H. Downing and O.H. Saverlender, 'Distribution Effects of Property Tax Equalization', *Proceedings of the Pennsylvania Academy of Science*, vol. 53, 1979, pp. 192-7.

5. Cmd. 1785, *A Survey of Palestine* 1945-1946, Jerusalem, pp. 279-89.

6. The land figures above include the share of public lands allocated to Arab Palestinians. These shares were based on the proportion of Arab private land holdings to total private lands in a given area. When population shares are used, the figures change slightly. The total land area rises to 56,530 dunums and the built-up area to 5,552 dunums.

7. Again, note that the lower estimate of losses is adopted. When population shares are used to allocate public lands, the Arab losses of urban real estate rise to £P120.2 million.

CHAPTER 21

1. Sir John Bagot Glubb, *A Soldier with the Arabs*, Hodder & Stoughton, London, 1957, p. 81.

2. *Yediot Aharonot*, 14 April 1972. See *The Journal of Palestine Studies*, vol. 1, n° 4, Summer 1972, pp. 142-6.

3. *Ibid*.